STARRY NIGHTS

Loose Can(n)ons

Edited by Bruce Kapferer
Editor: Bruce Kapferer, Professor Emeritus of Anthropology, University of Bergen, and Honorary Professor, University College London

Loose Can(n)ons is a series dedicated to the challenging of established (fashionable or fast conventionalizing) perspectives in the social sciences and their cultural milieux. It is a space of contestation, even outrageous contestation, aimed at exposing academic and intellectual cant that is not unique to anthropology but can be found in any discipline. The radical fire of the series can potentially go in any direction and position, even against some of those cherished by its contributors.

Volume 1
Starry Nights
Critical Structural Realism in Anthropology
Stephen P. Reyna

STARRY NIGHTS

CRITICAL STRUCTURAL REALISM IN ANTHROPOLOGY

Stephen P. Reyna

berghahn
NEW YORK · OXFORD
www.berghahnbooks.com

Published in 2017 by
Berghahn Books
www.berghahnbooks.com

© 2017 by Stephen P. Reyna

Library of Congress Cataloging-in-Publication Data

Names: Reyna, Stephen P., author.
Title: Starry nights : critical structural realism in anthropology / Stephen P. Reyna.
Description: New York : Berghahn Books, 2017. | Series: Loose can(n)ons ; volume 1 |
    Includes bibliographical references and index.
Identifiers: LCCN 2016053586 (print) | LCCN 2017000525 (ebook) | ISBN
    9781785334610 (hardback : alk. paper) | ISBN 9781785332449 (pbk. : alk. paper) |
    ISBN 9781785332456 (eBook)
Subjects: LCSH: Anthropology—Philosophy. | Critical realism.
Classification: LCC GN33 .R49 2017 (print) | LCC GN33 (ebook) | DDC 301.01—dc23
LC record available at https://lccn.loc.gov/2016053586

British Library Cataloguing in Publication Data

A catalogue record for this book is
available from the British Library.

ISBN 978-1-78533-461-0 (hardback)
ISBN 978-1-78533-244-9 (paperback)
ISBN 978-1-78533-245-6 (ebook)

DEDICATION

This book is dedicated to clear nights spent outdoors, mostly in the country. You rarely see the stars well in cities. Additionally, it is dedicated to Nina, family and friends—stargazers all.

Contents

Preface

No man is an island
Entire of itself,
Every man is a piece of the continent,
A part of the main
—John Donne, *Devotions upon Emergent Occasions*

There are certain academics who ride the wave of the latest scholarly trend. If only they can catch—gloriously posed—the curling crest at the right moment, they can ride it to fame and fortune (or that small portion of it that elites allow to those in the academy). Confession! I am not much of a beach boy, more a one-eyed fool—loitering (which, of course, is a misdemeanor).

No riding waves, just chilling, "a part of the main," mingled with folk—poor, middling, and the occasional rich plutocrat—in the forests, savannahs, and deserts of Africa; the subways, apartments, and skyscrapers of New York; or the reception rooms, manager's offices, or conference suites of global bureaucracies. Furthermore, when not with these peoples I have the unsanitary habit of hanging with old, dead thinkers (who were good enough to be remembered). The point of being a fool—recommended as an anthropologist's default position—is that loitering (another term for ethnography) among folk encourages learning about them. *Starry Nights,* the work of a fool, explores a few "main" things learned about human being.

There are many who have contributed to this text. I'm a New Englander. New England in former times was a hard land of forest and field. Every spring farmers' fields sprouted new crops of rocks that grew over the winter. So every April and May, farmers hitched teams of oxen to their sledges and harvested the rocks. These rocks seem to me to be like egregious blunders that grow in my texts. Those who have assisted with *Starry Nights* hitched up their intellectual sledges and labored at egregious blunder removal.

Over the years, helping in this work have been R.E. Downs, Eric Wolf, Abe Rosman, Marvin Harris, Conrad Arensberg, Jonathan Friedman, John Gledhill, Bruce Kapferer, Sarah Green, R. Brian Ferguson, Hastings Donnan, Don

Kalb, Hannah Lessinger, Martine Guichard, John Eidson, Olaf Zenker, Andrea Behrends, Joe Lugalla, Boris Nieswand, Patrick Heady, and Markus Hoehne. I thank them very much. Günther Schlee, director of the Conflict and Integration Department at the Max Planck Institute of Social Anthropology, has been a kind host and smart critic since 2001. Chris Hann, director of the institute's Resilience and Transformation Department, and Marie-Clare Foblets, director of the Law and Anthropology Department, have been intellectually alive and welcoming. The institute's librarians—Anja Neuner and Anett Kirchof—have been brilliant at tracking down hard to find documents.

Chapter 1 was originally published in *Man* 29 (1994): 555–581. Chapter 4 was originally published in *Identities* 4 (1998): 431–465.

Introduction

A wizened warrior
Wanders wonder wild.
Three vultures appear
And circle …
—Anonymous fragment. Possibly from Püt-Ni

pavane: *a slow processional dance common in*
Renaissance Europe during the 1500s

One evening, during my doctoral fieldwork, I slept outside on an old cot in the Chadian dry season. The temperature was above 100 degrees. Lying on my back, anticipating a breath of a cooling breeze, I faced the sky: ink-blackness in which stars gleamed diamond bright, the Milky Way bisecting the darkness. Constellations arrayed in place; Orion—the Hunter—always visible; shooting stars occasionally discernible; the moon—cool, dispassionate. During the night I awoke a number of times. Stars and moon moved. Awake again. They had moved more. Awake yet again. They had moved still more: a pavane of stars, constellations, shooting stars, the moon, and galaxies in a stately dance across darkness. Here was more than just a starry night. Here was "the main" thing: a masque of being, with human being a sparkling of heavenly bodies dancing out there, somewhere in the obscure empyrean.

Consider the state of "the main" now. At the end of the Middle Ages, Immanuel Wallerstein (1974) told us that there were economic problems, terrible disease, and grim war in feudal Europe. Things seemed to be falling apart. However, there was a modern world to be won and global capitalism, sailing the good ship imperialism, won it. The high tidemark of that modern world was during the years just prior to the beginning of World War II, when the vast bulk of the globe was in some way subject to Western capitalist domination. Now, according to some, like Slavoj Žižek, we are *Living in End Times* (2011) predated by the "four horsemen of the apocalypse." Žižek has horsemen. I have vultures, and really it only takes three to do the job: ecological calamity, economic dysfunction, and violence of global warring.

Europe's problems in late medieval times were regional. The same cannot be said of contemporary times. There is no world to be won. It was won and the circling vultures threaten it. The starry night of now is one where "the main" thing is that soon it may be lights out, creating a night sky with three vultures and no diamond-bright stars from the galaxy of human being. The topic of *Starry Nights* is to present in five essays an approach to help understand and explain the current nighttime of human being, with the goal of warding off circling vultures. This approach is termed critical structural realism (CSR). It is introduced next.

Critical Structural Realism

First, consider what CSR is for. The speculations of nineteenth-century unilinear, cultural evolutionary anthropologists—E.B. Tylor (1871) or Lewis Henry Morgan (1877)—were largely wrong, racist, and supportive of Western imperialism. However, the goals of their analysis were attractive: to study all expressions of humanity in all places and all times. During the first half of the twentieth century Franz Boas (1940) and his followers attacked the evolutionists' empirical findings, critiqued their racism, and challenged their legitimation of imperialism. However, they did not throw the baby out with the bathwater. Even if evolutionary studies had been mistaken in their substantive conclusions, they had been right in their insistence that anthropology should be an enormous field of studies. The Boasians introduced a four-field approach in which anthropologists investigated sociocultural anthropology, archeology, human biology, and linguistics to acquire knowledge about the vastness of peoples' escapades.

Since the Boasians, different anthropological waves have risen and crested. All tend to narrow anthropological boundaries, with the biological thrown out, and restrict the discipline to analysis of social relations or to culture, conceptualized narrowly as ideas. Think of Radcliffe-Brown (1952), who made social anthropology a subfield of sociology, or componential analysts, like Ward Goodenough (1981), who reduced it to gathering a few cultural terms, especially those of kinship. The former Boasian anthropology imagined human being to be a major galaxy dancing in the night sky.

Current anthropology sees human being as a few stars, twinkling here and there. More troublesome, a postmodern anthropological wave arose and became a rave starting in the late 1970s, especially in ethnography. I argue in this text that such an anthropology labors with an oedipal epistemology. Oedipus, it will be remembered, was the mythical king of Thebes who gouged out his eyes. Postmodern anthropologists, for the most part, take a vow to abjure science and, in so doing, eliminate the strongest tool humans have developed for knowing reality. As such, they are oedipal epistemologists, blind to the pavane of human being. It should be clear something fundamental is at issue here. Anthropology proposes to study the human condition, but if it has epistemologically blinded itself it cannot undertake this labor. CSR offers an alternative to the anthropologists riding the wave of oedipal epistemology.

CSR is for a neo-Boasian, big galaxy anthropology. It is for those who want to know about the economics, politics, social institutions, culture, and biology of humans everywhere, at all times, from the earliest homo sapiens populating Africa 300,000 years ago to the present "end times" actors doing their thing globally. "Human being," from this standpoint, is all places, times, and ways that humans are observed being humans. Some may worry that such an anthropology hurdles boundaries into other social sciences mashing sensitive, disciplinary toes. So be it. Big galaxy anthropology is a scholarly space in which other, scope-challenged human sciences may join in an intellectual quest specializing in cross-boundary observation—of the relationships of the economic to the political or the biological to the social— to seek fuller knowledge of the starry night of human being. Why do this? First, out of sheer wonderment at the stars pinwheeling across the empyrean. Second, to help against vultures—circling.

Next consider what CSR is not, and what it is. CSR is *not* the author's brilliant invention. It is *not* new. Numerous versions of it have existed, and continue to exist, since deep in antiquity, though it is possible that the present concatenation of it offers some novelty. Further, CSR is not a particular theory. One can imagine Marxist or Liberal theory in CSR, though my take on it is leftist. Rather, it is a tool for anthropologists, or other thinkers in the human sciences, for exploring the nature of being. In this sense, it is in Althusserian terms problematic, or in those of Kuhns a paradigm, capable of supporting a number of different theories.

For the fool who "wanders wonder wild" investigating being, CSR is their multipurpose jackknife with three blades. One blade is epistemological, the second is ontological, and the third is critical. The first blade helps intellectual workers to know *how* to go about knowing. The second helps to *define* their object of study: what is out there in the starry night of human being. The final blade, which needs to be the sharpest of all, is that of *knowing what to do* about what is. This blade is to be used against the vultures circling human being. Consider, first, epistemology.

Epistemology

The epistemology of CSR is based upon an old ontological view, realism. Realism is the notion, according to Fetzer and Almeder:

(1) that we inhabit a world whose nature and existence is neither logically nor causally dependent upon any mind; (2) that some of our beliefs about this world are accurate, even if incomplete, descriptions, and that thereby qualify as true; and (3) that our methods of inquiry enable us to discover that (at least) some of our beliefs about the world are true. (1993: 117).

There are many types of realism, which means that (realistically) thinkers have to make a choice. The realism I find attractive is scientific, where it is asserted that the world described by science is real—insofar as reality is knowable. What makes scientific realism interesting? Frankly, as is argued in the first chapter, it seems that there are simply no other *clearly* superior ways of knowing reality. If there were, thinkers would be utilizing them.

However, CSR's scientific realism is not that of Auguste Comte's or the Vienna Circle's positivism, though it will become clear that I both respect and utilize the latter group. In general, positivists tended to overly claim science's epistemic powers. Chapter 2 reviews postpositivist critiques of science's abilities; including issues of underdetermination, incommensurability, and theory-ladenness. While these appraisals helpfully show where the earlier positivists overly claimed science's powers, they do not argue for a rejection of science. Rather, they tend to concur with the view that there are not better alternatives for knowing human being than science.

CSR's view of science gives up knowing final truths. Rather, it understands science as the development and utilization of the most rigorous practices for knowing as truly as possible, that is, for achieving approximate truths about the starry night of being. The practice of "gaze/regard reflexivity" assists discovery of approximate truths. "Reflexivity," generally, is a person reflecting upon being. "Regard" is understood as the observer discerning some Other, with the Other broadly defined as "something observed and explained." Two sorts of regard coexist. The first concerns the nature of what is. Ontology is the study of the nature of Something Other.[1]

The second sort of regard is that of the scientist. It is less lofty than the first. She or he regards reality directly (or as directly as possible) and, in Kant's famous (1781) formulation, attempts to discover the truth about "the thing in itself" (*ding an sich*), that is, something. "Gaze," as understood here, pertains to some Other observing something and telling that something what they are. Scientific gaze refers to scientific Others observing a particular something, the supposed truths of another group of scientists. This means that what one group of scientists' regard as the truth about something is subjected to other scientists' gaze, with the gaze of the second group of scientists a confrontation of the first group of scientists' regard.

Science, thus, refuses to simply regard something said to be true as true but subjects it to the gaze of skeptics to validate whether something well regarded actually has any truth to it. What it regards as true is only as good as the last time it was subjected to scientific gaze. Because there is no final gaze, there is no final truth, which means all truths are approximate. Consequently, science, because of gaze/regard reflexivity, is skepticism.

Approximate truths involve two types of knowledge: what is and why. The first is knowledge of *istheit* (being itself), and not the nature of being, which is emergent from thinking about *istheit*.[2] The second knowledge is of warranted theory. Both are considered next.

Making Istheit *Knowledge*

One cannot directly know being itself. People know sensations of reality through the organs of perception (eyes, ears, nose, etc. and their connections, especially with the posterior cerebral cortex). "*Istheit* knowledge" is re-presentation of sensation of being as quantitative or qualitative symbols (i.e., concepts). Sensation is bodily reports of being itself, which have been carried to the body in the form of light waves, sound waves, touches, smells, and so on. Light waves and so forth are not *istheit,* but they have been directly in contact with it and so come bearing information about it. They enter the body through the sense organs and are re-presented as electrochemical currents that travel along neuronal networks to the brain (largely in the posterior cortex), where they become sensation. Then they travel further different neuronal networks, being re-presented again and again, until finally they are given symbolic re-presentation.

Such re-presentation can be stored in memory neurons that can be retrieved into consciousness. Symbolic re-presentation of *istheit* may be termed "measurement." See a big, furry something charging (sensation)! Call it a "bear" (qualitative measurement). Decide it weighs 300 kilos (quantitative measurement). One has taken the measure of an ursidae—run like hell (sensible thing to do).

Istheit knowledge is arrived at through the practice of "observation," symbolic re-presentation of sensations of reality, with re-presentation understood as the taking of something and presenting it as something else. Participant observation is important because it is observation that brings ethnographers closest to the actuality of human speech and actions, allowing fuller sensing of that reality and thereby, in principle, permitting more complete re-presentation of human being. Because the starry night of reality occurs in particular places over specific intervals, it is important to observe the spatiotemporal sequencing of human being. First, in time and space, the bear is pretty far away. Second, in time and space, it is alarmingly closer. Importantly, if anthropology is to be a big galaxy discipline, it needs additional observational techniques other than those of ethnography—especially those of history, semantics, archeology, and the life sciences. Attention turns to the question of quality. How good is *istheit* knowledge?

It is not perfect. Frailties in regard to knowing reality itself result from what can be termed "haecceity glitches." The term "haecceity" derives from the medieval scholastic Duns Scotus (1987). There are different understandings of it (see Rosenkrantz 1993), though generally it refers to the "thisness" of things—their singular qualities, properties, or characteristics that make them this as opposed to that other thing. The haecceity of something is the degree to which concepts re-presenting it get these qualities, properties, and characteristics correct. Qualities, properties, or characteristics are symbolic re-presentations of sensations produced by being. "Haecceity glitches" are situations in which symbolic re-presentations of things do not reveal their haecceity. Problems can occur for at least two reasons. The first of these has to do with difficulties of observation, in which sensations of reality for some reason do not accurately report it. A second reason for glitches has to do with preexisting conceptual bias, which hampers accurate sensing of reality.

Observational haecceity glitches flourish when sensation reveals too little, or too much, of something. Consider, for example, a case in which observation initially divulges too little. Lucretius, in *The Nature of Things* (2007), a century before Christ, asserted that being was composed of atoms, but he could reveal little about atomic properties because he believed they were imperceptible. Here was a situation of "conceptual thinness." Nineteen centuries later, at the end of the nineteenth and the beginning of the twentieth century, because improved observational methods made atoms perceptible, physicists such as Ernest Rutherford and Neils Bohr sensed that atoms had a structure, whose parts they gave the symbolic status of neutrons, protons, and electrons.

A century later, at the turn of the twenty-first century, with the invention of still better sensing devices that culminated in the Large Hadron Collider, it became possible to examine what went on in the parts of an atom and elementary particles were sensed, such as quarks, photons, mesons, and finally the Higgs boson. Now more of the properties of atoms were known, meaning there was a situation of "conceptual maturity." "Conceptual bloat" is the second observational haecceity glitch, occurring when inaccurate sensing leads to re-presenting some reality as being greater than it actually is. A god that is all things is a bloated concept. There is no way of knowing whether one has achieved complete haecceity. Reality is an infinity of space and time, and an observer simply does not know if she or he has sensed all there is to sense of what is out there pertaining to something, so it is not possible to know if all of something's properties have been known.

Preexisting conceptual biases can provoke haecceity glitches. Observers come to reality preloaded with a stock of concepts—10,000 to 20,000 words and numbers, variously formed into an unknown number of cultural messages, including those of her or his disciplinary specialty (Crystal 2002: 46). Different persons have different conceptual stocks. This means that an observer's sensations can be biased in favor of her or his symbolic store, especially those concepts that the observer's working memory has been primed to retrieve.

Conceptually biased haecceity glitches occur when the preexisting concepts assign properties to observations. For example, an Israeli settler in occupied territory sees a Palestinian youth throwing stones. She or he quite possibly may give this sensation the status of "terrorist," while if a Palestinian sees that same stone thrower, she or he may well place it in the category of intifada.[3] A second sort of conceptually biased haecceity happens when concepts are "broken," in the sense that they lack sensational hooks specifying how a concept is linked to the reality it is supposed to re-present.[4]

A "sensational hook" is a statement, or statements specifying properties of a concept of something so that observers may "hook" into—in the sense of make observations of—the something's reality. Elephants are defined as having tusks and a long nose. These properties are its sensational hooks. If one observes a tusked, long-nosed animal, one may additionally sense that it only eats certain vegetables, thereby discovering another property of its *istheit*. Sensationally hookless notions create "conceptual blindness," concepts unable to sense reality. Notions with too many or too few sensational hooks produced a "conceptual blur," concepts that can sense reality but in an incomplete, that is blurred, fashion.

Consider blur in a concept in which there were too few sensational hooks. Employment, for example, has often been defined as people working. The sensational hook here is "folks working." However, employment during neoliberal times has become part time, short term, and poorly paid. Just observing people employed does not catch neoliberal employment. For a while there was no term to re-present this reality, so that the instability of peoples' lives was blurred behind its non-re-presentation. Introduction of the notion of "precarity," which is concerned with the percentage of workers in part-time jobs, length of time in part-time jobs, and remuneration of these jobs, addresses the blurring of the realities of employment in neoliberal times. The sensational hooks in precarity are part-time jobs, time in these, and salary in them. Observation of them helps remove the blur obscuring growing human insecurity.

Often, conceptual blindness and blur occur in concepts high in abstraction and broad in generality, purporting to re-present vast areas of being. For example, Gilles Deleuze and Félix Guattari have a concept of a "machine" which they say, "may be defined as a system of interruptions or breaks (coupures)" (1983: 36). This definition may strike readers as gnostic. Deleuze and Guattari, perhaps to assist readers' grasp of what they meant by machine, elucidated the notion of "breaks" (in the sentence immediately following their formal definition of machine), stating:

> These breaks should in no way be considered as a separation from reality; rather they operate along lines that vary according to whatever aspect of them we are considering. Every machine, in the first place, is related to a continual material flow (hylé) that it cuts into. It functions like a ham-slicing machine, removing portions from the associative flow: the anus and the flow of shit it cuts off, for instance; the mouth that cuts off not only the flow of milk but also the flow of air and sound; the penis that interrupts not only the flow of urine but also the flow of sperm. (Deleuze and Guattari 1983: 36)

So a machine is "like a ham-slicing machine" that among other things "cuts off ... the flow of shit." Unspecified by the gentlemen are sensations that hook their machine up to reality, and the ham-slicing trope does not really help in this regard. The Deleuze–Guattari machine seems conceptually blind. The danger of such concepts is they make their users think that the starry night of being is well regarded, when they are delusional, stumbling about in a darkly clouded night.

In sum, the route to knowledge of what is (*istheit*) is through elimination of haecceity glitches due to conceptual thinness, bloat, and defective sensational hooks that produce conceptual blur or blindness. How should one proceed? Chapter 2 offers suggestions, of which, perhaps, the most useful is to be skeptical about reality. Be incredulous of those who award themselves absolute haecceity just because they have "been there." Knowing what is depends upon achieving conceptual maturity; this depends upon a number of observers sensing something, discovering all its properties amenable to observation, and re-presenting them conceptually. Of course, once people know what is, they need to know why. This leads to discussion of explaining why what is is, which involves theorizing.

Making Theory

Lamentably, some anthropologists' understanding of theory shades toward conceptual blur because they do not bother to articulate what they mean by the term, assuming that everybody knows what it is, just as they know what a fork is. Such inarticulateness may not be harmful when practicing with a fork. It may lead to big-time grandiloquence in theoretical practice, for the reason that the practitioner does not know what she or he is talking about. Chapter 2 reviews some questionable understandings of theory in anthropology.

"Theory," as the term is employed in CSR, takes the form of explicit generalizations that map, in the sense of stating, the relationships between abstract and general conceptual terms referring to different spaces and times of being in order to explain or understand why and how what is observed to occur in those spaces actually occurs. The making of explicit, abstract, and general generalizations is "theorizing." The most abstract and general generalizations are theories; less abstract and general generalizations can be hypotheses or empirical generalizations (Wallace 1971).

Theory formulation alone is only half the chore of explaining why what is is. Theory must be validated; that is, there must be news from the senses that what a theory states to go on in *istheit* is actually observed to go on. The validating of theory is science's observational, or empirical, practice. Unvalidated theoretical statements lack truth-value. Validated ones can be said to be approximately true knowledge, at least as far as there are observations to warrant them. Empirical work for the validation of theory is hard. It can require the development of observational techniques that allow more accurate and more representative, intersubjective viewing of realities that need inspection for validation. Be very clear about it, an intellectual discipline that does not develop rigorous validation practices is in the business of producing gobbledygook. In sum, CSR's epistemology seeks formulation of what is out there in the starry night of human being and explicit, validated theory in order to acquire an increasing fund of approximate truths concerning why it is out there. Consider next CSR's ontology.

Ontology

> The real: *it is structured ...*
> Althusser, *Reading Capital*

The text will now turn to the nature of "the real" following some preparatory discussion of ontology. Starting in the seventeenth century, at least in England, the concept of ontology began to be used as a substitute for metaphysics. In the nineteenth century, Auguste Comte (1975) critiqued the latter term. The criticism was influential, and the term "metaphysics" was increasingly replaced by that of ontology. Heidegger became a twentieth-century ontological icon. Recently, some in anthropology have taken an "ontological turn."[5] Eduardo Viveiros de Castro, a spear-carrier for this group, explains what he understands by ontology:

> Ontology, as far as anthropology in our understanding is concerned, is the comparative ethnographically-grounded transcendental deduction of Being (the oxymoron is deliberate) as that which differs from itself (ditto)—being-as-other as immanent to being-as-such. The anthropology of ontology is anthropology as ontology; not the comparison of ontologies, but comparison as ontologies. (2014)

This definition seems to have thrown caution to the wind and is something of a cocktail that might have been mixed by Voltaire's Professor Pangloss—a dollop of Heidegger (the "Being"), a jigger of Kant (the "transcendental" logic), spiked with a "deliberate" oxymoron and a piquant "ditto." What *is* the gentleman talking about? Who knows?

A lesson to be drawn from the above is not to simply terminate ontological inquiry as a bizarre cocktail of mind-numbing conceptual blur. Rather, a starting point of ontological inquiry might be appreciating that not all ontologies are equal. Crucially, they have different truth-values. This recognition is part of anthropology's debt to Franz Boas. During his time racist ontologies prevailed that understood human being as essentially divided into superior and inferior races. Boas and his followers, in the early part of the twentieth century, provided evidence suggesting such an ontology to be fallacious. Ontologists, oblivious to ontologies' truth-value, will not be disposed to distinguish Nazi from other ontologies. Anthropologists are advised to evaluate the truth claims of different ontologies, lest they career off the ontological turn into jungles of phantasmagoria.

In order to do so, CSR favors a scientific realist approach to ontology, understanding the term as asking "questions such as 'What is or what exists?.' 'What kinds of thing exists primarily?' and 'How are different kinds of being related to each other?'" (Bunnin and Yu 2009: 491). Ontological practice involves empirical discovery of *istheit*, specifying their similarities and differences and from this generalizing about the nature of what is. So what specifically is CSR's scientific ontology?

It is a form of "reism": "the doctrine that only things exist" (Woleński 2012: 1), because, by definition, nothing is nonexistent. Being is things. Reism is an ancient position favored by Stoics and materialists. CSR argues a materialism, noting that even things that appear immaterial are material. Ideas, for example, are the operation of brain systems, which are material things. However, CSR is a particular type of reism based upon its understanding of the nature of things. Things do not exist alone. Rather, they "go steady," in the sense of being connected with other things. Parts (things) connected to other parts (other things) are structures or forms or organizations or systems satisfying the condition that they exist over time. CSR's ontology then, the starry night, is a reism of structural time-being. How does human being fit into time-being?

Marshall Sahlins threw a damper on this topic when he claimed, "We live in an anti-structural age" (2013: xii). This assertion is right and wrong. The first five decades of the twentieth century saw the rise of Parsonian and British social anthropological structural functionalisms followed by French structuralisms, of which Lévi-Strauss's work was the crowning anthropological achievement. Then, in the 1970s these structuralisms were repudiated and poststructuralism proclaimed (Poster 1989). Thereafter, many anthropologists took the interpretive turn (Geertz 1973), declaring hostility to the notion of structure and devotion to the text, literary or other. In this sense, Sahlins is right.

But what was actually given up were the older structuralisms, in part because they seemed *istheit* challenged regarding organizational intricacies of twentieth-century human being. New structuralisms, however, immediately trooped in, conceptualized, in principle, to more truly re-present social being, especially a social being that had burst the boundaries of locality, tribe, and state and was utterly, if messily, global. By the 1990s, at least part of sociology as well as some areas of cybernetics and mathematics had taken a "complexity turn" (Urry 2005), proposing complexity theories, designed to accommodate analysis of local and global phenomena, with concepts, among other things, of fractals, black swans, chaos, and butterfly effects.

Certain geographers and sociologists by the turn of the twenty-first century had developed a "TPSN framework" to theorize sociospatial relations, especially to address questions of "polymorphy"—the organization of sociospatial structures in multiple forms (Jessop, Brenner, and Jones 2008). From postmodernism, supposedly a fortress of antistructuralism, came notions such as assemblage, rhizome, and actor networks, which au fond are structural concepts. So in this sense Sahlins is wrong. My judgment is that much as they desired it, human theorists could not completely jettison structuralism because in the end, "The real: it is structurd"(1970: 36)" What, then, distinguishes CSR's structuralism?

It is differentiated by two features. The trope of time-being as like a starry night helps to explicate the first of these. Two broad constellations of structure can be distinguished relative to human being—E- and I-space—roughly corresponding to certain usages of the terms "objective" and "subjective." However, these latter two terms are avoided because they are freighted with so many meanings as to invite confusion.

The "space" of E- and I-space is defined in terms of two dimensions. The first is that of structures practicing what they do in places. Places are the environment in which structures function. As such, place is a system of systems of particular structural forms. The second dimension of space is that of the time in which systems of systems operate in place. E-space in this perspective consists of all the different forms of structure external to peoples' bodies. E-space structures include life and nonlife forms. CSR is especially interested in a type of life-form termed "social." Social forms consist of human actors acting with other actors and things. Different social forms are connected with other social forms and, for that matter, other living and nonliving forms, which places may be thought of as the constellations in the galaxy of human being.

I-space is the constellation including structures internal to peoples' bodies, such as the circulatory, respiratory, or reproductive systems. However, CSR has concentrated upon the I-space structure that is most directly responsible for allowing actors to choreograph connections between antecedent events in E-space with their consequents. This structure is said to be located in the brain and is termed a "cultural neuroheremeneutic system" (CNHS). The CNHS is said to generate desires or, in the case of elites, *délires* (powerful desires able to affect a lot of people). Desires and *délires*, the combinations of emotion and understandings, help choreograph social forms, especially when they become public *délires*, institutionalized directions of how to organize human being. Of course, what is of great interest is how the CNHS in I-space connects with the different social forms of E-space. This leads us to the second feature of CSR's structuralism.

The different social forms in constellations of the E-space might be imagined as burning bright as fiery points of energy. This energy might be conceptualized as generated by "force/power dyads," the forces that cause powers in social forms. This is a second distinguishing feature of CSR's structuralism, its interest in the organization, function, and origin of force/power dyads. Force/power dyads connect with other force/power dyads, much as neuronal pathways link with each other and the different systems of the body. Further, just as neural networks direct the operation of the body's complex systems in I-space, so force/power dyads direct the operation of the constellations of social forms in E-space. How do they do it?

Neuronal pathways work by neurotransmission, which involves signal molecules, neurotransmitters, being released by a neuron (the presynaptic neuron) that activates the receptors of another neuron (the post synaptic neuron). The neurotransmitters of the presynaptic neuron may be said to have the force to cause effects with certain powers in the postsynaptic neuron. Social forms may be likened to neurons. The various force resources at the disposal of a social form might be conceived of as its neurotransmitter molecules. When these are exercised they can cause effects in other social forms. These effects are the powers consequent upon the exercise of force.

Neurotransmitters have either excitatory or inhibitory powers. They cause something to occur or they prevent it. Likewise, the effects of exercises of force may have excitatory and/or inhibitory powers. Campaigns for voter rights in the United States, such as that of Martin Luther King's marches on Selma, Alabama in 1965, involved peaceful force/power dyads exercising force to have the power of increasing the civil rights of African Americans. These campaigns had excitatory powers. President George W. Bush's 2003 invasion of Iraq employed violent force/power dyads to have the power of eliminating Saddam Hussein's regime and, as such, had an inhibitory power. Sometimes both exercises of force may occur concurrently. In an election campaign, for example, the competing parties marshal their forces—money, volunteers, strategy—to both have the power to win for themselves and to defeat their opponents.

Desires and *délires*, resulting in public *délires*, "choreograph"—in the sense of organizing in space and time—force resources so that they may have particular forces. Neurons are arranged in pathways. Force/power dyads are connected in strings, which exhibit "logics." Buying marijuana and then selling it again for a profit is a string with two force/power dyads (buying and selling) that exhibits a capitalist logic. The various force/power dyads in the marches on Selma, Alabama led by Martin Luther King during 1956 were strings whose logic was that of the extension of civil rights. Of course, different strings connect and when they do they produce "webs," strings connected with other strings. Bush's Iraq invasion involved force/powers dyads with strings involving security, military, and intelligence institutions that were linked with strings from economic institutions that supplied the military institutions with the force resources they needed, thus weaving a web exhibiting logics of the production and reproduction of violence.

So the structural reism of CSR is about structuring of force and power, positing that different social forms are parts of force/power dyads connected in strings strung into webs. Metaphorically, the movements of the stars in the night sky are the result of these webs of force and power. So for the time being, the work to be done is to accumulate scientific knowledge to explain the forces and powers immanent in the strings and webs of stars and constellations in the dark night of actuality. Attention now turns to considering what to do with such knowledge, which is about getting critical.

Getting Critical

> The philosophers have only interpreted the world, in
> various ways. The point, however, is to change it.
> —Karl Marx, "Theses on Feuerbach"

Knowledge may be used to maintain existing social forms, or to change them. Much social thought has been about the problem of order: figuring out what the order is (usually some form of exploitative inequality) and devising ways of keeping it that way. Ghassan Hage has said, "Critical thought is not 'radical' thought" (2012: 285). He is certainly correct. Kant, for example, was a critical theorist, and for him getting critical meant analyzing the utility of a faculty of knowing or body of knowledge, by discovering for the limits imposed on it by the fundamental it employed.

However, Robert Ulin (1991) noted two traditions of critical thought co-occur in anthropology; one influenced by political economy and the other by postmodernism. CSR's standpoint derives from the political economy position, in which getting critical is being radical. Specifically, it is influenced by Max Horkheimer and Theodor Adorno, whose position was itself an elaboration of Marx's view expressed above. The US government budgeted about $65 billion on military research (OMB 2014) to devise ways to defend the existing social order. Critical anthropology is applied anthropology putting science in service of acquiring knowledge to change the world. Of course, some things do not need altering, while others do. Critical anthropology's job is to help decide what needs change and how to do it.

Horkheimer helps in understanding what things in social being need alteration, with his remark, "The chief aim of" critical science "is to prevent mankind from losing itself in those ideas and activities which the existing organization of society instills into its members" (Horkheimer 1937). This is, as Adorno put it, because society is an "immense concentration of economical and administrative power [that] leaves the individual no more room to maneuver" and that leads "toward totalitarian forms of domination" (Adorno 1998: 298). Adorno and Horkheimer were writing of "society" just prior to World War II. There are those today who warn that the United States is moving toward totalitarianism (Wolin 2008) and fascism (Hedges 2006). In CSR, human being is a space–time of structures of force and power, and it is these that determine the direction of human being.

So, what Horkheimer and Adorno were saying is that the enormous concentrations of power in current capitalist and state institutions create an "elite" category of class actors, with mammoth amounts of force giving them power to make their "ideas" become public *délires* (laws, executive orders, administrative decree, etc.) to arrange the actions of ordinary persons. It is as if elites played God and arranged a slow, totalitarian pavane across the night sky. But the situation today is worse than in Adorno and Horkheimer's time, because in the sky are the vultures of economic dysfunction, ecological calamity, and global warring, born of the elite's operation of structures of force and power.

Under such a nighttime sky, critical anthropology has two chores. The first is the analysis of structures of force and power to know the points of entry in order to change them. The second concerns elites' ability to steal into peoples' brains and manipulate their minds so that they desire what is in elite interest. Such controlled desire may be said to be hermetically sealed into ordinary folks' emotions and perceptions of what is and procedures of what to do about it. Hermetic seals may not be 100 percent, but they certainly exist and are effective for many people.

Radical critical anthropology is a tool for learning where to concentrate intervention for arranging the galaxy of human being in ways that better benefit all such being. This may seem like a utopian chore. It certainly is one beyond the limited epistemic capabilities of postmodern critical anthropology, with its rejection of science. If you abjure science, your knowledge of what is will be frail, and you cannot know what to do about what is if you are ignorant of it. Time now to consider the essays and how they help make the case for a critical structural realism.

The Essays

Starry Night's text is divided into three parts. The first addresses the question of epistemology, the second applies CSR's ontology, and the third offers critical judgments. The following essay (Chapter 1) is "Literary Anthropology and the Case against Science."[6] It opens the epistemological part and makes a case for a scientific epistemology by documenting the frailties of antiscience opposition. This opposition includes scholars, variously termed literary or postmodern anthropologists. Postmodernity repudiates grand narratives (Lyotard 1984) and is skeptical of truth-seeking practice (Rorty 1991).[7] Given the latter attribute of postmodern thought, how could they possibly know that all grand narratives were to be rejected? Moreover, so sweeping a generalization of rejection is, ironically, a grand narrative of antigrand narratives, placing postmodern anthropologists in the position of being a local expression of the anti–grand narrative.

Clifford Geertz might be said to have been postmodern anthropology's iconic founder, with his *Interpretation of Cultures* (1973) and *Local Knowledge* (1983) providing a doctrinal base and the articles collected in James Clifford and George Marcus's *Writing Culture* (1986) offering amplification of the original doxa. Perhaps, the postmodernists' central tenet is that a people's culture is "an ensemble of texts" (Geertz 1973: 452), which meant that their epistemological job was "penetrating" the "literary text" (ibid.: 448). Penetrance was to be achieved through the observational prick of "thick description" (ibid.) (which was actually participant observation developed by Boasians and social anthropologists in the first half of the twentieth century). While thick description can be a powerful observational tool, it is not practiced in an especially scientific manner in postmodern anthropology due to indifference to truth-seeking techniques, for example seeking to ensure the representativeness of observation.

Chapter 1 contributes to this debate by exploring the grounds for taking antiscience positions. It does so by posing, and answering, two questions: first, whether there have been critiques of science so compelling as to warrant its rejection; and, second, whether more powerful modes of knowing have been revealed. Literary anthropologists', hermeneutic philosophers', and certain postpositivist philosophers' antiscience arguments are examined in the text, which concludes that none of these arguments compel the elimination of science. Further, the essay argues that the thick description alternative to science exhibits properties of gossip; and while he said, she said accounts can be entertaining, they are not especially useful for discovering the truths of things. Science, as indicated earlier, does not provide absolute, true knowledge. Far from it, investigators have to work long and hard to establish approximate truths. However, it remains the most formidable epistemological practice humans have, which justifies keeping it as the epistemological blade of CSR's jackknife.

While scientific theory has been tabooed within certain regions of anthropology, there has actually been little consideration of what has been prohibited. Chapter 2, "What Is Theory? Something, Time-Being, Art," offers an interpretation of such theory. The approach, though using elements of thought from the Vienna Circle, is postpositivist. Science is considered an art. Art is about creation. Science creates theory. Theory creation occurs through practices of theorizing and validating.

Theorizing is the crafting of generalization necklaces that explain, and understand, the way *istheit* appears to be. There is discussion of explicitness, scope, abstraction, and relationship formation in theoretical practice. Validating is the inspection of generalization necklaces to judge whether their explanation of *istheit* can be judged to exhibit some approximate truth. Here, the discussion considers the roles of fact and observation as well as those of objectivity, representativeness, and intersubjectivity in validating. In the chapter, we understand the theorist as a hero creating re-presentations of being that have the beauty of being approximately true.

Recall that the stars, constellations, and galaxies trace a pavane across the hours of the night sky. The second part applies CSR's ontology to formulate an understanding of social dynamics—a view, if you will, that explains the dance in the night sky. The part consists of a single essay, "Dialectics of Force: Contradiction, Logics, and Conservations of *Délires.*" It considers E-space structures. Recall that these are treated ontologically as organizations of force and power. These display logics of order or disorder. This E-space ontology, then, is put in service of a new "dialectics of force" theory of change dynamics, raising the question: what is this theory? This question is answered by suggesting that a dialectical theory does the job.

Of course, if one proposes to think dialectically, one needs to appraise the desirability of employing Hegelian dialectics. The essay makes just such an assessment and concludes that Hegel's dialectics are an animistic ghost story. Two problems are signaled as problematic. First, Hegelian contradiction is judged a conceptual blur. Second, its dialectics have a realization problem, in the sense that they lack a credible theory of how the effects of contradictions are realized in structural change. Consequently, the essay offers a "gang of four" (Hobbes, Hume, Nietzsche, and Godelier) reconceptualization of contradiction. It, then, formulates a realization theory based upon notions of individual and social reflexivity, hermeneutic politics, public *délires,* and conservation of *délires.* This theory encourages the conclusion that up there in the night sky, among the constellations of human being, the stars of E-space are moved by contradiction between plays of force in logics of disorder versus those of order.

The final part of the text contributes to the critical part of CSR. It contains two essays. To set the stage for the first of these, "Right and Might" consider that Foucault, in a number of publications, made clear that humans were not so much actors as subjects; specifically, they were subjected to the "effect" of different powers, which in modernity were often disciplinary (1977, 1982).[8] Foucault was saying that elites exercise their force to have the power of subjectification, transforming the many into the subjects of the mighty. What is to be done?

Many things, but critical among these is revelation, in the sense of revealing subjectification. Revelation is recommended because the elites do not send their subjects formal announcements to the effect, "Dear Sir/Madame, on Thursday last week you were subjectified." Consequently, a condition of releasing people from elite thrall is knowing they have been enthralled. A notion of hermeneuts is helpful in producing such knowledge. Hermes was the Greek god who brought messages from the gods on high to ordinary folk. The Greek gods are gone, replaced by their brethren "hermeneuts": (amply) rewarded media leaders (journalists, scholars, "experts") who inject economic and political elites' *délires* into ordinary blokes, the better to infect such subjects with elite delirium. Discovery of hermeneuts reveals those who subjectify.

"Right and Might" illustrates this point by taking up the case of one hermeneut, Professor Clifford Geertz. This might seem outrageous. He was, and remains for many, a champion who exorcised positivist demons, winning through to the bright light of cultural interpretation. "Right and Might" tells a different story of a hermeneut who brought elite *délires* from on high to anthropological subjects. Geertz's first research had been conducted on Indonesia. Grim massacres had occurred there in 1965–1966, the work of Indonesian military elites, who butchered 500,000 persons.

Of course, the generals who did the massacring offered a moral judgment legitimating their *délire*-ious work. Geertz in his *After the Fact* (1995) presented a view of these massacres that artfully legitimated the military's *délires*. So it might be said that he was in the business of communicating to ordinary readers the *délires* of mighty Indonesian generals. "Right and Might" makes a general point that discovering hermeneuts is an important part of a critical discipline, because it helps explain how elites transform people into their subjects. Attention now turns to the second essay in the critical part.

At least since the origin of the state, it has been a world of perpetual war. Permanent peace has seemed a dream. However, Immanuel Kant (1795) during the Enlightenment suggested that democratic states did not war with each other. The policy implications of this were immense. If all states became democratic, war would cease, making perpetual peace possible. Kant's view, accepted by many liberal political thinkers, is today known as democratic peace theory. In contemporary times, it has formed part of the rationale for warring, with President George W. Bush making his wars to bring democracies to bring peace. The second essay in the critical part, "Perpetual Peace?" applies critical science to examine democratic peace theory.

It is established in the essay that since the end of World War II the United States has made war frequently throughout the global. This is a global warring. When the structures of force and power of US "democracy" are examined, they reveal an imperial social being, an informal one based upon capitalism. Consequently, a theory is formulated, called "global warring theory" (GWT) to explain Washington's bellicosity. The theory explains global warring in terms of reproductive fixes, due to contradictions, that involve creation and implementation of public *délires*. The theory is validated with evidence from twenty-four US wars between 1950 and 2015. It is argued that global warring does not relax imperial contradictions and that insistence upon democratic peace theory as a way to eliminate war is dreaming—while the world marches onward to the sixth global extinction. The problem is capitalist empires.

Vultures Again

At the beginning of this introduction, three vultures of destruction soared in the night sky—ecological calamity, economic dysfunction, and global warring. There may be others out there; who knows? But the three we know about are no joke. Can critical structural realism assist in struggling against them? CSR works with science, which, after all is said and done, is the best epistemic practice humans have for knowing realities.

It applies science in a structural reist ontology pursuing knowledge of two structural possibilities. The first knowledge is of structural disordering and involves discovering forces with powers to create the three vultures. In particular, it examines those elites who are the vultures' myrmidons—pleasuring themselves at the expense of everyone else. It seeks to know the forces these elites have, how they exercise them, the better to know how to oppose them. The second knowledge is of structural ordering and involves learning how to organize. Its goal is information of the forces needed to articulate organizations into a complex system of systems spanning the globe satisfying human wants equally in a sustainable manner. Why not try CSR? The alternative might be that those vultures of destruction get their way, leaving starry nights with fewer stars because the galaxies of human being went missing.

Notes

1. Hegel, for example, proclaimed all sorts of speculations upon the nature of being (being he never observed); which is, perhaps, why his *geist* is a phantasmagoric form of animism presented as modernist ontology (as argued in Chapter 5).
2. Some may find the use of a German term for "being itself" pretentious. There was an English candidate: "Is-E-Tude." Unfortunately, it provoked in hearers the flapping of stiff upper lips indicating irrepressible guffaws.

3. Haecceity glitches due to preexisting conceptual biases are predictable when some-thing utterly new is observed. Consider, for example, when a boy—ignorant of bi-ological facts—performs certain manipulative acts culminating in his first seminal emission. Mazel tov! But he has no idea what he just did, though he is preloaded with concepts informing him that squirting fluids, save for urination, is not the way his penis works. Biased by this knowledge, he classifies the new pleasant sensation as the result of having "broken" something.

4. The notion of sensational hooks resembles Carnap's concept of reduction sentences (1936–1937), which were statements containing information about how the reality re-ferred to in a concept might be observed.

5. Holbraad, Pedersen, and Viveiros de Castro (2014) provide an introduction to the ontological turn. Descola's *Beyond Nature and Culture* (2013) is worthy of attention.

6. This chapter was originally published in *Man* (n.s.) 29 (1994): 555–82.

7. Ward (1996) provides a useful account of postmodern, including actor-network the-orists' attempts to challenge truth seeking. Critically, these attempts do not confront, and consequently cannot refute, various epistemologists' defenses of truth-seeking.

8. "Right and Might" was originally published in *Identities* 4–3, no. 4 (1998): 431–65.

References

Adorno, Theodor. 1998. *Critical Models: Interventions and Catchwords.* New Columbia Uni-versity Press.

Althusser, Louis and Etienne Balibar. *Reading Capital.* London: New Left Books, 1970.

Bandyk, Matthew. "Is Unemployment the Worst since the Great Depression?" *US News.com,* June 2, 2009, accessed June 2, 2015. http://money.usnews.com/money/business-econ omy/articles/2009/08/27/is-unemployment-the-worst-since-the-great-depression.

Baudrillard, Jean. *Simulacra & Simulation.* Ann Arbor: University of Michigan Press, 1994.

Boas, Franz. *General Anthropology.* Boston: Heath, 1938.

———. 1940. *Race, Language, and Culture.* New York: The Free Press.

Bunnin, Nicholas and Jiyuan Yu. *The Blackwell Dictionary of Western Philosophy.* Oxford: Blackwell, 2004.

Carnap, Rudolf. "Testability and Meaning." *Philosophy of Science* 3, no. 4 (1936): 419–47.

———. "Testability and Meaning—Continued." *Philosophy of Science* 4, no. 1 (1937): 1–40.

Clifford, James and George Marcus. *Writing Culture: The Poetics and Politics of Ethnography.* Berkeley: University of California Press, 1986.

Comte, Auguste. 1975. *Auguste Comte and Positivism: The Essential Writings,* ed. Gertrud Lenzer. New York: Harper Torch Books

Crystal, David. *The English Language,* 2nd ed. London: Penguin, 2002.

Deleuze, Gilles, and Felix Guattari. 1983. *Anti-Oedipus: Capitalism and Schizophrenia.* Min-neapolis, MN.: University of Minnesota Press.

Descola, Phillipe. *Beyond Nature and Culture.* Chicago: University of Chicago Press, 2013.

Fetzer, James, and Robert Almeder. 1993. *Glossary of Epistemology/Philosphy of Science.* New York: Paragon House.

Foucault, Michel. *Discipline and Punish.* Translated by Alan Sheridan. New York: Pantheon, 1977.

———. "The Subject and Power." *Critical Inquiry* 8, no. 4 (1982): 777–95.

Geertz, Clifford. *The Interpretation of Culture.* New York: Basic Books, 1973.
———. *Local Knowledge: Further Essays in Interpretive Anthropology.* New York: Basic Books, 1983.
———. *After the Fact: Two Countries, Four Decades, One Anthropologist (The Jerusalem-Harvard Lectures).* Cambridge: Harvard University Press, 1995.
Goodenough, Ward. 1981. *Culture, Language, and Society.* Menlo Park, CA: Benjamin Cummings.
Harvey, David. *A Brief History of Neoliberalism.* Oxford: Oxford University Press, 2005.
Hedges, Chris. 2006. *American Fascists: The Christian Right and the War on America.* New York: The Free Press.
Holbraad, Martin, Morten Axel Pedersen, and Eduardo Viveiros de Castro. "The Politics of Ontology: Anthropological Positions." *Fieldsights—Theorizing the Contemporary, Cultural Anthropology Online,* 13 January 2014, accessed 1 June 2015. http://www.culanth .org/fieldsights/462-the-politics-of-ontology-anthropological-positions.
Horkheimer, Max. (1937) 1972. "Traditional and Critical Theory." In *Critical Theory: Selected Essays of Max Horkheimer.* New York: Bloomsbury Academic.
Jessop, Bob, Neil Brenner, and Martin Jones. "Theorizing Sociospatial Relations." *Society and Space* 26 (2008): 389–401. DOI: 10.1068/d9107.
Kant. Immanuel. (1781) 1991. *Critique of Pure Reason.* London: J.M. Dent and Sons.
———. (1795) 2007. "Perpetual Peace: A Philosophical Sketch." In *Kant, Political Writings.* Cambridge: Cambridge University Press.
Latour, Bruno. *Reassembling the Social: An Introduction to Actor Network Theory.* Oxford: Oxford University Press, 2005.
Lucretius. 2007. *The Nature of Things.* New York: Penguin.
Lyotard, Jean-François. *The Postmodern Condition: A Report on Knowledge.* Minneapolis: University of Minnesota Press, 1984 [1979].
Marx, Karl. "Theses on Feuerbach." 1845. *Marxist Internet Archive,* accessed 2 June 2015. https://www.marxists.org/archive/marx/works/1845/theses/theses.htm.
Morgan, Lewis Henry. (1877) 1985. *Ancient Society.* Tucson: University of Arizona Press.
OMB [Office of Management and Budget]. "Special Topics: Analytical Perspectives." *Budget of the United States Government, Fiscal Year 2015.* Washington DC: Office of Management and Budget, 2014, accessed 26 September 2015. https://www.whitehouse.gov/ sites/default/files/omb/budget/fy2015/assets/topics.pdf.
Pereboom, Derk. "Kant's Transcendental Arguments." In *The Stanford Encyclopedia of Philosophy,* edited by Edward N. Zalta. http://plato.stanford.edu/archives/fall2014/ entries/kant-transcendental.
Poster, Mark. *Critical Theory and Post-Structuralism: In Search of Context.* Ithaca: Cornell, 1989.
Pullman, Bernard. *The Atom in the History of Human Thought.* Oxford: Oxford University Press, 1998.
Radcliffe-Brown, A.R. 1952. *Structure and Function in Primitive Society.* Glencoe, IL.: The Free Press.
Rorty, Richard. *Objectivity, Relativism, and Truth: Philosophical Papers,* vol. I. New York and Cambridge: Cambridge University Press, 1991.
Rosenkrantz, Gary. *Haecceity: An Ontological Essay.* Dordrecht: Springer, 1993.
Sahlins, Marshall. Forward. In *Beyond Nature and Culture,* edited by Phillipe Descola, xi-xiv. Chicago: University of Chicago Press, 2013.

Scotus, Duns. *Duns Scotus: Philosophic Writing, A Collection*. Indianapolis: Hackett, 1987.

Smith, Adam. *The Wealth of Nations*. New York: Modern Library, 1937 [1776].

Tylor, Edward Burnett. (1871) 1958. *Primitive Culture, Part 1: The Origins of Culture*. New York: Harper.

Ulin, Robert. "Critical Anthropology Twenty Years Later, Modernism and Postmodernism in Anthropology." *Critique of Anthropology* 11, no. 1 (1991): 63–89.

Urry, John. "The Complexity Turn." *Theory, Culture and Society* 22, no. 5 (2005): 1–14.

Wallace, Walter. *The Logic of Science in Sociology*. Chicago: Aldine, 1971.

Wallerstein, Immanuel. 1974. *The Modern World System I: Capitalist Agriculture and the Origins of the European World Economy in the Sixteenth Century*. New York: Academic Press.

Ward, Steven. *Reconfiguring Truth: Postmodernism, Science Studies, and the Search for a New Model of Knowledge*. Lanham: Rowman and Littlefield, 1996.

Weber, Max. *Economy and Society: An Outline of Interpretive Sociology*. New York: Bedminster Press, 1968.

Woleński, Jan. "Reism." In *The Stanford Encyclopedia of Philosophy*, edited by Edward N. Zalta. http://plato.stanford.edu/archives/sum2012/entries/reism.

Wolin, Sheldon. 2008. *Democracy Incorporated: Managed Democracy and the Specter of Inverted Totalitarianism*. Princeton; Princeton University Press.

Žižek, Slavoj. *Living in End Times*. London: Verso, 2011.

PART I

Epistemology

Literary Anthropology and the Case against Science

Literary anthropology arose in the late 1970s and 1980s. Most would agree that major figures in this project have been the contributors to the influential text *Writing Culture: The Poetics and Politics of Ethnography* (Clifford and Marcus 1986), including James Clifford (1988), Vincent Crapanzano (1992), George Marcus and Michael Fischer (1986), Paul Rabinow (1977), Renato Rosaldo (1989), and Steven Tyler (1987). These gentlemen were in certain ways enabled by Clifford Geertz, whose collected essays in *The Interpretation of Cultures* (1973) and *Local Knowledge* (1983) became something of a Vulgate. A central canon of these essays was that because people's culture is like "an ensemble of texts" (Geertz 1973: 452), cultural analysis must proceed as if it were "penetrating" the "literary text" (ibid.: 448).[1]

Clifford claims that literary anthropologists "draw on recent developments in the fields of textual criticism, cultural analysis, semiotics, hermeneutic philosophy, and psychoanalysis" (1986: 4). These diverse developments have taken a postmodern turn, which makes literary anthropologists believe themselves to be a vanguard of postmodernism in anthropology. Because "postmodern" has been defined as "incredulity toward metanarratives" (Lyotard 1984: xxiv), and because science is a vast epistemological metanarrative—the modern story of the stories of how people know—it is not surprising that many literary anthropologists repudiate science. Tyler, for example, announces that "the postmodern world is a post scientific world" (1987: 211), one in which "scientific thought is now an archaic mode of consciousness surviving for a while yet in a degraded form" (ibid.: 200). This is the topic of this article. How appropriate is it to reject science as degraded? Before proceeding, however, it might be useful to have some idea of the nature of science.

Approach

The view of science I shall present is influenced by Richard Miller's postpositivist *Fact and Method* (1987). I begin by offering an opinion about art. Art, among other things, is a creative, imaginative representation of experience. Science is an art. Like other art forms it is a manner of representing experience. The experience it represents is that of reality. Two goals of the art of science are to understand how and why reality is constituted as it is and to understand how well it is known how and why reality is constituted. Practices that contribute to the attainment of the former goal involve explanation, while those that contribute to the latter goal involve validation. At its most elemental science is explanation, and validation of explanations, concerning reality.

Where there is debate, and there is extremely lively debate, is over the nature of explanation and validation. For example, some believe that Hempel's deductive–nomothetic covering law model (hereafter D–N) is the only form of explanation, even though Hempel himself believed there to be other forms, such as probabilistic explanation (1966: 54–59).[2] Certain characteristics of explanation and validation are discussed below. Explanation involves the formulation of sentences, or propositions, containing concepts that are related to each other. For example, one might state a proposition that "the more a person occupies a prestige position, the greater that person's appearance of objectivity." This proposition consists of two concepts, *prestigious persons* and *aura of objectivity*, that exhibit a positive relationship between each other.

Sets of propositions that are high in abstraction and generality may be said to be theories. It is such propositions that are generally termed "laws." Sets of propositions that are relatively low in abstraction and generality may be said to be empirical generalizations or hypotheses. The related concepts in the sentences of theories, empirical generalizations and hypotheses, are representations of how and why reality is constituted. A value of explanation is that relatively few laws can cover (i.e., represent) enormous realms of reality.

It is through different practices of validation that the accuracy of explanation is tested.[3] It should be understood that the validation that occurs in science is a relative validation, which means that the type of truth arrived at is an approximate truth (Miller 1987: 177).[4] An explanation may be said to be approximately true and validated relative to other existing explanations if it conforms to the norms of simplicity, correspondence, and greater relative correspondence. A theory exhibits simplicity if it has been demonstrated to be more parsimonious than its rivals (Hempel 1966: 40–41). Parsimony refers to the number of concepts and the relationships between the concepts, as well as to the complexity of these relationships and concepts in a theory. The fewer the concepts and relationships, and the less complex they are, the greater the theory's parsimony.

A theory conforms to a norm of correspondence if the predictions or retrodictions formulated "on the basis of the theory are in fact fulfilled" (Kaplan 1964: 313). The concepts and the relationships between the concepts in a theory assert that something will, or did, go on in reality. These assertions are predictions or retrodictions. Observations are experiences of what does, or did, go on. They are the *facts*. If what is observed to occur corresponds to what is theoretically supposed to occur, then the theory *fits the facts*. The theory is not true if it has been shown not to fit the facts; it is not falsified if it has been shown on at least one occasion not to fit the facts. However, the more facts a theory fits in the absence of counterfactual observations, the greater its adherence to the norm of correspondence.

The notion of greater relative correspondence resembles Miller's (1987) and Feyerabend's (1984) approaches to validation. For both, validation is never that of a single theory and always that of alternative explanations of the same realities. This means that theories are always judged against other theories. It is a question, therefore, of a relative validation. A theory that accounts for more observations while encountering fewer counterfactual observations than its alternatives is of greater approximate truth than its rivals. Such relatively greater verisimilitude means that it better satisfies the norm of greater relative correspondence.

The view of science just presented is postpositive in at least two senses. First, science is not concerned with the production of what is universally true but with the construction of what is approximately true—explanations that last only until the imagination and creativity of scientists construct truer explanations. Second, the methods of science are not uniform. Rather, each scientific discipline relies upon the creativity and imagination of its practitioners to be able to craft its own validation procedures to arrive at approximately true explanations. If one rejects science, one rejects the art of explaining, and validating the explanation, of the experience of reality.

Prudent thinkers might be persuaded to reject science provided that two questions had been answered. The first of these is whether criticisms of science are compelling. The second is whether there is another, more powerful mode of knowing than science, so that investigators might turn to a replacement that would help them to address reality more adequately than has science. If the criticisms of science are valid, there is reason to be dubious about scientific metanarratives, and if there is a more powerful epistemology, then it is appropriate to abandon science.

Definitive answers to these two questions in all realms of inquiry would be a gargantuan task. I propose to consider the plausibility of certain literary anthropologists' attacks upon science. Further, certain of these anthropologists have suggested that the case against science has been made by philosophical hermeneutics and a relativist philosophy of science. I shall explore some of these critiques. Finally, an analysis will be made of *thick description*, suggested by some literary anthropologists to be an alternative to science in the sociocultural realm.

When Lyotard (1979) defines the postmodern as "incredulity toward metanarratives," he announces a postmodern skepticism. This essay suggests that the views of literary anthropologists extend well beyond skepticism to a doctrine that might be termed "Panglossian nihilism."

Literary Anthropology and the Case against Science

Literary anthropologists, though emphatic that they disapprove of science, do not devote large portions of their texts to arguing this view. Clifford, for example, in *The Predicament of Culture* (1988), offers no explicit arguments against science. Similarly, readers of Crapanzano's *Hermes' Dilemma and Hamlet's Revenge* (1992), subtitled *On the Epistemology of Interpretation,* a heading that promises the consideration of questions of knowing, discover that science plays no extended role in his arguments.[5] A review of the literature, however, suggests that there have been three general positions assumed by literary anthropologists when they reject science. The first of these is illustrated by Clifford Geertz.

Geertz was recently interviewed by Richard Handler about his life's work. At one point the two men discussed what Geertz refers to as the "science thing" (Handler 1991: 607). Geertz confides, "I never really bought it, but I entertained the idea—even tried to do it once in a while ... but gave it up" (ibid.: 608). In another part of this same discussion, Geertz says, "I came out of a nonscientific background," again divulging "and I never did buy this stuff" (ibid.: 607).

Geertz gave up science because he did not buy it. No other reasons are offered throughout the interview for repudiating science. The slang expression "to buy" something means "to believe" it. Geertz did not believe the "science thing" and so he rejected it. This is the first of the antiscience positions advanced by literary anthropologists. Science is simply dismissed without grounds.

It might be objected that this dismissal of science occurred in an interview during which Geertz was speaking only informally. Consider, then, the assertion made on the opening page of *Local Knowledge* that there was a "growing recognition" that science "was not producing the triumphs of prediction, control, and testability that had so long been promised in its name" (1983: 3).[6] In this case it appears that there is reason to dismiss science. After all, there was "growing recognition" that science was "not producing." Now social science may, or may not, have been working prior to 1983. However, *Local Knowledge* marshals no systematic and compelling evidence—in fact, it assembles no evidence—bearing upon the absence of prediction, control, and testability for a single study.

Possibly, when Geertz said that there was "growing recognition" that science was "not producing," he was alluding to a body of scholars who had made such discoveries. Yet these thinkers are not named. Their evidence is not presented. So there is no way of assessing whether, in fact, they had unequivocally demonstrated Geertz's point. Readers of *Local Knowledge* are led to believe that there was reason to reject science. However, the reason for making such a rejection is simply asserted, again without grounds.[7]

There is a second antiscience position that is illustrated by consideration of certain arguments of Renato Rosaldo. Rosaldo does appear in *Culture and Truth* to criticize a major aspect of science: its claims to objectivity, for he says, "This book argues that a sea change in cultural studies has eroded once-dominant conceptions of truth and objectivity" (1989: 21). My analysis of Rosaldo's treatment of objectivity begins by presenting his understanding of a major actor in debates over objectivity. Next, it offers the substance of his views concerning objectivity. Finally, it presents the terrain over which debates have actually swirled in the last four hundred years when scholars considered questions of objectivity.

Max Weber, at the turn of the twentieth century, introduced the question of the possibility of objectivity to the social sciences. As Mannheim observed, Weber was quite clear that there are "social conditions which are requisite to the genesis' of values, and that these values influence analysis" (Mannheim 1936: 81). This committed Weber to the belief that, "there is no absolutely 'objective' scientific analysis of culture … or … of 'social phenomena' independent of special and 'one-sided' viewpoints" (1968: 85).

Rosaldo is aware that "discussions of objectivity in the human sciences ritually invoke Max Weber as their founding ancestor" (1989: 169). He further asserts, "The Weberian tradition has legitimated research programs that attempt, in the name of value-free inquiry, to clarify the world rather than change it" (ibid.: 172). This statement implies that Weber—as founder of this tradition—believed in the possibility of value-free inquiry, which we have just seen was not the case. So, readers should recognize that Rosaldo does not appreciate the complexity of Weber's approach to objectivity.[8] Thus they might be on their toes concerning his own treatment of the topic.

Since objectivity is never formally defined in *Culture and Truth,* its meaning must be inferred from its usage in the text. At one point Rosaldo asserts, "Such terms as *objectivity, neutrality* and *impartiality* refer to subject positions once endowed with great institutional authority" (1989: 21, emphasis in the original). The notion of a *subject position* goes undefined in *Culture and Truth,* but it seems to refer to a social position, such as that of a professor or a student. Impartiality and neutrality are used in ways that suggest them to be similar in meaning to objectivity. If this is indeed the case, then perhaps what Rosaldo is implying is that social positions were endowed with objectivity. For example, there is the opinion, now in some disrepute, that professors are objective.

Later in the text Rosaldo announces, "I have argued that during the classic period … norms of distanced normalizing description gained a monopoly on objectivity" (1989: 48). His "classic" period was that of twentieth century anthropology prior to postmodernism. The "norms" he refers to were those of a writing style, which he terms "distanced normalizing," that "prescribed, among other things, the use of the present tense to depict social life ... and the assumption of a certain distance that purportedly conferred objectivity" (ibid.: 48–49). This second usage of objectivity resembles the first, in that it asserts that a style may be endowed with objectivity.

What Rosaldo seems to be suggesting in these two usages is that objectivity refers to thoughts and sentiments of impartiality or neutrality that can be provoked in people by certain social positions or styles. People who accept the impartiality of a person believe in that person's credibility. Thus, when Rosaldo analyzes objectivity, he is concerned with the conditions that confer credibility.

Almost four centuries ago, Francis Bacon, in *Novum Organum*, said, "The human mind resembles those uneven mirrors which impart their own properties to different objects ... and distort and disfigure them" (qtd. in Durant 1926: 143). Such distortions, Bacon believed, were due to idols. The archaic term "idols" might be glossed as "biases," and Bacon argued that these arose from different causes. One of the idols was produced by the marketplace. Here biases derived "from the commerce and associations of men with one another. For men converse by means of language, but words are imposed according to the understanding of the crowd" (ibid.: 145). If the phrase "the understanding of the crowd" is understood to be a precursor of the notion of *cultural values*, then Bacon's view that there are idols of the marketplace is a realization that values impose bias.

Objectivity is normally defined in science as the property of a proposition or a method that "accurately reflects ... phenomena that exist independently of our beliefs about them" (Boyd, Gasper, and Trout 1991: 779). Bacon posed the question of whether objective knowledge of the world was possible, even though thought is biased, and decided that it could be achieved through observation. Cambridge Platonists at the time disagreed with him, and their disputations might be said to have begun modern debates over objectivity.

Whether objectivity is possible has been vigorously contested throughout the twentieth century. Weber, as noted earlier, introduced this debate to the social sciences. Cunningham considered, and argued against, the pre-1970s antiobjectivist positions (1973). Hesse (1980) argued on different grounds a similar position. Brown, in *Observation and Objectivity* (1987), made a case for the possibility of objectivity, even though he accepted certain antiobjectivist premises. Recently, Greenwood has sought to demonstrate that objective classification and explanation are possible even though actions and practices are socially constituted (1990a: 196). *Culture and Truth* appears unfamiliar with these pro- and antiobjectivist positions, for they are not discussed in the text.[9]

The following conclusion may be drawn, given the preceding. When Rosaldo informs his readers that he will argue that objectivity has "eroded," his audience could assume that he is using the normal, scientific understanding of objectivity and that he is concerned with an epistemological matter, that of whether propositions can accurately reflect phenomena independently of beliefs about them. This, we have seen, is not the case. Rosaldo's topic is social psychological in nature and not epistemological. He is interested in the generation of thoughts and feelings that make something appear credible, that is, objective.

Rosaldo has nothing to say about objectivity for the simple reason that he is not talking about it. This, then, is a second antiscience position exhibited by literary anthropologists, one in which it appears that there is a case against science, though they really have nothing to say because they are addressing some other topic.

Certain pronouncements of Tyler as well as Rabinow and Sullivan illustrate a third antiscience stance adopted by literary anthropologists. Tyler asserts that science's practitioners think of it as a "game" (1987: 201) that has now "failed" but which continues to be played in a "degraded" state (ibid.: 200). Let us explore this claim of degradation. It is important to realize that the text from which this assertion is taken contains no analysis that unambiguously and explicitly details (1) what is degraded in science, (2) how much it is degraded, and (3) what the evidence is for the two previous assertions. In effect, Tyler says that science is degraded because it is. The philosopher Engel reminds us that the fallacy of begging the question "is to assume the point in dispute" (1981: 106). President Coolidge committed this fallacy in announcing that "When large numbers of people are out of work, unemployment follows." Tyler does the same when he asserts that science is degraded, because it is.

There is, however, a far more disturbing peculiarity of Tyler's position. He pushes his readers to accept his views by attributing emotionally malign qualities to opposing views. Tyler does not want you to accept science, because it is a "game" that has "failed" and is "degraded." Such a form of argumentation might be called that of *deceptive emotive emphasis,* because it uses words to convey feelings about arguments so that one accepts a conclusion on emotive grounds, regardless of its empirical or logical status. One rejects degraded things—like corpses and science—because they smell bad.

Tyler pursues this same form of argumentation later in the same essay when he characterizes "scientific rhetoric" as "inappropriate," "empty," "ridiculous," "simpleminded," and an "absurdity" (1987: 207). This is an argument by deceptive emotive emphasis that relies on what might be considered a form of echolalia. This latter is a literary device that involves repetition of words, or syllables in words, to achieve an echo effect. In this instance, by repeating in the short space of a single paragraph pejoratives such as "ridiculous" and "simpleminded," Tyler sets echoing in readers' minds feelings that science is not good. However, arguments that proceed by begging the question or by deceptive emotive emphasis are fallacious (Kaplan 1964).[10]

There is an additional problem with Tyler's handling of science. For example, in the essay just considered he says that a scientific investigation provides a representation of the world, while an ethnography—which he contrasts with and greatly prefers to science—provides an "evocation of the same reality" (1987: 200). A few pages further on he explains to readers why he prefers evocation to representation, announcing, "The whole point of 'evoking' rather than 'representing' is that it frees ethnography from mimesis and that inappropriate mode of scientific rhetoric which entails 'objects,' 'facts,' 'descriptions,' 'inductions,' 'generalizations,' 'verifications,' 'experiments,' 'truth,' and like concepts" (ibid.: 207). Regardless of the fact that Tyler again begs the question and does not demonstrate to readers why "objects," and so on, are inappropriate, what is important for the purpose at hand is his understanding of science that the quotation just presented reveals.

Consider first whether science seeks validation and truth. Rudolf Carnap, a logical positivist and arguably the most influential interpreter of science in the first half of the twentieth century, said in the 1930s, "If verification is understood as a complete and definitive establishment of truth then a universal sentence, for example, a so-called law … can never be verified, a fact that has often been remarked" (1953: 480). Carnap says that by the 1950s it had "often" been made clear that scientific practices did not seek to verify truths. There is no evidence that Tyler had, or has, any familiarity with the work of Carnap, Popper (1935), Lewis (1934), or Nagel (1934) that developed this position.

The claim that the adequacy of science depends upon a particular rhetoric might also be questioned. Rhetoric is "the deliberate exploitation of eloquence for the persuasive effect in public speaking or in writing" (Baldick 1990: 188). In the quotation from Tyler cited earlier, he states that there is a "scientific rhetoric which entails 'objects,' 'facts,' 'descriptions,' 'inductions,' 'generalizations.'" The contention that activities that result in the establishment of facts, descriptions, inductions, and generalizations are "deliberate" exploitations "of eloquence" is nonsensical. The propositions of an induction may be offered with considerable rhetorical fanfare. However, the persuasive effect of these statements depends upon whether canons of inductive or deductive logic have been appropriately applied and not upon their rhetorical ornamentation. Tyler has confused the communication of scientific practices with the practice. Such a representation of science is a misrepresentation of it.

Finally, the declaration that science is mimesis deserves scrutiny. Tyler defines mimesis in one place as "representations" (1987: 26) and in another place as "thinking as representation" (ibid.: 164). *Representation* goes undefined. However, it is possible to provide examples of common denotata of the term.

A statue of a woman is a representation of her, as are poems to her, paintings of her, and scientific theories of her gender. However, statues, paintings, poems, and theories are different from each other.

In short, the concept of mimesis as representation has enormous substantive scope, broader than that of science. But Tyler simply asserts that science is a form of mimesis. He adds no other information relevant to science and science alone. This is like defining economics as a part of culture, without explaining what it is that is economics. So Tyler's readers lack the information needed to distinguish the theory of a woman from a picture of one.

Tyler's case against science is made by begging the question, by arguments that convince by deceptive emotive emphasis, and, as has just been shown, by offering an understanding of science that is either incorrect or inexact. Thus Tyler's arguments are directed not at science but at a straw figure.

Attention now turns to Rabinow and Sullivan and their treatment of objective science. In the introduction to their *Interpretive Social Science: A Second Look* (1987), they appear to confront science directly. They announce that "the nineteenth century's conception of logical, cumulative progress through a purely objective science … has been progressively undermined" (ibid.: 4). A point might be made about the subject of Rabinow and Sullivan's deconstruction. The subsection of the introduction in which their critique of science is contained is titled "The Deconstruction of the Positivist Idea of Science." Thus what they are concerned with is a particular idea of science, specifically a positivist one. Some equate positivism with science, but though the concept is a broad one, this usage is incorrect. Rather, it is a particular body of doctrine about science. Rabinow and Sullivan tell their readers that what they are exercised about is the conception by the *logical positivists* of the *Comtean ideal* (ibid.: 10), but their arguments are directed against a particular attempt to explain and understand science.

There is a venerable lineage of philosophies of science ascending in generations from contemporary postpositivists to the logical positivists, from the logical positivists to Comte and earlier Kant, from Kant to Locke and other empiricists, from Locke to Bacon, and eventually winding from Bacon back to Aristotle in the ancient world. The growth in this lineage has resulted from later evaluations of earlier scientific paradigms. Bacon, for example, encouraged the forging of modern conceptions of science by railing against medieval philosophies of science that relied too much upon Aristotelian deduction.

However, and this is critical, science is science and not necessarily what philosophers may think it to be. This means that while the existence of problems with a particular philosophy of science—for example, logical positivism— may imply that there are difficulties understanding science, these problems imply nothing necessarily about the properties of science itself. This means that actually Rabinow and Sullivan offer no criticism of science per se. With this understood, let us explore whether Rabinow and Sullivan raise cogent questions concerning science itself when they make their case against the Comtean ideal.

Rabinow and Sullivan debate the Comtean ideal in the fourteen paragraphs that compose the "Deconstruction of the Positivist Idea of Science" section.[11] Their argument can be expressed in six propositions and begins with four propositions about logical positivism:

1. Logical positivism had an ideal of a "unified science" that included the natural and human sciences (1987: 10).
2. Logical positivism inclined human scientists to "formal models" (ibid.: 11).
3. The "cultural world could not meet this norm" (ibid.).
4. The structuralisms of Piaget and Lévi-Strauss were representatives of this logical positivist "project" (ibid.).

Then a fifth proposition is added, specifying a problem with these structuralisms. This problem is expressed in a quotation that Rabinow and Sullivan take from Ricoeur:

5. Structuralism "seals its formalized language off from discourse, and therefore from the human world" (Ricoeur, qtd. in Rabinow and Sullivan 1987: 12).

Finally, from the fifth proposition, Rabinow and Sullivan draw a sixth conclusion, which is that structuralism is:

6. "A high price indeed for the science of man" (1987: 12–13).

The crux of their position appears to be that structuralism does not seem able to account for certain types of phenomena, those involving the cultural world. Whether this is correct is debatable. However, even if it were true, the conclusion of their argument does not seem to follow from their premises. In effect, they contend that because a particular brand of science cannot account for certain types of phenomena, it follows that logical positivism, the Comtean ideal, and science are undermined. However, there is nothing in their first five premises that warrants such a conclusion.

Further, whether or not a particular science is successful is irrelevant to whether or not philosophies of science or science itself are correct. To insist upon this is like asserting that because Ptolemaic theory does not account for planetary motion or logical positivism, positivism and science are no longer credible. Such a position is based on a fractured logic. The inappropriate logics, the question begging, the deceptive emotive emphases, and the fuzzy straw figure arguments of Tyler, Rabinow, and Sullivan constitute a third, antiscience position of the literary anthropologists. This is one in which—as opposed to the two previous positions—there are actual assaults on science. However, they are specious.

Bluntly put, literary anthropologists have not made a cogent case against science. However, their works include references to certain hermeneutic philosophers, such as Richard Rorty, and philosophers of science, such as Thomas Kuhn, who have commented upon science and have perhaps pursued a more vigorous prosecution of the case against science. So it is to the hermeneutic philosophers that attention now turns.

Hermeneuticists and science

> *No one would dream of putting in doubt the immanent*
> *criteria of what we call scientific knowledge.*
> (Gadamer 1987: 111–12).

Among the different positions that hermeneuticists have adopted vis-à-vis science, three stand out, none of which is too menacing. In fact, the first position, far from attacking science, insists that interpretation is a variant of science. This view, of course, is that of Wilhelm Dilthey, who believed that interpretation was performed by the human sciences and, as is communicated by the title of one of his chapters, that "The human sciences form an independent whole alongside the natural sciences" (1989: 56).

This stance is also that of Jurgen Habermas. His project, characterized as a "struggle for the soul of science" (Wellmer 1974: 53), formulated a theory of *cognitive interests* in *Knowledge and Human Interests* (1972). These interests, according to Held, "give rise to the conditions for the possibility of three sciences: the empirical-analytic, the historical-hermeneutic, and the critical" (1980: 255–56). Habermas does dislike positivism. However, it should be remembered that positivism is not science, and there is certainly no insistence in Habermas that science is degraded. Nor is there any demand that it should defer to hermeneutics, for the latter is but one of people's scientific interests.

The doctrine that interpretation is a form of science has also been argued in the literary world by Hirsch. In *Validity in Interpretation* (1967), Hirsch set himself the task of demonstrating that "the much advertised cleavage between thinking in the sciences and the humanities does not exist" (1967: 264). This was because "the hypothetico-deductive process is fundamental to both of them" (ibid.). Hirsch accepted the "hypothetico-deductive" method, and he believed that he had used it, in the words of Madison, to establish "the basis of a science of interpretation" (1988: 3).

A second position that hermeneuticists have advanced concerning science is the opposite of the first, that is, that science is a form of interpretation. Such a thesis is entertained by Gadamer in *Truth and Method* (1975); at least this seems to have been his intent when he said, "Understanding must be conceived as a part of the process of coming into being of meaning, in which the significance of all statements—those of art and those of everything else that has been transmitted—is formed and made complete" (ibid.: 146). I interpret the phrase "everything else" to include science. Thus, science, along with everything else, is part of a dynamic of coming into understanding.

Gadamer hopes, then, to subsume science within interpretation. However, according to one commentator, Gadamer, by doing this, intended "not so much to attack science as to defend history, art and other forms of humane knowledge" (Weinsheimer 1985: 26). This explains why he is careful to inform his readers that science offers a "certainty" (1975: 446) and that "no one would dream of putting in doubt the immanent criteria of what we call scientific knowledge" (1987: 112). What Gadamer appears to mean by the "immanent criteria" of science are the canons of scientific methodologies.[12]

However, Weinsheimer (1985) reports that Gadamer devoted little effort to digesting either works of science or those of philosophers of science, so that his ability to actually understand these immanent criteria is limited. Gadamer does suggest "that ... the use of scientific methods does not suffice to guarantee truth" (1975: 446). Though he is quick to add immediately, "This does not mean a diminution of their scientific quality" (ibid.). Of course, as already noted in our discussion of Tyler, this was a similar view to that held by the logical positivists, suggesting—at least with regard to the question of the possibility of truth—that Gadamer's position resembled that of the foremost advocates of science.

We now discuss an American pragmatist in the largely continental hermeneutical community, Richard Rorty. In a major evaluation of Rorty's work, Taylor suggested that Rorty has argued "a new thesis of the unity of science," to wit that "all sciences are equally hermeneutic" (1980: 46). Rorty, at least in 1980, accepted this construction of his position (1980: 39). This acceptance meant that he, too, accepted Gadamer's contention that science is a form of interpretation.

Rorty has said some contentious things about "a demise of foundational epistemology" in *Philosophy and the Mirror of Nature* (1979: 311), and because epistemology was read by many to mean "science," it was believed that Rorty had argued in favor of a demise of science. This was not the case. Rorty's opponents were, as he himself states, realist philosophers who advocated a "representationalist problematic" (1991: 12). Further, close reading of *Philosophy and the Mirror of Nature* suggests, as Roy Bhaskar observes, that Rorty actually accepted a Hempelian version of logical positivism (1990: 199). Bhaskar shows in addition that Rorty believed that this scientific methodology was "in order and correct" and "compatible with the possibility of Geisteswissenschciften" (ibid.: 197).[13] In short, Rorty believes that "there is nothing wrong with science, there is only something wrong with attempts to divinize it, the attempt characteristic of realistic philosophy" (Rorty 1991: 34).

There is a third point of view that hermeneuticists have entertained concerning the relationship between interpretation and explanation. It acknowledges that there are two different modes of knowing but rejects the view that there is any "epistemological dichotomy" between the two (Strasser 1985: 31). Rather, it insists that they are interrelated. Perhaps the most influential proponent of this view is Paul Ricoeur, who communicated it to an English-speaking audience in the early 1970s in his essay "The Model of the Text" (1971).[14] Ricoeur expresses the relationship between explanation and interpretation as one of a "dialectic," insisting that the "status of hermeneutics is that defined by the very dialectic between these two attitudes" (1981: 36), that is, those of scientific explanation and hermeneutic understanding.

Rabinow and Sullivan represent Ricoeur's position as one that could not be "farther from positivist orthodoxy" (1987: 9). Ricoeur certainly has little interest in positivism; however, Rabinow and Sullivan seem unaware that such a position is not incompatible with an appreciation of science. Ricoeur, for example, characterized his efforts in *Hermeneutics and the Human Sciences* as attempting to "take another step in the direction of this reconciliation between explanation and interpretation" (1981: 161). Further, Ricoeur says that one of the "epistemological concerns of hermeneutics" is to be "scientific" (ibid.: 44).

A reading of *Hermeneutics and the Human Sciences* suggests that Ricoeur had not done extensive reading in the sciences, that he had done almost no reading in the postpositivist philosophy of science that had been developing rapidly since the 1960s, and, finally, that he hoped hermeneutics could be elevated to the "status" of a science (1981: 44). Thus, even though Ricoeur was not especially knowledgeable about science, he was interested in "reconciliation" between the two modes of knowing and in making hermeneutics "scientific."

The following remarks seem pertinent to the philosophers of interpretation we have just considered. First, when they consider science, it is generally not so much to invalidate it as to place it in some relationship with hermeneutical analyses. Second, they do not appear deeply grounded in either science or the philosophy of science. Third, perhaps because of the preceding observations, all are respectful of science.

Rabinow and Sullivan have said, "The philosophers of interpretation have been important figures in the undermining" of the "Comtean ideal" (1987: 10). The Comtean ideal was, of course, positivistic, and to the degree that positivism asserted that the only valid form of knowledge was scientific, the hermeneuticists have sought to suggest that this is incorrect.[15] However, such a view is compatible with an acceptance of science. After all, as Gadamer said, "no one would dream of putting in doubt the immanent criteria of ... scientific knowledge."

The Relativists and Science

> Science can stand on its own two feet.
> —Paul Feyerabend, *Against Method*

The most cogent evaluation of science has been that of a group of philosophers of science—including Duhem, Quine, Feyerabend, and Kuhn—called "relativists" (Hesse 1980).[16] An understanding of this critique requires familiarity with positivism, with certain specifics of what was rejected in positivism by the relativists, and, finally, with a recent alternative to relativism. This alternative position—advanced in diverse forms by Glymour (1980), Miller (1987), Harre (1986), Suppe (1989), Dretske (1969), Salmon (1989), and Ziman (1978)—is scientific realism (Boyd, Gasper, and Trout 1991: 780).[17]

Before proceeding, however, two points should be clear. The relativists have been opposed to a particular scientific paradigm: logical positivism. However, they further presume that if it were corrected, a science would bloom that "is one of the most wonderful inventions of the human mind" (Feyerabend 1984: 4).

Positivism, as formulated by Comte, was the doctrine that the central methodological notions, especially those of explanation and confirmation, could be applied "according to rules that are the same for all sciences and historical periods" (Miller 1987: 1). The dominant school of positivism in the first half of the twentieth century was logical positivism.[18] Central to logical positivism was the tenet that observation can provide a neutral, that is, objective, means of evaluating theory. Kuhn and Feyerabend "rejected this view" (Suppe 1989: 301). Their arguments against objectivity were complex and involved judgments about whether theory can be confirmed by facts and whether one theory can be shown to be better supported by observation than others. Below I explicate aspects of the relativist antiobjectivism and then present certain realist counterarguments to their position.

Kuhn (1970) and Feyerabend's (1984) case against objectivity is based upon their interpretation of what is known as the Quine–Duhem thesis (Quine 1953; Duhem 1906). This thesis emphasized the supposedly weak links between theory and observation. Such frailty was asserted to result because theories only make contact with observation through a network of connecting, auxiliary theories or hypotheses.

The full implications of the weak theory/observation links will become apparent following explication of the nature of logical positivist theory. A theory involves both enormously general and abstract propositions and others that are less general and abstract. The former propositions, often termed "laws" or "explanatory theories," are composed of abstract and general concepts, called "theoretical terms," which exhibit relationships between each other, and in so doing ultimately specify what the relationships should be between events in the world.

The latter propositions are variously called "exploratory" or "auxiliary" theories or hypotheses, as well as "correspondence rules" (Suppe 1977: 77).[19] Certain concepts in these latter propositions are called "observational terms." Theoretical terms are so abstract as to have no direct observational referents. Observational terms refer to directly observable referents. Correspondence rules and connecting or auxiliary hypotheses specify which observational terms will qualify as being about which theoretical terms. The logical part of logical positivism comes about because exploratory, or auxiliary, theories or hypotheses are deduced from an explanatory theory based in good measure upon which theoretical terms are said to represent which observational terms.

Carl Hempel, as earlier noted, suggested that such a theory follows a deductive–nomological form of explanation (1966). This explanation includes proposition(s) stating what is to be explained, the explanandum (E), as well as those that do the explaining, the explanans (Ln). The explanandum contains an auxiliary theory or hypothesis. There are two types of propositions in the explanans: those consisting of explanatory theories, called "Hempel laws" (Ln), and those called "correspondence rules" or "operational definitions," connecting laws with events that may be observed in reality (Cn). In a deductive–nomological explanation the explanandum is deduced from the explanans, that is, from the laws and correspondence rules that compose it. When this occurs, the laws in the explanans may be said to "cover" what is being explained in the explanandum, in the sense that the latter is logically entailed by the former.

Durkheim's theory of suicide may be expressed in D–N form. The explanans consists of one covering law and three correspondence rules. The covering law is Ll; deviance is inversely related to solidarity.

The correspondence rules are:

> Cl: Suicide is a form of deviance.
> C2: Catholics have higher solidarity.
> C3: Protestants have lower solidarity.

The auxiliary hypothesis in the explanandum is:

> E: Catholics commit suicide less often than do Protestants.

If the propositions in the preceding are correct, then the following syllogism illustrates a D–N explanation of suicide:

L1
Cl. C2. C3 therefore, E

One is now in a position to grasp why observational/theory links might be thought to be weak in such an explanation. Duhem and Quine claimed that such theories only made connections with observations via the network of auxiliary theories, hypotheses, and correspondence rules (Duhem 1906: 187; Quine 1953: 43). This meant they believed that an explanatory theory, that is, a covering law, can always be protected from falsification by the alteration or substitution of auxiliary hypotheses or correspondence rules employed in the derivation of the falsified prediction, or as Quine bluntly put it, "Any statement can be held true …, if we make drastic enough adjustments elsewhere in the system" (1953: 43). If this is the case, then facts cannot confirm theories, because the correspondence rules and auxiliary hypotheses can always be altered to fit the observations, that is, the facts.

For example, it might be the case in the postmodern United States that Protestants no longer commit suicide more frequently than Catholics but that positivists throw themselves off bridges far more often than do hermeneuticists. Such facts would appear to disprove Durkheim's theory of suicide. However, Duhem and Quine might say, "All that needs to be done to sustain the original covering law is to change the auxiliary hypothesis to 'Hermeneuticists commit suicide less than positivists' and the last two correspondence rules to 'Hermeneuticists have higher solidarity' and 'positivists have lower solidarity.'" When this is done, Durkheim's law again covers the facts.

Kuhn and Feyerabend accepted the Quine–Duhem thesis and suggested that it had implications for objectivity. For them the Quine–Duhem thesis meant that all observations were "theory-laden" or "theory-informed." Observation is theory-laden in the sense that what a scientist "sees" is dependent upon what an existing theory directs the scientist to observe. Durkheimians see deviance everywhere. Marxists see exploitation. So a Durkheimian view of civil disturbances might be heavily laden with observations of deviant rioters, while a Marxist's view of the same reality might be equally heavily laden with observations of oppressed revolutionaries. This means that theory biases observation, making objectivity impossible.

If the preceding is correct, Kuhn and Feyerabend argued further, then scientists attached to different theories are obliged to make different observations in support of their theories. Two consequences follow from this claim. The first is that a theory can be confirmed only relative to the observations that apply to it. The second is that if each theory has its own observations by which it is evaluated, then there is no basis for judging contending theories. Theories are, in effect, incommensurable. Such relativist contentions appear to devastate science.

However, largely in the 1970s and 1980s, scientific realists responded and, as the title of one of their works suggests, sought to have *Relativism Refuted* (Siegel 1987). Suppe argues that their work has been so thorough that today the relativists are but "influential relics of the history of the philosophy of science" (1989: 300). The following bears upon the plausibility of Suppe's claim.[20]

First, it must be realized that even if the relativist claims are correct, the implications for scientific praxis—what scientists actually do—are not that great. The Quine–Duhem thesis seemed to imply, as Feyerabend put it, that "theories cannot be refuted by fact" (1984: 113).[21] However, even if this assertion is accepted, it does not mean that one stops evaluating theories in terms of whether what is observed (the facts) conforms to what has been said will be observed (the theory). Quine and Duhem both realized that theoretical knowledge was more dependable if supported by observation and that the more it was supported by fact, the more reliable it was. This means that theoretical knowledge unsupported by observation is unreliable, while such knowledge supported by great bodies of fact is far more reliable, and, of course, one prefers the latter to the former (Ziman 1978). This implies that even if the Quine–Duhem doctrine is judged correct, the canon of logical positivism, the norm of correspondence—that is, that theory must fit the facts (Kaplan 1964: 313)—still guides research.

Similarly, even though competing theories may be incommensurable, it does not mean, according to either Kuhn or Feyerabend, that one stops using evidence to evaluate them. Feyerabend, in fact, actually suggests procedures for formulating new theories on the basis of observations from older ones. He says that scientists might make observations that bear upon an existing theory, dividing these observations into those that support and those that do not support the old theory. Then, on the basis of these facts, a search for a new theory begins with the capacity to account theoretically for both the confirming and falsifying facts of the old theory (Feyerabend 1984: 158–59). Three points should be clear if one follows Feyerabend's procedures: (1) facts are absolutely critical in the evaluation of old and new theories, (2) theories are commensurable in terms of the numbers of confirming and falsifying facts, and (3) there can be theoretical progress because new theories possess fewer false and more supporting facts.

Recently Greenwood, working with a notion of a *developing spiral* of theories formulated by Enc (1976), has suggested "that there is something fundamentally wrong" with the relativist "conception of the relation between explanatory theories and the exploratory theories and other auxiliary hypotheses upon which many observations depend" (1990b: 569–70). He has tried to show how alternative theories are, indeed, tested by observation and are thus commensurable.

In sum, both relativist and scientific realist paradigms regard science as a powerful mode of knowing, which they are concerned with understanding better. Further, it is far from clear that relativist doctrines can be sustained. Rather, their positions are claimed to be relics. However, everyone, including the relativists, insists that theories should be supported by evidence. In fact, both relativists, like Feyerabend, and his critics, like Greenwood, suggest methods for evaluating alternative theories on the basis of observation.

Nowhere in the major texts of literary anthropology is there an extended analysis of the logical positivists, the relativists, or the scientific realists. There is neither identification of the different doctrines that define these approaches nor consideration of their cogency. Literary anthropologists have no idea what the philosophers of science have actually said about science. This means that when Tyler says that science is degraded he does so in ignorance of Feyerabend's claim that "science can stand on its own two feet." It is time now to turn to the second part of the analysis of the case against science and to consider a literary anthropology alternative to science.

Thick Description

> *Anthropologists strive for "thick description."*
> Ohnuki-Tierney, *Culture through Time*

The object of study in literary anthropology is "the web of language, symbol and institutions that constitutes signification" (Rabinow and Sullivan 1979: 4). Understanding this web is a central task of analysis and has been so since Geertz, in *The Interpretation of Cultures,* declared, "Believing with Max Weber, that man is an animal suspended in webs of significance … I take culture to be those webs" (1973: 5). This declaration prompted the question of how one studies culture, and it was in response to this that Geertz first formulated his views concerning thick description.

This Geertz did in the introductory essay to *The Interpretation of Cultures* when he proposed that "the analysis of" culture was "interpretive" (1973: 5), that anthropologists analyze culture through ethnography, and finally that "ethnography is thick description" (ibid.: 9–10). These statements equate thick description with interpretation, which prompts three questions. What precisely is thick description, is it in any way problematic, and to what extent is it Weberian?

Geertz says it is a "sorting out of structures of signification" (1973: 9), which to him "is like trying to read (in the sense of "construct a reading of") a manuscript" (ibid.: 10). Insofar as other literary anthropologists, with a notable exception, have not questioned this definition of thick description, and as it has informed the studies of many both in anthropology and beyond, it may be taken as a fundamental methodological practice of both literary anthropologists and those interested in cultural analysis. The notable exception to this enthusiasm for thick description is Crapanzano, who claims, at least when it is practiced in Geertz's classic essay "Deep Play," that it "offers no understanding of the native from the native's point of view" (1992: 67). I concur with this assessment.

There appear to be two problems with thick description. The first has to do with its vagueness. Geertz said that interpretation "is like trying to read (in the sense of 'construct a reading of') a manuscript" (1973: 10). Consider, for example, the term "reading." Geertz never divulges what he means by a reading. One common understanding of it is as the attribution of meaning to concepts in language X by assigning to them meanings from other concepts in language X. By this definition, call it number 1, the statement "Love is a feeling of caring about somebody" is a reading.

However, Geertz is talking about reading meanings in other cultures. This would imply, as Rabinow suggests it does, that interpretation, insofar as it involves reading, is a "process of translation" (1977: 151). If this is the case, and Geertz is talking about reading as translation, then what is meant by reading is the mapping of the meaning of concepts in language X onto those in language Y. By this definition, call it number 2, the statement "Love is l'amour" is a reading. Definitions 1 and 2 are plausible, nonidentical understandings of reading. Other definitions are entertainable, yet Geertz does not indicate whether he wants readers to do number 1 or number 2, or something else. Thus the nature of reading, or perhaps translation, is left unread, or perhaps untranslated.

Geertz is clear, however, that in a reading one must construct the meanings of natives. Unfortunately, again there is little examination of the notion of construction by Geertz, though it appears for him to involve a "sorting out of the structures of signification" of the natives (1973: 9).[22]

There are two concerns with such a definition of construction. The first is that the notion of structure of signification is enormously complex. There are many types of meanings. So presumably there are many types of structures of signification, and it might have been useful if Geertz had enlightened his readers as to just what sorts of structures of signification he was talking about.

Second, the phrase "sorting out" is not very informative. One's imagination runs riot contemplating different techniques of sorting out signification. Definitions that leave crucial properties unspecified of what they are about may be said to be ambiguous. A definition of construction as undisclosed sortings of unspecified significations would appear to qualify as ambiguous. If thick description involves notions of reading and construction whose meaning is left unclear, then those performing this practice may not know what they are doing when they are constructing a reading. This would imply, as Geertz makes a matter of principle, that thick description "is (or should be) guessing at meanings" (1973: 20).

A second, related problem with thick description has to do with the validity of its attributions of meaning. Again it is Crapanzano who has a helpful insight. He realizes that what Geertz does in "deep play" is to offer "the constructed understanding of the constructed native's constructed point of view" (1992: 67). This suggests that thick description involves readings of readings. These include the following:

> Reading 1: what natives think they mean
> Reading 2: what native informants think the natives mean
> Reading 3: what ethnographers think the informants mean
> Reading 4: what ethnographers think audiences want to know about what natives mean

Geertz acknowledges that thick description involves multiple translations, stating, "Anthropological writings are themselves interpretations, second and third order ones to boot" (1973: 15).

The crucial epistemological question is: does thick description provide analysts with ways of making multiple readings valid? Crapanzano, for his part, believes that Geertz "offers no understanding of the native from the native's point of view" because Geertz's "constructions of constructions appear to be little more than projections or blurrings of his point of view with that of the native" offered in the absence of "specifiable evidence" (1992: 67). This is a serious charge. Anticipating the charge, Geertz's apparent answer to it is "You either grasp an interpretation or you do not, see the point or you do not" (1973: 24). Such a response may be construed in two ways. Either he is asserting that it takes intuition to make reliable interpretations, or he is saying that you "see the point or you do not," but I am not going to explain how this is done. Either construal arrives at the same conclusion. Geertz does not detail in a systematic manner how to arrive at valid interpretations. Therefore, as Abner Cohen states, his attributions of meaning are frequently "conjectural, unverifiable" (1974: 5).[23]

Max Weber, unlike Geertz, believed that "every interpretation strives to achieve utmost verifiability" (1968: 36). Weber meant by verifiability roughly what is meant by validity. Thus for him there were more and less valid interpretations in the sense that there were appropriate and inappropriate attributions of meaning to action. Further, Weber suggested certain procedures involving "verification of interpretation by its results" (ibid.: 37) to evaluate the adequacy of meanings. Essentially, these involved the comparing of observed action, the results, with the attributions of the meaning of the action, the interpretations. If the results are consistent with their interpretation, then verification has occurred.

Though one may not agree with the adequacy of Weber's techniques for achieving validity, the point remains that he believed it worthwhile to establish such procedures. This means that when Geertz informs readers that he is a Weberian, he is only partially correct. Geertz tells his readers that they "will not find very much in the way of 'the theory and methodology of interpretation'" in *Local Knowledge* (1983: 5). Gone from Geertz is a Weberian concern with validity. Below, Tyler's, Rabinow and Sullivan's, and Clifford's views are explored concerning the possibility of valid interpretations.

Tyler suggests that "evocation" (1986: 123) occurs when somebody like Geertz constructs his readings and that perhaps in evocation can be found a way of making accurate interpretations. Normally tropes are used to evoke something. Consider, for example, the fetching conceit "My love is like a red, red rose." Here what is being evoked is love, and this is done by metaphorically saying that it is like a rose.

Tropes describe things not in terms of their own attributes but in terms of other things' attributes. In the example given above, love is not described in terms of what it is, but in terms of what it is not—a plant. Tyler seems to realize this, because he says that what is constructed in such exercises is "an emergent fantasy" (1986: 125), which is "reality fantasy of a fantasy reality" (ibid.: 139). This means that thick description, at least when it is based upon an evocation, appears to be a technique for the construction of meaning in which the denotata of terms are explicitly not those of the native.[24] Such a procedure would appear to hinder discovering valid interpretations.

Tyler appears to accept such a judgment when he says, "The point is not 'what counts as reliable representation of experiences and culture' … The point is the irrelevance of these issues" (1989: 566). This is because he is interested in "poetry" (1987: 202), and poetry in the form of "postmodern ethnography is a cooperatively evolved text consisting of fragments of discourse intended to evoke in the minds of both reader and writer an emergent fantasy of a possible world of common sense reality, and thus to provoke an aesthetic integration that will have a therapeutic effect" (ibid.: 202). "Reliable interpretation" is irrelevant for Tyler because he wants to use thick description to indulge in "fantasy" therapy.

Rabinow and Sullivan, for their part, say, "Ambiguity is an inherent aspect of all interpretation" (1979: 13). This is a strong assertion. "All" interpretation exhibits uncertainty because "the text is plurivocal, open to several readings and several reconstructions" (1987: 13). However, they tell readers, "It is not infinite. Human action and interpretation are subject to many but not indefinitely many constructions. Any closure of the process through external means is violence and often occurs" (ibid.). Some may be relieved to find that, though there are "many" interpretations, these are not "infinite." This raises the possibility that some interpretations are more valid than others, which prompts the question: by what procedures does one arrive at them?

However, Rabinow and Sullivan, like Geertz and Tyler, never offer methods for distinguishing between more and less valid interpretations. Rather, they warn that "external" stopping of interpretation "is violence." What the word "external" might mean here is never specified. Nor is it made clear why the stopping of interpretation might be "violent." Clearly, simply ceasing to interpret the meaning of an action is not violent in the normal sense of the term. So, perhaps they are talking about some metaphorical violence. If they are, their text does not inform readers what this might be. What, however, seems to be implicit in the preceding quotation warning against "closure of the process" of interpretation is that to ward off violence one must keep on interpreting, like a religious person chanting over and over again a magical verse.

Clifford's approach to the question of the possibility of achieving valid interpretation is influenced by his enthusiasm for a passage from Nietzsche in which he asks, "What then is truth?" to which he responds, "[a] mobile army of metaphors, metonyms, anthropomorphisms—in short, a sum of human relations, which have been enhanced, transposed, and embellished poetically and rhetorically, and which after long use seem firm, canonical" (Nietzsche, qtd. in Clifford 1988: 93). Such truth is not about accurate representations or images of beings but about those that just "seem firm." This doctrine of truth was untenable and, as has been noted, Nietzsche himself later repudiated it (Clark 1990; Westphal 1984).

If accepted representations are truth, then Clifford believes, "It is more than ever crucial for different people to form complex, concrete images of one another" (1988: 23). Further, he believes it is the calling of ethnographers to formulate these images in their ethnographies. These should be the result of "a constructive negotiation" (ibid.: 41) between the ethnographer and informants of the Other in which the resulting text will be a "dialogue and polyphony" (ibid.) of interpretive images. Clifford never explains what he means by "negotiation." However, ethnographic representations are not supposed to provide an accurate translation of meaning. This is because "no sovereign scientific method or ethical stance can guarantee the truth of such images" (ibid.: 23), an assertion that seems based more on his admiration for a doctrine disavowed by Nietzsche than on any close analysis of science that he has performed.

In sum, the response to the question "how does one validly interpret?" has been as follows. Geertz says you either get it or you do not. Tyler argues that "reliable" interpretation is irrelevant when your goal is to write therapeutic poetry. Rabinow and Sullivan suggest that it is being "violent" to look for valid methods of interpretation. Clifford is interested in negotiating a polyphony that "seems firm" and whose truth he cannot "guarantee." After investigating the same literature that we have just considered, Spencer concludes that literary anthropology has abandoned "*any* consideration of problems of validation" (1989: 159, emphasis in the original).[25] This rejection of validation by these literary anthropologists is not characteristic of all students of meaning.

Scholars as diverse as Eco (1990), Goodenough (1965), Habermas (1972), Mannheim (1936), Ricoeur (1971: 544–51), and Schutz (1967) have followed Weber in struggling to develop procedures for arriving at valid interpretations. Interpretations arrived at in the absence of validation procedures do not include attempts to discover if they are in conformity with the norms of correspondence or of relative correspondence. This means that such interpretations are not proposed on the basis of evidence. They are "fantasy realities" of what the anthropologist says the informants say the natives say. Plainly spoken, they are gossip. So the literary anthropologist's final product seems to be her or his impressions of Others' gossip. Gellner, perhaps exasperated, called one such discourse "metatwaddle" (1992: 41).

Conclusion

Nihilism is "the doctrine that nothing, or nothing of a specific and very general class exists, or is knowable" (Runes 1942: 210). Literary anthropologists' demands for the repudiation of science, and for its replacement with a thick description innocent of validation, means that they hold a doctrine that allows them to know next to nothing. As a result, theirs is a de facto nihilism. However, it is a special variety of nihilism.

Doctor Pangloss was the character in Voltaire's *Candide* who specialized in talking intellectually pretentious nonsense. Neither the literary anthropologists, hermeneutical philosophers, or relativist philosophers of science have provided compelling critiques of science. This means, as Rorty (1991) said, "There is nothing wrong with science." Further, Geertz proposes to replace science with gossip. Science is not degraded, and gossip is not a substitute for it.

This means that literary anthropologists know little, not because they have shown that little is knowable but because they have chosen, without reason, not to know. Having made such a choice, and hence knowing little, but believing themselves to be an intellectual vanguard, theirs would appear to be a Panglossian nihilism. A danger with nihilism is that it stops practices that lead to the acquisition of knowledge of how to proceed in all realms. A Panglossian nihilism is one that encourages people to proceed not on the basis of knowledge but on that of bombast. It is agents with the power to make the most noise who tend to prevail in such a situation.

Notes

This chapter is dedicated to L.J. Reyna, whose views made it possible. N. Glick Schiller and R.E. Downs have been exacting supporters. Versions of the argument were presented at the New York Academy of Sciences, Brandeis University, and the University of New Hampshire. I am indebted to those who read early drafts and who corrected shortcomings, especially V. Dusek, K. Westphal, and E. Wolf.

1. Literary anthropology was also influenced by V. Turner (1982). There are other anthropologists besides those identified in the essay who might appropriately be called literary, such as Fernandez (1991) and Tedlock (1983). However, the authors of *The Interpretation of Culture and Writing Culture* are those who are frequently said to truly represent literary anthropology. When I refer to literary anthropologists it will be to these authors.

2. Thorton, for example, equates D–N explanation with science when he says, "The scientific, or nomothetic deductive method, achieves explanation through appeal to formulae that are regarded as 'established' through either empirical or logical means" (1992: 19). Miller has argued that ultimately explanation is causal (1987: 60).

3. The terms "confirmation" (Miller 1987) or "verification" (Reichenbach 1953) are often used in place of validation. Kaplan (1964) uses the latter term and I prefer it. This is because, at least in English, the first two terms more strongly connote that a proposition has been confirmed or verified once and for all, which is never the case. The notion of validation includes the sense that a theory may have been validated, though not necessarily universally or absolutely.

4. Miller has propounded explicitly a doctrine of approximate truth.

5. Science is not mentioned in the index of either *The Predicament of Culture* (Clifford 1988) or *Hermes' Dilemma and Hamlet's Revenge* (Crapanzano 1992).

6. It is not clear to what science Geertz was referring when he said it was "not producing." Certainly he was disposed to believe in the failure of scientific anthropology à la Radcliffe-Brown, Lévi-Strauss, Harris, or Goodenough. This disposition was shared by many of his American colleagues in the 1970s and may account for the popularity of his views. However, the failure of particular instances of science is not evidence that science itself is a failure. It is, in fact, evidence of the reverse when explanations of greater approximate truth come to replace those of lesser accomplishments.

7. Geertz's oeuvre is extensive. Nowhere in it does he construct his own compelling critique of science.

8. Exploration of Weber's views concerning values in science can be found in Anderson (1992).

9. Rosaldo does not reference anthropological literature that is favorable to objectivity, for example, Beattie (1984) and Jarvie (1986).

10. Other literary anthropologists have used argument by deceptive emotive emphasis. Rabinow, for example, in a comment upon an essay critical of literary anthropology, implied that those opposed to literary anthropology might be "moral majoritivists" and that the essay's argument was suspect because its author cited a source with connections to "the Brazilian military" (1988: 430). Geertz has said that "many" behavioral scientists have "engaged" in "collective autism" (1973: 57).

11. Actually, their argument occurs in the first eight paragraphs of the "Deconstruction" section. The remaining six paragraphs of the section describe how interpretation

might deal with discourse, action, and understanding and are, thus, irrelevant to the argument.

12. Gadamer does have concerns about the extent to which empirical–analytic science is relevant (Nuyen 1990).

13. Bhaskar's interpretation of Rorty is based upon his reading of passages on pages 347, 356, and 359 of *Philosophy and the Mirror of Nature*.

14. Strasser (1985: 31) suggests that Apel (1976), von Wright (1971), and de Boer (1983) take positions similar to that of Ricoeur, as do the later Dilthey (1989: 31) and Rickman (1980: 311).

15. The assertion that positivism has been undermined has been contested, i.e., by J. Turner (1992), who expresses propositivist sentiments.

16. Relativists are also called postempiricists (Hesse 1980) and neoempiricists (Greenwood 1990b). However, the term "relativist" seems to catch the type of empiricism they propose because of their belief that knowledge and its justification "are accessible only relative to some set of background principles which do not themselves admit of any neutral evaluation" (Siegel 1987: 537).

17. Scientific realism is the view that the subject matter of scientific research and theories exists independently of our knowledge of it and that the goal of science is the description and explanation of both the observable and unobservable aspects of this independently existing world (Boyd, Gasper, and Trout 1991: 780).

18. Logical positivists, prior to World War II, were members of the Vienna Circle. Following the war, most logical positivists were either in the United States, where Nagel and Hempel were major spokespersons, or in England, under the influence of Ayer, Brathwaite, or Popper. Popper and his followers, one of whom was Feyerabend, emphasized that theories were best tested by falsification than confirmation.

19. Correspondence rules are referred to variously in the literature as operational definitions, epistemic correlations, coordinating definitions, and rules of interpretation.

20. Criticism of Kuhn and Feyerabend comes from Hesse (1980: 167–87), Shaphere (1966), and Suppe (1977: 617–49, 1989: 313–54).

21. Carnap had noted in the 1930s, "Even if each single instance of the law were supposed to be verifiable, the number of instances to which the law refers, e.g., the space–time points is infinite and therefore can never be exhausted by our observations which are always finite in number" (1953: 48). This meant that logical positivists did not believe that laws could be verified with facts. Popper, however, insisted that theories could be falsified (1959), and it is this that Feyerabend says is also impossible.

22. Construction appears to have begun as a logical positivist notion (see Carnap 1953). Lutz (1988: 5) and Gergen and Davis (1985: 266), respectively, offer cultural and social approaches to construction.

23. Spencer says that Geertz, on page 30 of *The Interpretation of Cultures*, expends "considerable energy on the problem of the validation of differing interpretations" (1989: 159). My reading of that page is that it offers no procedures for arriving at valid attributions of meaning.

24. I am not asserting that metaphors are irrelevant to culture and society. Fernandez makes it clear that this is not the case (1991).

25. Other studies of literary anthropology have arrived at critical conclusions (see Carrithers 1990; Friedman 1987; Polier and Roseberry 1989; Roth 1989; Sangren 1988; Spiro 1992; Ulin 1991). There has also been support for this kind of anthropology (Pool 1991).

References

Anderson, Perry. "Science, Politics, Enchantment." In *Transition to Modernity: Essays on Power, Wealth and Belief,* edited by John A. Hall and I.C. Jarvie, 187–212. New York: Cambridge University Press, 1992.

Apel, Karl-Otto. *Analytic Philosophy of Language and the "Geisteswissenschaften."* Dordrecht: Reidel, 1976.

Baldick, Chris. *The Concise Oxford Dictionary of Literary Terms.* Oxford: Oxford University Press, 1990.

Beattie, John H.M. "Objectivity and Social Anthropology." In *Objectivity and Cultural Divergence,* edited by Stuart C. Brown, 9–20. New York: Cambridge University Press, 1984.

Bhaskar, Roy. "Rorty, Realism, and the Idea of Freedom." In *Reading Rorty: Critical Response to Philosophy and the Mirror of Nature,* edited by Alan R. Malachowski, 198–232. Oxford: Blackwell, 1990.

Boyd, Richard, Philip Gasper, and John D. Trout, eds. *The Philosophy of Science.* Cambridge, MA: MIT Press, 1991.

Brown, Harold I. *Observation and Objectivity.* Oxford: Oxford University Press, 1987.

Carnap, Rudolf. "Testability and Meaning." *Philosophy of Science* 3, no. 4 (1936): 419–47.

———. "Testability and Meaning." *Philosophy of Science* 4, no. 4 (1937): 1–40.

Carrithers, Michael, Andrew Barry, Ivan Brady, Clifford Geertz, Roger M. Keesing, Paul A. Roth, Robert A. Rubinstein, and Elvi Whittaker. "Is Anthropology Art or Science?" *Current Anthropology* 31 (1990): 263–82.

Clark, M. Nietzsche. *On Truth and Philosophy.* New York: Cambridge University Press, 1990.

Clifford, James. "Introduction: Partial Truths." In *Writing Culture: The Poetics and Politics of Ethnography: A School of American Research Advanced Seminar,* edited by James Clifford and George E. Marcus, 1–26. Los Angeles: University of California Press, 1986.

———. *The Predicament of Culture: Twentieth Century Ethnography, Literature, and Art.* Cambridge, MA: Harvard University Press, 1988.

Clifford, James and George E. Marcus, eds. *Writing Culture: The Poetics and Politics of Ethnography: A School of American Research Advanced Seminar.* Los Angeles: University of California Press, 1986.

Cohen, Abner. *Two-Dimensional Man: An Essay on the Anthropology of Power and Symbolism in Complex Society.* Los Angeles: University of California Press, 1974.

Crapanzano, Vincent. *Hermes' Dilemma and Hamlet's Revenge: On the Epistemology of Interpretation.* Cambridge, MA: Harvard University Press, 1992.

Cunningham, Frank. *Objectivity in Social Science.* Toronto: University of Toronto Press, 1973.

de Boer, Theodorus. *The Foundations of Critical Psychology.* Pittsburgh: Duquesne University Press, 1983.

Dilthey, Wilhelm. *Introduction to the Human Sciences.* Edited by Rudolf A. Makkreel and Frithjof Rody. Princeton: Princeton University Press, 1989.

Dretske, Fred I. *Seeing and Knowing.* Chicago: University of Chicago Press, 1969.

Duhem, Pierre. *La Theorie physique: son objet et sa structure.* Paris: Chevalier and Riviere, 1906.

Durant, Will. *The Story of Philosophy.* Garden City: Garden City, 1926.

Eco, Umberto. *The Limits of Interpretation.* Bloomington: Indiana University Press, 1990.

Enç, Berent. "Spiral Dependence between Theories and Taxonomy." *Inquiry* 19 (1976): 41–71. DOI: 10.1080/00201747608601786.

Engel, S. Morris. *The Study of Philosophy.* New York: Holt, Rinehart and Winston, 1981.

Fernandez, James W., ed. *Beyond Metaphor: The Theory of Tropes in Anthropology.* Stanford: Stanford University Press, 1991.

Feyerabend, Paul. *Against Method.* London: New Left Books, 1984 [1975].

Friedman, Jonathan. "Beyond Otherness: The Spectacularization of Anthropology." *Telos* 71 (1987): 161–70. DOI: 10.3817/0387071161.

Gadamer, Hans-Georg. "Hermeneutics and Social Science." *Philosophy and Social Science* 2, no. 2 (1975): 307–16. DOI: 10.1177/019145377500200402.

———. "The Problem of Historical Consciousness." In *Interpretive Social Science: A Second Look,* edited by Paul Rabinow and William M. Sullivan, 82–140. Los Angeles: University of California Press, 1987.

Geertz, Clifford. *The Interpretation of Cultures.* New York: Basic Books, 1973.

———. *Local Knowledge: Further Essays in Interpretive Anthropology.* New York: Basic Books, 1983.

Gellner, Ernest. *Postmodernism, Reason and Religion.* New York: Routledge, 1992.

Gergen, Kenneth J. and Keith M. Davis. *The Social Construction of the Person.* New York: Springer-Verlag, 1985.

Glymour, Clark. *Theory and Evidence.* Princeton: Princeton University Press, 1980.

Goodenough, Ward H. "Yankee Kinship Terminology: A Problem in Componential Analysis." *American Anthropologist* 67, no. 5 (1965): 259–87. DOI: 10.1525/aa.1965.67.5 .02a00820

Greenwood, John D. "The Social Construction of Action: Objectivity and Explanation." *Philosophy of Social Science* 20, no. 2 (1990a): 195–207. DOI: 10.1177/0048393190020 00204.

———. "Two Dogmas of Neo-empiricism: The 'Theory-Informity' of Observation and the Quine-Duhem Thesis." *Philosophy of Science* 57, no. 4 (1990b): 553–74.

Habermas, Jürgen. *Knowledge and Human Interests.* London: Heinemann, 1972.

Handler, Richard. "An Interview with Clifford Geertz." *Current Anthropology* 32, no. 25 (1991): 603–13.

Harre, R. *Varieties of Realism: A Rationale for the Natural Sciences.* Oxford: Blackwell, 1986.

Held, David. *Introduction to Critical Theory: Horkheimer to Habermas.* Los Angeles: University of California Press, 1980.

Hempel, Carl G. *Philosophy of Natural Science.* Englewood Cliffs: Prentice Hall, 1966.

Hesse, Mary. *In Defense of Objectivity,* 2nd ed. Chicago: University of Chicago Press, 1980.

Hirsch, Eric D. *Validity in Interpretation.* New Haven: Yale University Press, 1967.

Jarvie, Ian C. *Thinking about Society: Theory and Practice.* Dordrecht: Reidel, 1986.

Kaplan, Abraham. *The Conduct of Inquiry: Methodology for Behavioral Science.* San Francisco: Chandler, 1964.

Kuhn, Thomas. *The Structure of Scientific Revolutions,* 2nd ed. Chicago: University of Chicago Press, 1970.

Lewis, Clarence I. "Experience and Meaning." *Proceedings and Addresses of the American Philosophical Association* 7 (1933): 125–146. DOI: 10.2307/1483038.

Lutz, Catherine A. *Unnatural Emotions: Everyday Sentiments on a Micronesian Atoll and Their Challenge to Western Theory.* Chicago: University of Chicago Press, 1988.

Lyotard, Jean-François. *The Postmodern Condition: A Report On Knowledge*. Minneapolis: University of Minnesota Press, 1984 [1979].

Madison, Gary B. *The Hermeneutics of Postmodernity*. Bloomington: Indiana University Press, 1988.

Mannheim, Karl. *Ideology and Utopia*. New York: Harcourt, Brace and World, 1936.

Marcus, George E. and Michael M.J. Fischer. *Anthropology as Cultural Critique: An Experimental Moment in the Human Sciences*. Chicago: University of Chicago Press, 1986.

Miller, Richard W. *Fact and Method: Confirmation and Reality in the Natural and Social Sciences*. Princeton: Princeton University Press, 1987.

Nagel, Ernest. "Verifiability, Truth and Verification." *Journal of Philosophy* 31, no. 6 (1934): 141–48. DOI: 10.2307/2015426.

Nuyen, A.T. "Truth, Method, and Objectivity: Husserl and Gadamer on Scientific Method." *Philosophy of the Social Sciences* 20, no. 4 (1990): 437–52. DOI: 10.1177/0048393190 02000402.

Ohnuki-Tierney, Emiko. *Culture through Time: Anthropological Approaches*. Stanford: Stanford University Press, 1990.

Polier, Nicole and Roseberry William. "Tristees Tropes: Post-modern Anthropologists Encounter the Other and Discover Themselves." *Economy and Society* 18, no. 2 (1989): 245–64. DOI:10.1080/03085148900000012.

Pool, Robert. "Postmodern Ethnography." *Critique of Anthropology* 11, no. 4 (1991): 309–33. DOI: 10.1177/0308275X9101100402.

Popper, Karl. *Logik der Forschung*. Vienna: Springer, 1935.

———. *The Logic of Scientific Discovery*. London: Hutchinson, 1959.

Quine, Willard Van Orman. *From a Logical Point of View: 9 Logico-Philosophical Essays*. Cambridge, MA: Harvard University Press, 1953.

Rabinow, Paul. *Reflections on Fieldwork in Morocco*. Los Angeles: University of California Press, 1977.

———. "Comment on 'Rhetoric and the Authority of Ethnography: "Postmodernism" and the Social Reproduction of Texts' by P. Steven Sangren." *Current Anthropology* 29, no. 3 (1988): 429–30.

Rabinow, Paul and William Sullivan, eds. *Interpretive Social Science: A Reader*. Los Angeles: University of California Press, 1979.

———. *Interpretive Social Science: A Second Look*. Los Angeles: University of California Press, 1987.

Reichenbach, Hans. "The Verifiability Theory of Meaning." In *Readings in the Philosophy of Science*, edited by Herbert Feigl and May Brodbeck, 93–102. New York: Appleton-Century-Crofts, 1953.

Rickman, H.P. "Science and Hermeneutics." *Philosophy of the Social Sciences* 20, no. 3 (1980): 295–316. DOI: 10.1177/004839319002000302.

Ricoeur, Paul. "The Model of the Text: Meaningful Action Considered as a Text." *Social Research* 38, no. 3 (1971): 529–36.

———. *Hermeneutics and the Human Sciences*. New York and Cambridge: Cambridge University Press, 1981.

Rorty, Richard. *Philosophy and the Mirror of Nature*. Princeton: Princeton University Press, 1979.

———. "A Reply to Dryfus and Taylor." *Review of Metaphysics* 34, no. 1 (1980): 39–47.

————. *Objectivity, Relativism, and Truth: Philosophical Papers,* vol. I. New York and Cambridge: Cambridge University Press, 1991.

Rosaldo, Renato. *Culture and Truth: The Remaking of Social Analysis.* Boston: Beacon Press, 1989.

Roth, Paul A., Michal Buchowski, James Clifford, Michael Herzfeld, P. Steven Sangren, David Sapire, Marilyn Strathern, and Stephen A. Tyler. "Ethnography without Tears." *Current Anthropology* 30, no. 5 (1989): 555–69.

Runes, Dagobert D. *The Dictionary of Philosophy.* New York: Philosophical Library, 1942.

Salmon, Wesley C. "Four Decades of Scientific Explanation." In *Scientific Explanation,* 3–219. vol. 13. Minneapolis: University of Minnesota Press, 1989.

Sangren, P. Steven. "Rhetoric and the Authority of Ethnography: 'Postmodernism' and the Social Reproduction of Texts." *Current Anthropology* 29, no. 3 (1988): 405–35.

Scheffler, Israel. *Science and Subjectivity.* New York: Bobbs-Merrill, 1967.

Schutz, Alfred. *The Phenomenology of the Social World.* Evanston: Northwestern University Press, 1967.

Shaphere, Dudley. "Meaning and Scientific Change." In *Mind and Cosmos,* edited by Robert Garland Colodny [np]. Pittsburgh: Duquesne University Press, 1966.

Siegel, Harvey. *Relativism Refuted.* Dordrecht: Reidel, 1987.

Spencer, Jonathan. "Anthropology as a Kind of Writing." *Man* 24 (1989): 145–64. DOI: 10.2307/2802551.

Spiro, Melford E. "Cultural Relativism and the Future of Anthropology." In *Rereading Cultural Anthropology,* edited by Enrique Mayer and George E. Marcus [np]. Durham: Duke University Press, 1992.

Strasser, Stephen. *Understanding and Explanation: Basic Ideas Concerning the Humanity of the Human Sciences.* Pittsburgh: Duquesne University Press, 1985.

Suppe, Frederick, ed. *The Structure of Scientific Theories.* Urbana: University of Illinois Press, 1977.

————. *The Semantic Conception of Theories and Scientific Realism.* Urbana: University of Illinois Press, 1989.

Taylor, Charles. "Understanding in the Human Sciences." *Review of Metaphysics* 34 (1980): 25–38.

Tedlock, Dennis. *The Spoken Word and the Work of Interpretation.* Philadelphia: University of Pennsylvania Press, 1983.

Thorton, Robert J. "The Rhetoric of Ethnographic Holism." In *Rereading Cultural Anthropology,* edited by George E. Marcus, 15–31. Durham: Duke University Press, 1992.

Turner, Jonathan. "The Promise of Positivism." In *Postmodernism and Social Theory,* edited by Steven Seideman and David G. Wagner, [np]. Oxford: Blackwell, 1992.

Turner, Victor. "Dramatic Ritual/Ritual Drama: Performance and Reflexive Anthropology." In *From Ritual to Theatre: The Human Seriousness of Play.* New York: Performing Arts Journal Publications, 1982.

Tyler, Stephen A. "Post-modern Ethnography: From Document of the Occult to Occult Document." In *Writing Culture: The Poetics and Politics of Ethnography,* edited by James Clifford and George E. Marcus, 122–40. Los Angeles: University of California Press, 1986.

————. *The Unspeakable: Discourse, Dialogue, and Rhetoric in the Postmodern World.* Madison: University of Wisconsin Press, 1987.

————. 1989. "Comment on 'Ethnology without Tears,' by Paul A. Roth." *Current Anthropology* 30, no. 5 (1989): 566–67.

Ulin, Robert C. "Critical Anthropology Twenty Years Later: Modernism and Postmodernism in Anthropology." *Critique of Anthropology* 11, no. 1 (1991): 63–89. DOI: 10.1177/0308275X9101100104.

Wacquant, Loic J.D. "Toward a Reflexive Sociology: A Workshop with Pierre Bourdieu." *Sociological Theory* 7, no. 1 (1989): 26–63.

Weber, Max. "'Objectivity' in Social Science." In *Readings in the Philosophy of the Social Sciences,* edited by May Brodbeck [np]. New York: Macmillan, 1968.

Weinsheimer, Joel C. *Gadamer's Hermeneutics: A Reading of Truth and Method.* New Haven: Yale University Press, 1985.

Wellmer, Albrecht. *Critical Theory of Society.* New York: Seabury Press, 1974.

Westphal, Kenneth R. "Was Nietzsche a Cognitivist?" *Journal of the History of Philosophy* 26, no. 3 (1984): 343–63. DOI: 10.1353/hph.1984.0042.

Wright, G.H. von and Hennik Georg. *Explanation and Understanding.* London: Routledge and Kegan Paul, 1971.

Ziman, John M. *Reliable Knowledge: An Exploration of the Grounds for Belief in Science.* Cambridge and New York: Cambridge University Press, 1978.

chapter two

What Is Theory?

Something, Time-Being, Art

> *In the room the women come and go.*
> *Talking of Michelangelo.*
> —T.S. Eliot, "The Lovesong of J. Alfred Prufrock"

I—a stately plump anthropologist nearing my "use by" date—bustle about the rooms where anthropologists perform their rituals of conferences, workshops, and symposia. There people come and go, talking, not of Michelangelo, but of theory. They do so because theory is "the core," don't you know (McGee and Warms 2000: iii). But their conversations are flat—like a glass of Chateau Latour without the bubbles. A goal of this essay is to craft CSR's understanding of scientific theory, arguing its virtues to anthropology. This approach seeks to eliminate a dualism between art and science. Theory is an art! To develop this view, it will be necessary to tramp through fields of theorizing and validating to discover the sense of five notions: something, time-being, art, representation, and, finally, theory. The essay is not *the* last word about theory. It merely seeks to inject a few bubbles back in conversations in rooms where anthropologists come and go, talking theory.

Something: Time-Being and Human Being

Recall that Immanuel Kant, hero of modern idealism, proclaimed in *Critique of Pure Reason,* "If I remove the thinking subject, the whole material world must at once vanish because it is nothing but a phenomenal appearance in the sensibility of ourselves as a subject, and a manner or species of representation" (1781: 383A). I will return later to "representation," but contemplate the generality Kant asserts: remove the thinking subject and the material world is gone. The old idealist concedes there is a material world.

What is this world? It is the "thing-in-itself" (*ding an sich*), *noumena*, reality. Recall in the introduction that we termed reality *istheit*. Earlier in his text Kant had confided, "Reality is *something*" (1781: 207, emphasis in the original). Why not reconceptualize the "thing-in-itself" as "something": the better to emphasize that reality (being), of which we know only its "phenomenal appearance," is something—out there.

However, there is more to something than just being, and the conduct of a thought experiment helps clarify what this is. Return to the trope of the starry night introduced in the introduction. Put yourself there on a clear, starry night. It is a marvelous spectacle. Remember the stars as different kinds of being, with the galaxies and constellations different regions of roughly similar sorts of being. Over there, high in the sky is chemical being; down low on the horizon is geological being. As the night continues the constellations pinwheel across the sky—before, they were here; after, they were there. Reality happens over time. So it is appropriate to remember that being is something occurring between X and Y times. "Something," so conceptualized, is always for the time-being. Anthropologists doing theory might be envisioned as stargazers whose art is that of a particular way of representing particular regions of time-being—that of the human something. In order to know more of this, representation and art are conceptualized.

Western thinkers have been aware that humans make representations since the times of Plato (2000), who distrusted them, and Aristotle (1998), who believed them to be a distinctive human activity. The approach adopted here is more Aristotelian. Representation became a debated topic when Richard Rorty (1979) declared that since the seventeenth century philosophers have had an insalubrious fixation on representation as the mind operating like a mirror reflecting (i.e., representing) reality. I understand it differently, as literally any re-presenting of being in some other form for some end. One goal of re-presentation is aesthetic, which brings us to the topic of art. Different arts have different aesthetics. Music takes something of sound and re-presents it as melodies and harmonies. Painting takes something of color and shape and re-presents them as compositions. Music seeks aural beauty. Painting seeks visual beauty.

Art is not the elegant commodity that the rich purchase to hide their moral seediness. Art is sweaty, best done in sturdy work boots. It is practices at the forge of creation: the craftsperson at work—creating something from something else. Art practice is the hammer of creation pounding against the anvil of obdurate something, re-presenting it for the time-being as something with beauty. Theory, from this standpoint, is a representational art of something for the time-being. Anthropological theory is a representational art for the time-being of humanity at all times and all places. Certain basics of the theoretical art are explored below.

Theory as Scientific Practice

> *Science is at no moment quite right, but it is seldom quite wrong,*
> *and has, as a rule, a better chance of being right than the theories of*
> *the unscientific. It is therefore rational to accept it hypothetically.*
> —Bertrand Russell, *The Problems of Philosophy*

We will consider the above quotation at the end of this section, but allow me to state the view I argue: the hammer of theory is scientific practice. The insistence that theory is about science may provoke projectile counterassertions, such as Steven Tyler's in the influential *Writing Culture*, that "scientific thought is now an archaic mode" that has already "succumbed" (1986: 123). If science is dead, it certainly gives new meaning to the phrase the "dead weight of theory," which makes it important to discover how it is possible to claim that science has "succumbed" and why this is untrue.

The Science Grudge Match

Tyler never explained why he believed science was dead. Perhaps, however, his judgment resulted from battles over science that began in the late 1950s pitting proscience against antiscience pugilists. There have been two rounds of science battles.[1]

Round 1 began in the late 1950s, following publication of C.P. Snow's *Two Cultures* (1959), in which he announced that two cultures of sciences and humanities had emerged and dominated twentieth-century intellectual life. He further declared that the two cultures lacked an understanding of each other (an understatement) and—taking the scientific side—suggested humanists indulged fascist tendencies, pointing to the Nazi flirtations of Yeats, Pound, and Wyndham-Lewis. This was scandalous, and within a few decades humanists would be declared not fascist but leftist. Nevertheless, Snow was a persuasive gentleman, and it might be said that round 1 of the match went to science.

Round 2 was a real grudge match, crowding everybody into the ring with an antipathy toward science—especially social and philosophical thinkers. There have been four general sorts of grudge holders: postpositivist philosophers of science, postmodernists, science studies folks, and feminists. The judgments of postpositivist philosophers of science—importantly Willard Quine, Hilary Putnam, Thomas Kuhn, and Paul Feyerabend—were made by scholars with expertise in induction, logic, and particular branches of science. Postmodern views on science come from philosophers—including Francois Lyotard, Jean Baudrillard, Richard Rorty, and Gilles Deleuze and Félix Guattari—with greater expertise in the humanities than science. Postmodernists tend to deny "the possibility of truth" (Lyotard 1984) because they see it as "either meaningless or arbitrary" (Culler 1982: 22).

Science studies, influenced by the postmodernists, have been performed importantly by Barry Barnes, David Bloor, Steven Shapin, and Bruno Latour. Important feminist positions on science were formulated by Sandra Harding and Evelyn Fox Keller. These brawlers landed telling blows. Scientific knowledge was shown to be less absolute than had been argued by positivists from Auguste Comte to the Vienna Circle. Certainly, science is deeply influenced by social phenomena, which limits its objectivity. Equally certainly, one aspect of this influence is that it has been a patriarchal enterprise. So Tyler might be excused following round 2 if he surmised that science was out for the count. But he was wrong!

Noretta Koertge assembled a group of authors who found "flaws" (1998) with the denigration of science, while Paul Boghossian claimed that none of the science critiques "uncovered powerful reasons for rejecting" it (2006: 131). Moreover, since the 1990s the criticisms of science have themselves been critiqued. Imre Lakatos and Larry Laudan, respectively, defended science as the evolution of what they termed research "programs" or "traditions." More recently Susan Haack, Philip Kitcher, John Zammito, Paul Boghossian and Alan Sokal, and Jean Bricmont have provided more technical defenses of science.

Consider that some supposed critiques of science are simply not critiques. Kuhn's epochal *The Structure of Scientific Revolutions* (1970) is not an argument against science but an argument in support of a particular understanding of how scientific changes occur through paradigm shifts. Sandra Harding wrote in *The Science Question in Feminism* that science's "modes of defining research problems and designing experiments, its way of constructing and conferring meanings are not only sexist but also racist, classist, and culturally coercive" (1986: 9).

However, a reading of both Harding and Evelyn Fox Keller suggests that they believe a feminist science would remove these maladies. As Keller put it, one cannot ignore "the undeniable successes of science" (1995: 11). Harding and Keller appear not so much against science as against nonscientific social and cultural factors that inhibit its performance. Similarly, certain science studies grandees do not see themselves as antiscience. Rather, they see themselves as providing a scientific understanding of science itself, one that seeks to "honor science by imitation" (Barnes, Bloor, and Henry 1996: viii). We now discuss the postpositivist philosophers of science.

They have been the heavyweights in the antiscience battle and have advanced three general criticisms of science. The first of these is the thesis of underdetermination of theory by evidence, associated with Quine, reviving Pierre Duhem's older position, which argued that the content of scientific theory was always greater than its empirically confirmable consequences, which implied that theories, however well tested, were never absolutely validated. Quine's thesis has not gone unchallenged (Leplin 1997: 153–63; Kitcher 1993: 250; Boghossian 2006: 119–22). Significantly, the thesis does *not* argue that there is anything wrong with validation per se. What it does assert, against the positivism of those like Auguste Comte, is that validation is never absolute. A theory is only as true as the evidence bearing upon its validation; hence, it is never absolutely true. Consequently, even if the thesis of underdetermination is accepted, its implications are this: a validated theory is truer than an unvalidated one—so validate on, because the more a theory is validated, the greater its approximation of the truth.

A second critique of science has been Thomas Kuhn's and others' views on the incommensurability of paradigms. This is the position that different scientific paradigms often cannot be understood in terms of each other. Kuhn's paradigms were composed of theories, and he was claiming, If one cannot conceptualize two theories using the same concepts (i.e., they are incommensurable), then the theories cannot be comparatively validated, which means that it is not possible to know which is the more validated theory, and hence the truer one. This position has been criticized (Weinberg 2001: 196–97; Boghossian 2006: 120–25; Sokal 2008: 191–97). A point of this criticism is the appreciation that theories that often appear mutually incomprehensible often turn out to not be so. Moreover, Kuhn's position is not an argument in favor of cessation of the validation of theory—a validated theory is always preferable to an unvalidated one—it is, rather, that it may be difficult to recognize which validation of two or more incommensurable theories is the preferred one.

Finally, a third critique, termed the "problem of the theory-ladeness of observation," was formulated by Kuhn, Quine, and Hanson. Roughly speaking, it is this view: don't trust your senses, because observations are imbued with theoretical bias. In its strongest version, the theory-ladeness of observation thesis suggests that theoretical bias in concepts overrides observation, which implies that observations do not validate theory. There has been lively debate over the theory-ladeness of observation position. Part of the controversy has been over the vagueness of the notion of "theory-laden" (Kitcher 1993: 222–33).

Something is laden if it is "heavily weighted" with something else. But the postpositivists are using the term metaphorically, which raises this query: just how does observation become "laden" with theory? There is some consensus that the position, even if accepted, "by no means undercuts the epistemic claims of science" (Sokal 2008: 8). To understand why this might be true, consider that theories are laden (i.e., biased) in the sense that their concepts ask those using them to observe reality in terms of those concepts. For example, in 1703 Georg Stahl, chemistry professor in Halle, theorized that all burnable material had phlogiston in it that was liberated during burning. Such a theory obliged one to look for the phlogiston. Observation led to the discovery of no phlogiston and to the recognition that it was an explanatory fiction. Stahl's theory was abandoned. It was no longer a phlogiston-laden world. The key here is the recognition that observation can produce liberation from concept bias.

Three conclusions emerge from the preceding. First, when examined more closely, a number of the apparent criticisms of science are not simply not so. Second, the postpositivist philosophers' claims about science's imperfections—underdetermination, incommensurability, and theory-ladeness—do illuminate limitations of scientific knowledge, but these are never so damaging as to warrant the rejection of scientific practice. Third, science's detractors, as argued in the preceding chapter, raise concerns about the limitations of scientific knowledge, but none offers superior alternatives. This reiterates Russell's judgment, expressed in the quotation at the opening of this section, that scientific inquiry is a "better" way of knowing "something" than unscientific speculation. What scientists know—because their practice creates it—is theory. In this optic, theory, like a painting or a piece of music—is a thing of art. The hammer forging theory is science practice. The anvil is anything of something, for the time being. What precisely theory is can be clarified by distinguishing it from its fuzzier conceptualizations.

Fuzzy Theory

The understanding of theory can shade toward the "fuzzy," by which is meant theory is either not comprehended or it is not comprehended well. Actually, for many social and cultural anthropologists, the concept of theory goes utterly undefined. They are doing ethnography, so why bother, or they are doing theory without examining what it might be. Certain anthropologists innocent of theory have been known to mimic the practice of intellectual authorities. Lévi-Strauss was iconic during the 1960s, so everybody digested *The Raw and the Cooked* (1964). Clifford Geertz was iconic in the 1980s, so it was off to the cockfights. Tim Ingold achieved a certain eminence in the 2000s; subsequently, for some it became time to imitate his lines of thought. Aside to reader: mimesis is not a way of doing theory. Doing theory without understanding the practices that make it is like children "driving" cars by mimicking what they see their parents do—wiggling the steering wheel and going "beep, beep."

Certain existing anthropological definitions of theory do exude fuzziness. Consider, for example, the proclamation that "theories may be both implicit and explicit" (Moore and Sanders 2006: 4). Sounds plausible, but think again. Implicit theories are those that are suggested for some reason, though not actually expressed. Why be explicit? Because it is never really clear, that is, it is fuzzy, what the actual theory is if it goes unspoken. Moreover, if what is theorized is vague, it is uncertain what needs to be observed to validate it.

Encouraging implicitness is not the only example of fuzziness in the an-thropological conceptualization of theory. Consider the following definition: "By 'theory' I mean a range of thought-frames—narratives, maps, categories, perspectives, positionalities—that operate as the conditions for allowing us to see and talk about social and cultural phenomena at all" (Ortner 2006: 90). At the heart of this definition is that theory is "a range of thought-frames." Now Ortner does not specify how she is using "thought-frames." Presumably, the term comes from Erving Goffman's seminal *Frame Analysis* (1974), where it denotes schemas of interpretation. For Ortner such schemas may include "narratives," "maps," "categories," "perspectives," and "positionalities." Let us be clear, theories *are* a type of narrative, a theoretical one, that maps different categories (theoretical ones) from different perspectives and positionalities.

Nevertheless, this definition of theory exhibits fuzziness due to conceptual bloat. Remember from the introduction that "conceptual bloat" refers to terms that contain more reality than they should. If an arm is defined as "the body," then the concept is bloated, because it now includes legs, heads, shoulders, and legs, which are not arms. Ortner's definition of theory is vague because it is a "range" of "thought-frames," with their range unspecified. Moreover, it is bloated because actually theory is a particular thought frame, not an unspeci-fied collection of them, suggesting the query: what is the specificity of theory?

Theory Defined

Specifically, "theory" is considered a type of thought frame composed of explicit generalizations that map, in the sense of stating, the relationships between abstract and general concepts referring to different aspects of some-thing, in order to explain or understand why and how what is observed to occur in that something actually occurs. "Generalizations" are propositions that certain concepts exhibit specific relationships. If there is only one concept, then there is no generalization. If relationships between the concepts go un-stated, there is no generalization. Generalizations can be obtained by inference from specific instances of something, but they pertain to the entire time-being of that something. For example, what is known as democratic peace theory, first proposed by Kant in his *Perpetual Peace* (1690), states:

Democracies do not war against other democracies.

The something represented in this theory is the time-being of democratic governance. There are two concepts in the theory "democracy" and "occur-rence of warfare." They are related in such a manner that the existence of democracy deters the occurrence of warfare between democracies. It is a gen-eralization because it pertains to the entire time-being that is in the realm of democratic governance.

Three sorts of generalizations can be distinguished, with generalizations themselves imagined as resembling necklaces hammered on the forge of reality. Theories are generalizations that are the most abstract and general. Because they are so abstract and general they might be thought of as multistranded necklaces. Empirical generalizations are generalizations resulting from observation, that are less abstract and general, and by which induction can be incorporated in a theory. Hypotheses, also less abstract and general, are deduced from theory.[2] Empirical generalizations and hypotheses might be conceived of as strands, which can be added to a multistranded theory. I will refer to theory, empirical generalization, and hypotheses as "theoretical necklaces." It is time to learn more of the art of representing something theoretically.

Practice Makes Theory

Two practices of theorizing and validating—operating reciprocally, in that each practice sets the other in motion—make theoretical necklaces. How these practices work is explored below, but first, it is helpful to distinguish theory from paradigms.

Paradigms (sometimes called "problematics" or "research programs") might be thought of as like murals. They provide the broadest picture of whole realms of something. Paradigms, with distinctive ontological stances, employing their own observational tools, are used to formulate numbers of empirical generalizations, hypotheses, and/or theories. For example, there are Marxist or structural–functional paradigms in the study of human being. Marxists consider conflict to be immanent within social forms, while structural–functionalists believe stability is immanent within them.

For Marxists "contradiction" is an important term concerning conflict, while "equilibrium" is a concept for structural functionalists regarding stability. Theory, then, is a component of paradigms. It is helpful to distinguish paradigms from narratives, worldviews, cultural hegemonies, and doxa. Narratives are *any* human story. Paradigms in this sense are a type of narrative. Worldviews are grand narratives. Like paradigms they have their own ontologies and picture enormous spaces and times of something. Christianity has a worldview. Cultural hegemonies, as understood here, are worldviews in service of class domination in the sense that they are understandings promulgated by, and beneficial to, dominating classes that are more or less taken for granted by dominated classes. Christianity was culturally hegemonic in medieval Europe.

Paradigms are a particular type of worldview, one that tells theoretical stories formulated using scientific practice. Paradigms do not invariably work in service of dominant classes. The global warming paradigm, for example, threatens certain economic and political elites. Critical science, as presented in the introduction, is a paradigm functional to cultural hegemonies. Finally, doxa is understood as "common opinion" (Childers and Hentzi 1995: 90) and is not arrived at through scientific practice. Doxa are particular understandings composed of worldviews and cultural hegemonies. Christ walking on water is a Christian doxa. What passes for theory in many nonscientific, scholarly narratives is doxa. It is time to examine the reciprocating practices that forge the necklaces of theoretical generalization.

Theorizing

Theorizing practice is the taking, or making, of concepts normally within a particular paradigm, the expressing of relationships between these concepts, so they explain or understand something in some being—with, for anthropologists, that being human being. The something being explained or understood is commonly referred to as the "explanandum." The something doing the explaining or understanding is the "explanans." For example, an important theory in Marxism has been this:

> Change is caused by intensification of contradictions within modes of production.

There are four main concepts in the theory: *change, intensification, contradiction,* and *mode of production.* Change is the explanandum

The other three concepts are the explanans. The mode of production is the something in which change is occurring. Intensification indicates the state of a contradiction, and it is intensified contradictions that explain how change occurs. The key relationship between the concepts is causation. Intensified contradictions within modes of production cause change. The following five sorts of activities are employed by those practicing the art of theorizing.

Explicitness

As argued earlier, a theoretical artist who does not make explicit her or his theory is no theorist. Generalizations need expression in sentences or equations, with, perhaps, a nice diagram to help visualize how it works. Sentences, equations, and diagrams are theorists' theoretical necklaces; they are their works of art.

Scope and Abstraction

Concepts in theoretical necklaces vary in scope and abstraction. *Scope* is the spatiotemporal dimension of the amount of being a concept includes. An arm has less scope than a body. *Abstraction*—a more difficult and contested notion—might be considered as the closeness of a concept to observation of being, with closeness as the degree to which something can be directly observed. *Speedy* is a less abstract concept. You can observe a person zipping along. *Acceleration* is a more abstract conception. It is the rate of change of velocity of something over time.

You have to first observe speed of something, that is, the distance moved over time, next calculate the velocity of the something at the different times, and finally subtract the initial velocity from the final velocity and divide by the time over which this occurred. Speedy may be a less abstract notion, but it is a bit of a blur because its sensational hook is seeing a person "zipping along," so it is unclear what qualifies as zipping. Acceleration is a less blurred concept. First you sense how long it takes for something to get from A to B, then you calculate the initial and final velocity, finally you calculate acceleration.

The larger the scope and the greater the abstraction of concepts, the more of being they are able to explain and/or understand. Recall generalizations, largely arising from observation, that are relatively low in scope and abstraction were said to be "empirical generalizations"; those derived through induction from empirical generalizations, exhibiting greater scope and abstraction, were said to be "theories"; and those deduced from theory were said to be "hypotheses."

Concept Formation

Concepts are the jewels in theoretical necklaces. No concepts in relationships, no theoretical necklace. Certain concepts are not jewels; though they may have glitter, they are fool's gold. Such concepts are conceptually blurred or blind, as understood in the introduction. Conceptual jewels not alloyed with blur or blindness are rare and precious. How does one form such gems?

Concept formation has been a major topic in disciplines ranging from psychology to education to philosophy. Schlick (1910) authored an early, influential logical positivist approach to scientific concept formation. Hempel (1952) provided a mid–twentieth-century, logical empiricist overview of the subject. Outhwaite (2011) discusses it in the social sciences. Fine et al. (2009) illustrate the work done in neuroscience on concept formation. One way of forming concepts relatively free of blur is to seek to understand why certain notions poorly represent the reality. In the 1670s, Anton van Leeuwenhoek, a Dutch lens maker, peering through a microscope made with his lens, saw something not seen before—invisible (to the naked eyes) living organisms. There was no term for them. Reaching into his knowledge of Latin, and of how words can be formed in Latin, he termed his invisible friends "animalcules." Over the years animalcules came to be known as "germs."

The world in which van Leeuwenhoek lived was dominated by a miasma disease theory, which asserted a causal relationship between noxious bad air (the miasma) and disease, with the former causing the latter. A problem with this generalization was that nobody ever actually observed miasma producing illness. However, the Italian Agostino Bassi showed in a series of experiments between 1808 and 1813 that a disease in silkworms known as *calcinaccio* was caused by a microorganism. In the later part of the nineteenth century, Louis Pasteur in France and Robert Koch in Germany showed how different germs produced different diseases. The inability to detect miasmas provoking illness led medical researchers to observe if the newly discovered germs did the job, and when this was seen to be correct a new concept was formulated: germs, microorganisms with the property of triggering illness.

Logical positivists had insisted on the role of inference in concept formation. The concepts in theory derived from empirical generalizations were made into new, broader in scope, and higher in abstraction concepts by inductive inference, while the concepts in hypotheses were made into new, narrower in scope, and lower in abstraction terms by deductive inference. My sense is that thinkers, in the hurly-burly of theorizing practice, just "see" the new concept, that is, they "get it" through intuition. Then, if there is any logical work it is after the fact, with the thinker showing that the generalization she or he is working on has concepts derived from inductive or deductive inference. Though there is recognition that intuition plays a role in all thought, though there is research into the role of intuition in scientific practice (Medwar 1969; Osbeck and Held 2014), and, finally, though there is increasing analysis of the neuroscience of intuition (Volz and von Cramon 2006; Chandrasekharan 2014), intuition itself remains something of an unknown.

Regardless of how a concept is formed—through examination of concepts that do not work, inference, or intuition—a key to concept formation is development of sensational hooks. Such hooks possess two parts: those that specify what reality to observe, and those that inform about what to do with the sensations once they have been recorded. Take, for example, the concept of mean height, in which the hook is, first, to sense the individual heights and then, second, sum those heights and divide by the number of individuals whose heights were sensed. Attention turns to the activity of making relationships between concepts.

Relationship Formation

If theoretical generalizations are imagined as necklaces, with concepts the necklace's jewels, then strings in theoretical generalizations are the relationships between the concepts. A *relationship* is something that links one concept, or group of concepts, with another concept, or group of concepts. A single concept cannot be a theory. *Agency* is an interesting concept, but there is no theory of agency unless there is some relationship between it and other concepts. Deleuze and Guattari (1991) defined philosophy as the discipline that creates concepts. Such a definition takes philosophy out of the business of making theory, if it means that all that philosophy does is invent concepts without specifying their interconnections, a move that may fill some philosophers with dismay.

Linkages are obtained—a bit like individuals in dating games—when two or more concepts are known to be "going steady." For example, among the Barma in Chad a fair number of women had no children and a fair number of marriages terminated in divorce. Here were two concepts *infertility* and *divorce*. How were they related? I further saw that many infertile marriages ended in divorce, while the fertile ones were more likely to continue. This suggested the two concepts were going steady in a relationship. Specifically, one in which:

Infertility produced divorce.

Because this statement arose directly from observation of fertility and divorce—"I see you have no children. I see you are divorced"—it was an empirical generalization. Since the arrival of postmodern anthropology with its doxa that science, as Tyler (1986) put it, has "succumbed" there has been little motivation to create generalization necklaces.

Explanation and Understanding

Theoretical necklaces explain or understand different somethings. There has been a sulphurous debate over the relative virtues of explanation versus understanding. Hempel (1965) articulated a covering law (sometimes called a hypothetico-deductive) model of explanation, which was for a long time in the twentieth century a staple view of scientific explanation.[3] Explanation has its merits. A first virtue of it is the vastness of the realms of something accounted for. Physicists currently seek a theory of everything to explain all physical aspects of the universe. A second, dangerous and fickle, virtue is the power produced over being. The same physicists on the quest to explain atoms created nuclear weaponry, which gave humans the power to transform themselves, and everybody else, from something to nothing.

Since the nineteenth century, hermeneuticists—Schleiermacher, Heidegger, Gadamer, von Wright—have argued that at least with regard to humans there was an ugly flaw in explanation, which was that the action component of human being could not be addressed by explanation and needed hermeneutic understanding. Føllesdal responded, by demonstrating how "the so-called hermeneutic method is actually the same as the hypothetico-deductive method applied to materials that are 'meaningful'" (1979: 319).

Similarly, Stegmüller, as claimed by Connolly and Keutner, showed that "interpretations" were "to be taken as methodologically equivalent to hypotheses in, say, astronomy or biology" (1988: 2–3). Thus Stegmüller and Føllesdal had argued understanding to be a form of explanation. My position in the explanation versus understanding debate is to cool it. Perhaps understanding can be understood to have explanatory powers. But the crucial point is that *both* are important. This is especially so because attributing meaning about what is and what to do about it is a crucial part of the way humans maneuver through reality. This means human being cannot be fully accounted for unless there are explanations of why people make the interpretations they do.

A third merit of explanations, and for that matter understandings, is that they answer the question of why: why answers explicate "for or what reason" something is the way it is. The explanandum in an explanation is that something about which the analyst wants to know why it is the way it is. The explanans is that which accounts for why the explanandum is as it is. Consider one explanation in which the explanandum was suicide. Emile Durhkeim had a friend who committed suicide, the shock of which appears to have moved him to explain why such a grim thing would occur (Lukes 1973). In *Suicide* (1898), he presented theoretical generalizations that explained why a person might be driven to terminate his or her own life.

The explanation began with observations of something about human being in nineteenth-century France—suicide and religious affiliation. It appeared that Catholics did away with themselves less frequently than Protestants. Conceptually, self-destruction is suicide, and Catholic and Protestants are examples of religious affiliation. Further, the two concepts are observed to be related by association:

Levels of suicide are associated with forms of religious affiliation.

Durkheim found two concepts (suicide and religious affiliation) linked by one relationship (association). Because the concepts and relationship were observed to be widespread, at least in France, they were a generalization. Because they were of relatively low scope (only nineteenth-century France) and abstraction (suicide and religious affiliation are fairly directly observable), and because they were arrived at subsequent to observation, the generalization may be said to be an empirical generalization.

But Durkheim did not stop with his empirical generalization. Using induction he sought to discover of what suicide and religious affiliation were specific instances. The former he inferred to be an instance of *deviance*, because, after all, killing oneself is taboo behavior. The later he inferred to be a type of *integration,* with different forms of integration providing different levels of support, or solidarity, to individuals and less-supported persons less protected from harmful urges. Crucially, Durkheim believed Protestants were less well integrated than Catholics (a belief that many have challenged). This belief suggested a relationship between integration and deviance: the less integrated individuals were (Protestants), the more likely they were to be deviant and, conversely, the more integrated individuals were (Catholics), the less likely they were to be integrated. In other words, the relationship between integration and deviance seemed to be an inverse one: as integration diminished, deviance increased. This can be expressed as follows:

$$D = F(^1/_I),$$

where D stands for deviance and I stands for integration. Because the concepts of deviance and integration are at a fairly highly level of scope and abstraction, and because they and their relationship were arrived at through induction, the preceding generalization is a theory.

Enterprising theorists might utilize Durkheim's theory of suicide to deduce hypothesizes concerning something else about human being. For example, resistance, understood as actions opposing a social order, might be deduced to be a form of deviance, and poverty level a form of integration, with it recognized that in capitalist societies as poverty increases the less actors can participate, that is, be integrated into social life. This suggests the following:

In capitalist social forms, as poverty increases, so does resistance.

There are two concepts in a positive relationship in this generalization—*poverty* and *resistance*—that are less abstract than the notions of integration and deviance from which they are deduced in Durkheim's theory. Resistance and poverty are also of lower scope than the concepts from which they are deduced, being restricted to capitalist realms. Finally, the resistance/poverty theoretical statement is a hypothesis because it is produced purely by deduction.

Each of the generalizations presented above results from explanation, a practice that accounts for why something in human being is the way it is. Why does change occur in modes of production? Because of the intensification of contradictions. Why does suicide occur? Because of lesser integration. Why does resistance occur? Because of greater poverty.

In sum, theorizing is activity that explicitly creates generalizations whose explanans explain, or understand, why some explanandum is as it is. These activities work by concept and relationship formation at different levels of scope and abstraction. Theorizing, in this optic, is a blow on the forge of reality crafting the necklace of generalization. Theorizing that does not check for fake necklaces is corrupt, while validating is in a reciprocal relationship with theorizing.

Validating

Validating is observational (i.e., empirical) practice. It is checking for fakes, which it does by providing information concerning whether what a theoretical generalization says occurs actually does or does not occur. It is the activity of confronting re-presentation with reality. Confrontation is the observation (i.e., sensing plus assignment of symbolic status to sensation) of whether what a theoretical generalization (a re-presentation) states occurs in something actually happens.[4]

Such observations are *facts*. Facts provide evidence. Generalizations whose theorizations of what occurs have been observed to occur are supported by factual evidence and validated. Generalizations whose theorizations of what occurs have been observed to not occur are unsupported by factual evidence and invalidated. Trofim Lysenko was a Ukrainian geneticist, dear to Stalin's heart, who rejected Mendelian genetics in favor his own Michurinism, a form of Lamarckism that insisted upon the heritability of acquired characteristics. Experiments with fruit flies were devised to validate Mendel's explanations. Soviet geneticists performing such experiments were denounced as "fly lovers" (Agazzi, Echeverría, and Rodriguez 2008: 149), and Stalin obligingly had them liquidated. However, Mendelian ratios and heritability were observed to occur as predicted in Mendelian theory. Experiments made by Lysenko and his associates to show inheritances of acquired traits were shown to be bogus. Lysenko, and his Michurinism, was a fake.

Observing and theorizing can work in tandem in two ways. Either, a set of observations is to be made that sense happenings in reality seemingly "going steady." This sets in motion theorizing practice. The happenings are given a symbolic status designed to represent them. This symbolic status takes the form of empirical generalizations, with their concepts and their relationships derived from the observers' paradigms and doxa. Empirical generalizations, then, through intuition or induction, are shown to be instances of the more abstract and broader in scope generalizations called theories.

Or, a theory exists and through intuition or deduction a less abstract and lower in scope hypothesis is produced, with their concepts and relationships retrieved from the observers' paradigms and doxa. This sets in motion observational practice, in which there is a sensing of whether what the hypothesis states to occur in reality indeed happens. Distinctive of scientific practice is a deep skepticism, a presumption that all theoretical necklaces are potential fakes and consequently require getting the facts to provide the evidence needed for validation. There are those, however, who are skeptical of validation, believing observation to be either an unemployed or flawed tool for revelation of fakes. Examination of these skeptics' views will lead us to matters of fact and assertions of truth.

Observation and Facts

During the 1880s, in his *Nachlass* (unpublished writings) Nietzsche took a hard line on facts, declaring, "There are no facts, only interpretations" (qtd. in

Wicks 2011). Hermeneuticists, social constructivists, and postmoderns were gratified by this proclamation, because it appeared to have buried science in the graveyard of "succumbed" (to return to Tyler's term) intellectual practices. The reasons for this burial are as follows. If there are "no facts," only squabbles over interpretation of sensations, then observation does not validate theoretical generalizations, which means there is no way to distinguish true from forged theoretical necklaces. Notice that Nietzsche's "no facts" proclamation reposed in unpublished notebooks, perhaps because he felt it was a hunch needing further development, which never occurred. Nevertheless, antifactism has become doxa for some, who can be said to be in(doxa)cated with it, and it has even expanded into popular culture where, as the subtitle of a recent book puts it, "the Facts Aren't the Facts" (Weinberger 2014).

Perhaps, this antifactism exists because certain scholars have argued that theoretical generalizations are *not* accepted on the basis of the facts of observation. Thomas Kuhns, Shapin and Steven Schaffer, and Bruno Latour are seen by some as exemplars of this view, so their claims are examined next. Kuhn researched one of the biggest theoretical transformations in astronomy, the Copernican Revolution. Recall that this "revolution" was literally about what revolved about what in the solar system, with Ptolemaic theory, geocentrism, insisting that the sun revolved around the earth and Copernican theory, heliocentrism, proclaiming the reverse. Writing in *The Structure of Scientific Revolutions* about these two theories, Kuhn insisted that, "Available observational tests ... provided no basis for a choice between them" but that there was increasing acceptance of Copernicus's view (1970: 75–76). Kuhn may be factually correct: that initially there were no empirical grounds to accept either of the two positions.

Copernicus wrote in the sixteenth century, without compelling evidence. Galileo defended Copernicus in the early seventeenth century, still without strong evidence of heliocentrism, and for his pains was punished by the Inquisition. Opponents of Copernicus's views insisted that for the Copernican solar system to be accepted there be evidence of a stellar parallax. It was only in the nineteenth century that such observations were made. Nevertheless, it is important here to recognize that initially there may have been scant observational supportive of Copernicus, but as the years went by it became clear there was evidence to forget Ptolemy and accept Copernicus. Kuhn's position does not so much justify an antiobservation position as it shows how difficult it may be to make observations.

Shapin and Schaffer (1985) in *Leviathan and the Air-Pump* examined seventeenth-century British science and a debate between the absolutist political philosopher Thomas Hobbes and Robert Boyle, younger son of an earl and a father of chemistry and physics. They fought over the role of evidence in deciding upon acceptance of theoretical generalizations. Boyle argued that truth in science was to be arrived at by observations made during the conduct of experiments. Shapin and Schaffer emphasized the role gentlemanly codes of conduct, rather than observation, had in Boyle's and his colleagues' decisions to accept theoretical generalizations. After all, you could trust a gentleman to tell the truth. Even today in the United Kingdom, members of the upper middle and upper classes are more likely to believe anything a toff with a Cambridge accent speaks over owt (slang for "anything") a bloke with a nice Mancunian (Manchester) twang might say. So it is not surprising that in the seventeenth century, when codes of class hierarchy were far stronger, Shapin and Schaffer found that gentleman, like Boyle, trusted other gentlemen.

There are some who argue that *Leviathan and the Air-Pump*'s argument rests upon inaccurate conceptions of Boyle's work (Principe 1998) as well as erroneous historical evidence (Horstmann 2012). Sargent has concluded that Shapin and Schaffer provided only a "superficial" discussion of Boyle's "methodology" (1995: 211). I am struck by two elements in Boyle's work: the enormous care he took to devise "mechanical contrivances" (Boyle 1662: 13) to make observations and his making those observations. This aspect of Boyle's research is actually documented in Shapin and Schaffer's text.

In 1661 Boyle contrived a J-shaped tube (not the famous air pump) to explore the relationship between the "spring" and the "weight" of air. He published the results of this research the following year, reporting that he had observed a generally inverse relationship between the spring and the weight of air. In our terms, the formulation of the generalization of an inverse relationship between air's spring and its weight is an empirical generalization. Over the years, further observations replicated Boyle's findings, though with the understanding that Boyle's air should be understood as "gas" and that his spring and weight are "pressure" and "volume," so that currently physicists speak of Boyle's Law: that the pressure and volume of a gas have an inverse relationship when temperature is held constant.

A second element in Boyle's work that I am impressed with is the effort he took to formulate and propagate "a new way of knowing," which he termed "experimental philosophy" (Sargent 1995: 1). This epistemology emphasized the conduct of experiments and the reliance upon observations from them to arrive at true generalizations. Further, Sargent in her study shows that Boyle, "More than most of his contemporaries … appreciated the problems involved in compiling observations" and especially—with the air pump experiments— being able to "replicate" them (1995: 208, 4–5). He even wrote an essay seeking to understand the unsuccessfulness of certain experiments (see Boyle 1661).

Boyle was a complicated person, who, like most persons, held conflicting beliefs. In addition to his scientific practice, he was a pious Puritan, was interested in witchcraft, and dabbled in alchemy. Furthermore, he sought through experiments to make observations to get the facts, and he sought to create an epistemology that explained why true knowledge was based upon observation. So, to further complicate the earl's younger son, he might be thought of as a class rebel who spent much of his intellectual life developing a way of knowing that did not depend upon gentlemanly trust.

Consider now the case of Latour and the *Pasteurization of France* (1993; *POF*). Louis Pasteur was the great microbiologist of the late nineteenth and early twentieth centuries whose observations greatly added to validation of the germ theory of disease. Moreover, his understanding of how microbes produce illness led to the development of different ways—from vaccinations to hygienic measures—to combat illnesses. Latour may have become interested in Pasteur because his family had been involved for generations in wine growing in Burgundy. Fermentation is crucial to the making of wines, and Pasteur's research uncovered how fermentation worked, thereby helping the Latour family to better produce fine wines. Pasteurization, as used in *POF*, refers not merely to the sterilization of milk but to all the effects, and these were enormous, produced by development of sterilization. *POF*'s text has two parts. The first seeks to account for pasteurization in France; the second is a contemplation of the significance of Latour's research. The analysis of pasteurization is based on articles published between 1870 and 1919 in the journals *Revue Scientifique, Annales de l'Institut Pasteur,* and *Concours Médicale.* The second part speculates about the ontology of the first. Stylistically, it evokes Spinoza's and Wittgenstein's tractatuses and is dominated by gnostic outcries, such as, "Nothing is known—only realized," "Time does not pass," "There are no theories" (Latour 1993: 159, 165, 178). I find this presentation of Latourian metaphysics unconvincing. Consequently, in what follows I focus upon the text's first part.

In our terms (not Latour's), the explanandum in his analysis is pasteurization. This is produced by an "assemblage of forces" (Latour 1993: 41). This assemblage is what he would term a network, which he likens to a "macramé" (ibid.: 206). The actors in the network, termed "actants," are agents. Microbes are "essential" agents (ibid.: 39), as are the various scientists, including especially Pasteur, who studied microbes, as well as hygienists, politicians, farmers, and medical doctors allied with Pasteur. The agency of the microbes in this network is to wreck illness upon humans and animals. The role of Pasteur, and microbiologist followers, was as "the revealer of microbes" (ibid.: 38). As the revealer of microbes, Pasteurians exposed a hidden microbial enemy. As allies of the Pasteurians, the doctors, hygienists, farmers, and politicians did the actual warring against the microbial hordes. The results of this war were the pasteurization of France. Let us term this "assemblage of forces" the "pasteurization network." It was the explanans of Latour's analysis, which consequently might be presented as:

The pasteurization network produced "pasteurization."

I am not entirely comfortable with this generalization because I am not certain whether what Latour argued in the first section *POF* is actually tautological and he was actually reporting:

> The pasteurization network is "pasteurization."

What are the implication of Latour's position in the first section of *POF* for the use of facts and observation to warrant generalizations?

None at all! Actually, he tells his readers, "I, too, love the solidity of facts " (Latour 1993: 147), and his analysis is full of facts from the journals he used as his data source to support his observations. Further, in no place in the text does he specifically argue either that the observations are irrelevant to germ theory or that observations in general are irrelevant to validating generalizations.

In sum, Kuhn's analysis of the Copernican Revolution did not show that observation was irrelevant to accepting generalizations. Rather, it revealed that the making of observation was no easy task and that it could take centuries before it was possible to get the facts bearing upon theory. Shapin and Schaffer certainly exposed the role of gentlemanly codes in seventeenth-century science. But what they and other Boyle scholars equally discovered was how Boyle and others in his network labored both to develop methods of observation suitable for their research and to provide arguments in favor of observation as the source of true knowledge. Finally, there is Latour, who confessed his "love … of facts" and whose account of the pasteurization of France was based upon the creation of a database from the three journals that chronicled the history of the Pasteur network and from this database to make observations that supported the position that he argued. Kuhn, Schapin and Schaffer, and Latour provide no reason to stop looking for the facts of the matter

In 2004, Latour confessed in something of a mea culpa essay, "I myself have spent sometime in the past trying to show 'the lack of scientific certainty' inherent in the construction of facts" (2004: 227). He acknowledges that such a position has legitimated some attempts "to destroy hard-won evidence that could save our lives" (ibid.: 227), and insists, "The question was never to get away from facts but closer to them, not fighting empiricism but, on the contrary, renewing empiricism" (ibid.: 231). The proceeding argues that those studying human being should get the facts to provide evidence to validate their positions, which prompts the question: how do you make observations and get the facts?

Methodology and Tactics

One answer to this is that when validating generalizations you need explicit research methodologies and tactics. Both methodology and tactics are about how to make observations to get the facts. *Methodologies* are the strategies of observation of different somethings. *Tactics* are the particular observational activities of different strategies. Together methodologies and tactics establish the boundaries of what can be observed, and by doing so they set limits to what can be validated, thereby establishing the limits to what is knowable. Anthropology has generally relied upon ethnographic methods that employ fieldwork tactics of participant observation and interviewing. Michael Herzfeld reports that within anthropology there has been a "disillusionment with fieldwork that began to appear in the 1960s" (2001: 4).

There are many reasons for this "disillusionment." Perhaps one of them is a violation of rule number 1 of methodology: don't forget to practice validation! Observation without validation leads researchers into re-presentation of being without connecting the dots of what being is interrelated, foreclosing the ability to know why or how it is the way it is. If all you do is make observations without discovering what something is observed to be related to something else and what concepts are appropriate for re-presenting the somethings in relationship, you cannot explain anything. Anthropology prior to the 1970s, for the most part, understood itself to be a science and implicitly, and sometimes quite explicitly, favored validation. However, when postmodern anthropologists arrived and, especially with the *Writing Culture* network, science was rejected, which meant that validation as a matter of principle was abandoned, which *is* disillusioning.

Methodologies specify the realms of something to be observed and how it is possible to perform observations. A major difference in methodologies is whether they are purely observational or experimental. *Observational* strategies identify a particular realm of something to be sensed and then sense it. *Experimental* strategies organize sensing of reality to observe relationships by designating certain portions of reality to be *independent* variables, other portions of it to be *dependent* variables, and then sensing whether if there are changes in independent variables then these are associated with changes in dependent variables.

Methodological advance has been a function of the technology available to make observations. Biological research strategies were revolutionized by invention of first the microscope and then the electron microscope. In neuroscience research until the 1980s, a key method was to observe what happened to brain function after different pathologies struck. Then in the late 1980s devices were invented that allowed researchers to observe what was happening in the brain roughly as it was happening (PET and MRI scans) that increased the ability to know how different brain regions interacted.

Research tactics concern the actual observational activities that occur in a particular research project. For example, E.E. Evans-Pritchard detailed his tactics when he told readers of *The Nuer*: "What I describe is almost entirely based upon direct observation and is not augmented by copious notes taken down from regular informants, of whom, indeed, I had none" (1940: 9). Observer's research tactics display their artistry because they display his or her inventiveness and skill in applications of methodology. Charles Darwin (1859), in his travels on the HMS Beagle, for the most part employed a natural history methodology that was distinctive in what chunk of something it observed. Natural history was concerned with the knowledge of living forms—plants and animals. Prior to the eighteenth century, natural history methods tended to involve finding different life forms and sensing their particular characteristics. However, Alexander von Humboldt (2014) in the eighteenth century offered an altered natural history methodology that emphasized observing organisms within their contexts.

Darwin was a naturalist influenced by the Humboldtian tradition when he sailed on the Beagle. His particular observational tactics were to apply the methodology to the analysis of animal types to circumscribed areas with distinctive different environments. His art was to see that when he did this, a category of birds on an island—the finches of the Galapagos Islands off Ecuador—had different beaks that were associated with the different foods they fed upon in their different environments, which observations would prove crucial in his theory of evolution based upon natural selection. In certain ways ethnography, which seeks to examine human being within its different contexts, has been an application of the Humboldtian tradition.

Different intellectual disciplines may be characterized as cosmopolitan or fundamentalist with regard toward methodologies. A *cosmopolitan* discipline is one in which there is encouragement and development of alternative observational methodologies and tactics. A *fundamentalist* discipline is one in which the discipline sticks to one methodology that it believes is fundamental for its success, while exhibiting tendencies of methodological cleansing. *Methodological cleansing* is the discouragement and/or elimination of alternative research practices in favor of preferred ones. Ethnography is a purely observational methodology that has been fancied in social and cultural anthropology since the days of Malinowski and Boas.

However, prior to the cresting of the postmodern wave in anthropology, there was the development of methodological alternatives. For example, cultural anthropologists in the 1950s and 1960s, working with Ward Goodenough, E. Hammel, and Floyd Loundsbury, developed methods of componential analysis based upon observational practice in semantics (Goodenough 1971). Murdock introduced statistical methods into the analysis of social structure (1949). Fred Eggan (1954) and British social anthropologists, especially in *African Political Systems* (1941) and *African Systems of Kinship and Marriage* (1950), introduced different comparative methods. This anthropology exhibited a more cosmopolitan methodological orientation.

Postmodern anthropology has sought to arrest this tendency. *Writing Culture* was influential in doing this. It sought to implement Clifford Geertz's desire for anthropology to be on the "the side of 'literary' discourses" (1988: 8) by constructing an alternative to a scientific anthropology. Ethnography figured importantly in this construction, because it was, as Tyler confided, "the discourse of the postmodern world" (1986: 123). Tyler suggested ethnography was "a cooperatively evolved text consisting of fragments of discourse intended to invoke in the minds of both reader and writer an emergent fantasy of a possible world of commonsense reality, and thus to provoke an aesthetic integration that will have a therapeutic effect" (ibid.: 125). Such ethnography was "in a word, poetry" (ibid.).

Moreover, as Geertz himself recognized, ethnography is about having "been there," which tends to encourage its practitioners to specialize in "incorrigible assertion" (1988: 5). *Writing Culture* espoused what might be termed "fundamentalist ethnography," whose fundamental heart was that anthropologists should get with "the discourse of the postmodern world," forgetting science, and asserting "poetry" to achieve a "therapeutic effect."

Kim Fortun, riding the wave of fundamentalist ethnography, has proposed a recent iteration of it. Continued is the doxa that ethnography should be therapy, but added is the assertion that it "can be designed to bring forth a future anterior" (2012: 450). It is not entirely clear what is meant by "future anterior." The concept is actually a grammatical term indicating tense. I think she means by it that fundamentalist ethnography can "bring forth" what happens in the future. The phrase "bring forth" implies causation. Terrible war can bring forth, that is, cause, refugees. So I think she is claiming that postmodern ethnography can cause the future, prompting the question: how?

According to Fortun, this will be through a "design process" that appears to involve three steps: "First ... the ethnographic work of discerning discursive gaps and risks, ... next the ethnography must loop," which is "leveraging ethnography not only to describe what is at hand but also to the discursive gaps and risks ...," and finally, "through the design of an experimental ethnographic system, to provoke new idioms, new ways of thinking" (Fortun 2012: 252–53). Thinking it is so does not make it so. Setting aside that "loop" and "experimental ethnographic system" are conceptual blurs, there are two problems with this ethnography.

First, it proposes no analysis of the structures of force and power among the actors in which discursive gaps and risks are found, and surely these structures will influence the future. Second, more epistemologically, Fortun nowhere affirms that her brand of fundamentalist ethnography will involve validation, so its users will know little of the truth of their ethnographic assertions. George Marcus, a postmodern elder, who has thought long and hard about ethnography, sounded a pessimistic note in a recent article, when he worried, "The classic ethnographic textual form, even as amended since the 1980s … is a very partial and inadequate means of composing the movements and contest of fieldwork" (2013: 202). Is it textual form that is inadequate, or is it ethnographic fundamentalism itself?

Boundary maintenance is important work in fundamentalisms—the better to keep people confined to the fundamentals. The problem with boundary maintenance—be it along the Mexican/US border or an intellectual tradition—is that it favors cleansing, ethnic in the case of the Mexican border and methodological in that of research disciplines. Of course, cleansing is a nasty business. With regard to any large intellectual tradition, such as anthropology, different topics require different observational procedures. No one size methodology fits all in any empirical research.

Ethnography is appropriate for the observation of many actions and verbalizations of a few people over a relatively short time and space. However, what happens if one proposes to observe global systems? This requires a huge set of observations over the entire world for long time periods. Not unsurprisingly, given the spatiotemporal enormity of their global systems project, Jonathon and Kajsa Friedman argue the "inadequacy of the local ethnographic field" and insist upon the importance of "history" as "a necessary component of the social reproductive approach" (2008: 31, 58). Broadly speaking they are urging the application of historical methods within anthropology, and in so doing making a plea for a methodological cosmopolitanism.

On the other hand, methodological cosmopolitanism has the virtue in observational practice of encouraging innovation in methods and tactics, which can lead to a more decisive role for observation in validating theorizing. Consider the case of Thomas Piketty's *Capital in the 21st Century* (2014). For the most part economics employs quantitative, mathematical methodologies. However, it is a fairly cosmopolitan discipline and also employs historical methods. Piketty acknowledges that *Capital's* success "is heavily indebted to recent improvements in the technology of research" (ibid.: 20).

This improved "technology" concerned historical observation. Influenced by historical work on Parisian estate tax records, he, in collaboration with colleagues, created the World Top Income Database (WTID), which allowed observations concerning income and wealth inequality as well as capital accumulation for a longer period (starting in the eighteenth century in France and in the early twentieth century in the United Kingdom and the United States). These novel research tactics allowed him to see more, in the sense that he could observe over a long time period, about the something involved in capital accumulation and inequality, and what he saw was relevant to existing theorizing.

Simon Kuznets's (1955) paper established the orthodox theoretical position concerning capital accumulation and inequality, which was:

Regardless of policy alternatives, in developed economies, as capital accumulation occurs, market forces first increase and then decrease economic inequality.

Unfortunately for Kuznets, Piketty's observations were over a longer period than those that had validated Kuznets's view. Specifically, they showed that over the longer time frame, capital accumulation and inequality were positively related. In other words, the facts suggested that what Kuznets theorized happened in the something of developed economies was absent.

Rather, the facts from the WTID report was consistent with another theoretical generalization: as capital accumulation occurred, the rate of returns on capital was greater than the rate of economic growth, which meant that economic inequality increased, with growing inequality further observed associated with social instability. In sum, Piketty's evidence supported the generalization:

Capital accumulation leads to inequality, which leads to instability.

Of course, this had been Marx's general position in the nineteenth century, except that for Marx capital accumulation intensified the capitalist/proletarian contradiction, producing greater inequality, which leads to instability in the form of revolution. Piketty was generally supporting Marx. It remained to be observed whether intensified contradictions or the ratios of the rate of return of capital to the rate of economic growth were more important in provoking instability, but Piketty's position was an alternative formulation of Marx's theory of the effects of capital accumulation.

This section has argued the importance of explicit methodologies and tactics when making observations to reveal the facts of the matter. Further, it has suggested that a methodological cosmopolitanism is preferred over a fundamentalism, as a way of developing more powerful forms of observational practice. It laments the antiscience stance introduced by postmodern anthropologists promoting abandonment of rule number 1 of methodology. It is time to see whether such practices can be in any way imagined to be objective and whether they can establish truths.

Objectivity

If theoretical generalizations are validated by observation guided by methodologies and tactics, can these generalizations be said to be objective? Here, reader, is a terrain of strife. Let us explore it.

There are numerous definitions of objectivity, but the one I prefer, due to its inclusiveness, is that of Helen Longino, who states, "Objectivity is a characteristic ascribed variously to beliefs, individuals, theories, observations, and methods of inquiry. It is generally thought to involve the willingness to let our beliefs be determined by 'the facts' or by some impartial and non-arbitrary criteria rather than by our wishes as to how things out to be" (1990: 170). At the time that Longino was writing that there was a growing consensus that belief in complete objectivity should be replaced by recognition of "situated knowledges," as the title of Donna Haraway's (1988) article put it. This cognizance implied that theoretical generalizations were not objective because they were "situated" in social, cultural, political, and methodological biases. Objectivity, then, is currently a contested possibility, raising the question of what should be done with it?[5]

My sense is that visions of absolute objectivity should be eliminated. *Absolute objectivity* is a situation in which observers have acquired the facts and these provide knowledge of the way something is, rather than how it ought to be. Consider the following argument against the possibility of such a situation: objectivity is based upon getting the facts, getting these involves making observations of reality, observations of reality are re-presentations of sensations of something—so what we know are those re-presentations of something, that is to say, we know the re-presentations report what reality ought to be, not what it is.

If it is not sensible to claim absolute objectivity; it is plausible to recognize that some knowledge is more objective than some other knowledge. A Nazi insisting on Jewish racial inferiority is less objective than Boas disputing this view. Another way of saying this is that some knowledge is relatively more objective than other knowledge. The goal, then, is to seek "relatively objective" knowledge, which is a formulation of theoretical generalizations that are relatively more objective than their alternatives. One way of doing this is to check for, and eliminate if found, biasing, while providing facts that are representative and intersubjective bearing upon generalizations. *Biasing*, as it pertains to validation, concerns factors prejudicing observational practices so that they favor certain theoretical generalizations, while rejecting others.

Two broad sources of biasing exist—that which is external to observational practice but, nevertheless, influences it and that which is internal to observational practice and influences it. Two major sources of external biasing exist—the first is social/cultural; the second is individual. An extreme example of social biasing has to do with Soviet genetics during Stalin's regime. Because of the regime's support for Lysenko's brand of genetics it was against the law to research the field in any other manner. If one did, one's life was forfeit. Unsurprisingly, Soviet genetics at this time was biased in favor of Lysenko. Cultural biasing involves prejudices people have due to their positions within populations, for example, partialities they have consequent upon being affluent, poor, of particular "races," of gender, or religion. Nineteenth-century anthropology, for example, was formulated by affluent, white, male Christians, who judged that the social forms populated by affluent, white, male Christians were "civilized" and that all other social forms were "savage" or "barbaric."

Individual biasing results from the singularities of a person's life, what they have experienced that is unique to them and not part of social or cultural position. My own experiences in Chad illustrate an individual biasing. A number of times a fighter plane flew over the village in which I was conducting fieldwork at strafing altitude. One evening I waited with the villagers to be attacked by rebels. At other times I heard the sounds of small arms fire, and everywhere people were in fear. Since those times it has seemed to me important not to grasp at the latest wave of anthropological doxa but to address people's fear and to study war.

Just as there are two major sorts of external biasing, there are equally two sorts of internal biasing—those that are conceptual and those that have to do with activities that pertain to the intersubjectivity and representativeness of observations. Biases that are inherent in terms influence observation in one of two ways. The first results from the fact that when validation occurs, the only observations to be made are those bearing up those concepts. For example, if there is a generalization that "values determine family structure," then a researcher is biased because she or he must observe values and family structure. The absence of concepts, Fortun's discursive gaps, is a second way that concepts can bias observation. Foucault reported that a concept of *homosexuality* did not exist prior to the nineteenth century (1998: 101). This meant that in the absence of a notion of male sexual bonding, many whispered of "the love that dare not speak its name."

Intersubjectivity and representativeness refer to how observations bearing upon generalizations are made. Observations may be more, or less, intersubjective and representative. More intersubjective and representative observations reduce bias, thereby improving objectivity. Let us begin with a discussion of intersubjectivity. This notion has featured in phenomenology, psychology, neuroscience, and the philosophy of science. Broadly, intersubjectivity is the capacity of two or more persons' subjectivities (in our terms, their E-space states) to be in consensus, unanimity, or agreement, that is, to share subjectivities.

Debate exists as to how much can be shared and the nature of the sharing—with a sense that intersubjectivity involves partaking of common cognitive, intentional, affective, and conative states. Intersubjectivity makes reliability possible, the ability for research findings to be replicated. Reliability is the situation in which different observers, with different biases, sensing the same something, observe it in the same manner. There is a belief that "the intersubjective," and the resulting reliability of observation, is "the mark of objectivity" (Kaplan 1964: 128).

Clearly, intersubjective observation is enhanced if clear and precise procedures—recipes, if you like—for observing something are communicated to, and followed by, researchers. Such recipes include concepts with clear sensational hooks. For example, if a researcher is interested in the average weight of Americans, she knows that the observational operations include get their individual weights, sum the weights, divide by the numbers of those weighed, and multiple by one hundred. This ensures that different researchers can observe something the same way, because they are following the same recipes, unbiased by their particular prejudices. This is *operational intersubjectivity*, and if it occurs, then observations are "uncontaminated by any factors save those common to all observers" (Kaplan 1964: 128). If there is no operational intersubjectivity, observers do not know how to observe the same something, encouraging biases to flourish.

Current social and cultural anthropology generally ignores questions of operational intersubjectivity. Concepts—highly abstract and ambiguous ones—are used without instructions as to how make observations bearing upon them. For example, certain anthropologists have taken a Heideggerian turn, which implies that they need to work with Heidegger's main concept *Da-sein*. Here is his explication of the term:

> Da-sein is a being that does not simply occur among other beings. Rather it is ontically distinguished by the fact that in its being this being is concerned about its very being. Thus it is constitutive of the being of Da-sein to have, in its very being, a relationship of being to this being. And this in turn means that Da-sein understands itself in its being in some way and with some explicitness. (1927: 10)

For there to be some operational intersubjectivity concerning this definition, there needs to be an explication of what you do to sense *Da-sein*. *Da-sein* is "being ... concerned about ... being" that is constituted "in its very being, a relationship of being to being." What then is being? A few pages earlier Heidegger said, "Being is the being of a being" (1927: 7). Is Heidegger hypnotizing his readers through repetitive chanting of the word "being?" This places those riding a Heideggerian wave to make reliable observations bearing upon *Da-sein* without instructions on how to do it. A popular textbook explaining ethnographic methods acknowledges, "Critics often argue that lack of replicability is a serious problem for ethnographers," which its authors dismiss as an "unwarranted" criticism (Schensul and LeCompte 2013: location 6320). I worry about reliability. How can anthropologists make Heideggerian arguments if they are unable to know how to reliably observe his key concept? Next consider representativeness.

The notion of *representativeness* refers to the degree to which observations sufficiently and accurately characterize something. The more observations do so, the less their sufficiency and accuracy is distorted by some bias. Consider, for example, that one proposes to study the ontology of an Amazonian group, and one makes observations of a group of ten or so young men. Such observations would be unrepresentative, because absent from the sensing are a fair number of the group's members, including middle-aged men, older men, as well as young, middle-aged and older women, plus a certain number who no longer speak its language and have been raised as Catholics. Postmodern ethnography, because it is antiscience, is indifferent to establishing the representativeness of observations, and while it is not entirely the case, if one consults journals publishing ethnographic articles, one notes little attention is paid to demonstrating that the observations forming the basis of articles' positions are representative.

Currently, when people come and go, discussing theory, they may well be discussing the boldest work in anthropology since Lévi-Strauss's *Elementary Structures of Kinship* (1949). This is Phillipe Descola's *Beyond Nature and Culture* (2013), which—taking an ontological turn—theorizes that in all places and all times humans have had only four different ontologies: animism, naturalism, totemism, and analogism. However, while Descola examines an enormous literature to get the facts to establish his point, he nowhere demonstrates that this literature constitutes a representative sample, with certain reviewers suggesting ways that it is not (Lapinski 2014; Frandy 2014). Bluntly put, unknown sample representativeness, conclusions notional.

At this point it is possible to state the requirements for relatively more objective observational practices. They are those that have been checked for, and sought to eliminate, external social, cultural, and individual biasing as well as internal conceptual biasing, while seeking to be as intersubjective and representative as possible. Such a research methodology is not developed or influential in the current postmodern anthropology. Finally, if a researcher has performed the practices to make her or his researches relatively more objective, and she or he has validated generalizations, has she or he found truth?

Truth

Sort of—though the establishment of truth is challenging. First, consider the view of some extreme cultural relativists who argue that there are truths, that these are relative to different cultures, and, consequently, if in a particular culture some idea is believed true, then that culture must be "respected" and its truth accepted. Such a view confuses what the notion of truth is about. Truth pertains to something, not what people may think about it. Thinking something is so does not make it so. Something is, or is not, some way. Something's *actuality* is its truth. For example, a canon of Nazi culture was that Jews were an inferior race suitable for extermination. But the actuality is that Jews are no more, or less, inferior than anybody. It seems irresponsible to insist that one must respect Nazi belief just because it is a belief. The only way one can establish any sort of truth, as is discussed below, is to validate belief. Consequently, first validate, then respect—though maybe not.

There is another difficulty. On one hand, a number of postmodern scholars are skeptical of the utility of the notion of truth. Consider, for example, Baudrillard declaiming, "The secret of theory is, indeed, that truth doesn't exist" (1986: 141). Postmodern anthropologists tend to scrape and bow allegiance to this doxa. A fulsome bashing of truth in anthropology was performed in *Writing Culture*. Tyler insisted anthropology is "beyond truth" (1986: 123), Rabinow said, "The production of truth is epiphenomenal(1986: 240)." Crapanzanno thought truth was "not the whole truth" (1986: 53). But even logical empiricists like Hempel seem to join truth skeptics when they assert, "We can never establish with certainty that a given theory is true" (1966: 81). On the other hand, few people would be skeptical of the assertion that "crocodiles are dangerous" is truer than the contention that "crocodiles are not dangerous." Further, few people would deny that knowledge of this truth is vital if you reside in crocodile territory. Pragmatically, then, a notion of truth seems useful, even life preserving. How does one proceed in such a situation?

First, I think it is important to make a distinction between absolute and approximate truth. Hempel, I believe, was talking about absolute truth: knowledge that some generalization about something is true "with certainty" forever. Such truths do seem beyond grasp. Forever is the fly in the ointment. It is a very long time. Actually it is infinity. If it is observations that form a basis of a generalization's truth, then, due to the endlessness of time, there are always observations that could be made but have not been made, so that it is impossible to know "with certainty" that the generalization is true.

However, generalizations can be approximately true. The notion of approximate truth has been developed to reveal what can truthfully be known about something, assuming that knowledge of its absolute truth of something is unavailable. Conceptualization of approximate truth has "proven challenging" (Hunt 2011: 159). Nevertheless, useful understandings of the term can be found in Niiniluoto (1987), Weston (1992), and Psillos (1999). The position about approximate truth I have taken, a "hard truth" approach, relies upon comparing the validation of competing generalizations pertaining to the same something (Reyna 2004, 2010).

Specifically, a generalization can be approximately true in one of three ways. First, it may be true judged relative to the number of times it has been validated. A generalization that has been validated many times can be said to exhibit a high degree of approximate truth. This is the case with Darwin's theory of natural selection. Second, a generalization may be relatively truer regarding the scope of something that it has been validated to explain or understand. The more of something a generalization has been validated to account for, the greater its relative truth. So understood, quantum physics is relatively truer than its Newtonian counterpart, though they both have their approximate truths.

Third, a generalization may be relatively true judged in comparison with other generalizations seeking to account for the same something. Confrontation between competing generalizations is judged in terms of the amount of something validated and the number of times it has been validated. Consider, for example, two empirical generalizations concerning the consequences of military occupation:

1. Military occupation leads to resistance.
2. Military occupation leads to acquiescence.

There appear to be at least two instances validating the second generalization (those of Japan and Germany after World War II). While there seem to be more instances validating the first generalization. Think of the creation of the minutemen militia in response to King George III's occupation of the colonies in the 1770s, the resistance movements that formed to oppose Nazi occupations throughout Europe during World War II, plus, more recently, Palestinian resistance to Israeli occupation, Iraqi resistance to the US occupation of Iraq, and the Taliban's resistance to the US occupation of Afghanistan. All of these suggests that generalization 1 is approximately truer than generalization 2.

However, it should be clear. As the preceding example reveals, both generalizations 1 and 2 have their approximate truths. This means that the establishment of the approximate truths of generalizations accounting for the same something can lead to situations of multiple truths. For example, by the turn of the twenty-first century there were on the order of ten theories that sought to explain the functioning of the prefrontal cortex (Miller and Cohen 2001). All were supported by some evidence and so all had their approximate truths. Here was a situation of clamoring multiple truths. What does one do? What one does *not* do is throw up her or his hands and lament that truth is "inherently partial" (Clifford 1986: 7).

Rather, it is at this point that one realizes that the search for truth is hard work—very hard work. Researchers need to design research to look at the validation histories of different generalizations that account for the same something. They need to establish what generalizations explain the most reality and have longer histories of successful validation. They need to establish whether different generalizations that account for different aspects of the same something can be integrated into a common explanation of that something. For example, the two generalizations about the consequences of occupation might be brought into a common set of generalizations if the effects of the occupation upon the welfare of those occupied was considered, with it understood that if welfare declined under occupation, resistance occurred, and if it increased under occupation acquiescence occurred. So there is now the generalization:

3. Under occupation, if the occupied peoples' welfare increased, acquiescence is probable, while if occupied peoples' welfare decreased resistance is probable.

The general point that has just been argued is that the quest for the Holy Grail of Absolute Truth should be put aside in order to get down to the nitty-gritty of sorting out approximate truths. This, assuming that the most objective observational techniques available have been employed, is a matter of validation—first, validation of particular generalizations and, second, examining the validation histories of different generalizations accounting for the same something to discover which generalizations have the most robust validation histories.

This concludes the presentation of CSR's theoretical approach and returns us to the question, so what is theory?

So What *Is* Theory?

Sapere aude!
—Kant, "Answering the Question: What Is Enlightenment?"

To answer this question it is necessary to know what theory is about, and what it is. Theory is about something. Something is *istheit* (what is) at particular times and places, that is, at specific time-beings. Actually, theory is about any something, which means it is about anything. So, when doing theory, to co-opt the great philosopher of science Paul Feyerabend's pronouncement (and give it a different meaning), "anything goes" (1975). What "goes" in theory is the performance of two artistic practices: theorizing and validating—re-presenting anything as generalizations and observing whether these generalizations are approximately true.

Theory in this optic is not a mirror of reality but a re-presentation of a not completely knowable something. Theorizing is the explicit formulation of generalizations, of which there are three main types (empirical generalizations, theories, and hypotheses). The making of generalizations is the fabrication of generalization necklaces. This involves discarding the fool's gold of blurred or blind concepts and the acquisition of concepts with clear sensational hooks. Such concepts are the necklace's gems that need to be strung, in the sense of showing the relationship between the jewels.

Validating is the hammering out of the approximate truth of generaliza-tion necklaces upon the anvil of anything for the time-being. It is the confron-tation of re-presentation with reality, which involves acquisition of knowledge of whether what is theoretically said to occur, occurs. Attainment of such knowledge depends upon making observations to get the facts to provide the evidence bearing upon whether theoretical necklaces are for real. There are a number of requirements for making competent observations. These include rigorous methodologies and tactics to guide observations, which are encour-aged by a discipline's having a tradition of methodological cosmopolitanism. Such methodologies will also operate to eliminate as far as possible internal and external biasing while strengthening observational representativeness and intersubjectivity. It is time to return to anthropologists coming and going at their ritual performances.

Why has the conversation been flat as anthropologists come and go, talking theory? Perhaps, it is because they are caught in a bind that literally leaves them speechless. They know theory is the core, but they don't know what the "core" is. They are not great at fabricating generalization necklaces, especially at making them explicit and in stringing concepts together in neck-laces. They tend not to explicitly validate generalizations. They are not good at making intersubjective or representative observations, so their objectivity is pretty much an unknown quality. Kant (1784), in his famous essay "What Is Enlightenment?" suggested heroes were those whose art was to "*Sapere aude!*" (Dare to know!). Perhaps what anthropology needs is artists who "dare to know" scientific theory. This might just put some bubbles back in the cham-pagne consumed as anthropologists come and go, chatting about theory.

Notes

1. The grudges in the science wars have been serious. Bruno Latour, for example, was proposed for a position at Princeton's Institute for Advanced Study by Clifford Geertz. This angered certain mathematicians and physicists at the institute (possibly because Latour was said to study them as if they were a bunch of tribalists). They blocked his appointment (McMillen 1997).

2. Empirical generalization, hypothesis, and theory are employed "in a variety of ways" (Kaplan 1964: 88). Their definition in the text follows the usage of Wallace (1971). Hypotheses are often referred to as "any claim that is put forward as a plausible con-jecture" (Curd and Cover 1998: 1298). Hypotheses deduced from theory initially lack validation but are plausible due to their deductive origin.

3. There are different models of explanation. Curd and Cover (1998) present a number of these. Kitcher and Salmon (1989) and Salmon (2006) provide useful accounts of the history and variety of approaches to explanation.

4. Validation is sometimes called "confirmation." I prefer the former to the latter term, because confirmation more strongly implies that some generalization has been con-

firmed, once and for all, which I do not believe to be the case. There are different theories of validation, with Bayesian confirmation theory being popular. It is supposed to compute the conditional probability of a generalization given certain evidence (for a discussion of Bayesian approaches, see Curd and Cover 1998: 549–674).

5. Discussion of objectivity can be found in Megill (1994), Douglas (2011), and Gaukroger (2012). Daston and Galison (2010) discuss the historical development of the term.

References

Achinstein, Peter and Stephen Barker, eds. *The Legacy of Logical Positivism*. Baltimore: Johns Hopkins University Press, 1969.

Agazzi, Evandro, Javier Echeverría, and Amparo Gómez Rodríguez, eds. *Epistemology and the Social*. Amsterdam: Rodopi, 2008.

Aristotle. *Poetics*. Chicago, University of Chicago Press, 1998.

Barnes, Barry, David Bloor, and John Henry. *Scientific Knowledge: A Sociological Analysis*. Chicago: University of Chicago Press, 1996.

Baudrillard, Jean. "Forgetting Baudrillard." *Social Text* 15 (1886): 140–144.

Boghossian, Paul. *Fear of Knowledge: Against Relativism and Constructivism*. Oxford: Oxford University Press, 2006.

Boyle, Robert. *A Continuation of the Experiments Physico-mechanical Touching the Spring and Weight of Air, and Their Effects*, 1662, Observatorio da Marina de San Fernando, accessed 11 July 2015. http://bvpb.mcu.es/en/consulta/resultados_navegacion.cmd ?posicion=1&forma=ficha&id=805.

Chandrasekharan, Sanjay. "Becoming Knowledge: Cognitive and Neural Mechanisms That Support Scientific Intuition." In *Rational Intuition: Philosophical Roots, Scientific Investigations*, edited by Lisa M. Osbeck and Barbara S. Held, 307–37. Cambridge: Cambridge University Press, 2014.

Childers, Joseph, and Gary Hentzi. *Columbia Dictionary of Modern Literary Criticism*. New York: Columbia University Press, 1995.

Clifford, James. *The Predicament of Culture: Twentieth Century Ethnography, Literature, and Art*. Cambridge, MA: Harvard University Press, 1988.

Connolly, John and Thomas Keuter. *Hermeneutics Versus Science? Three German Views. South Bend: University of Notre Dame Press, 1988.*

Crapanzano, Vincent. "Hermes' Dilemma: The Masking of Subversion in Ethnographic Description." In *Writing Culture,* edited by James Clifford and George Marcus, 51–77. Los Angeles; University of California Press, 1983.

Culler, Jonathan. *On Deconstruction: Theory and Criticism after Structuralism*. Ithaca: Cornell University Press, 1982.

Curd, Martin and Jan A. Cover. *The Philosophy of Science: The Central Issues*. New York: Norton, 1998.

Darwin, Charles. *On the Origin of Species by Means of Natural Selection, or the Preservation of Favoured Races in the Struggle for Life*. London: John Murray, 1859.

Daston, Lorraine and Peter Galison. *Objectivity*. Cambridge, MA: MIT. 2010.

Deleuze, Gilles and Félix Guattari. *Anti-Oedipus: Capitalism and Schizophrenia*. Minneapolis: University of Minnesota Press, 1983 [1972].

———. *What Is Philosophy?* New York: Columbia University Press, 1994.

DePaul, Michael R. and William Ramsey, eds. *Rethinking Intuition: The Psychology of Intuition and Its Role in Philosophical Inquiry.* Lanham: Rownam and Littlefield, 1998.

Descola, Philippe. *Beyond Nature and Culture.* Chicago: University of Chicago Press, 2013.

Douglas, H. "Facts, Values, and Objectivity." In *The SAGE Handbook of Philosophy of Social Science,* edited by I. Jarvie and J. Zamora Bonilla, 513–529. London: SAGE Publications, 2011.

Durkheim, Emile. *Suicide.* New York: Free Press, 1998 [1966].

Eggan, Fred. "Social Anthropology and the Method of Controlled Comparison." *American Anthropologist,* no. 56, no. 5 (1954): 743–63. DOI: 10.1525/aa.1954.56.5.02a00020.

Feyerabend, Paul. *Against Method: Outline of an Anarchistic Theory of Knowledge.* London: New Left Books, 1975.

Fine, Eric, Dean Delis, David Dean, Victoria Beckman, Bruce Miller, Howard Rosen, and Joel Kramer. "Left Frontal Lobe Contributions to Concept Formation: A Quantitative MRI Study of D-KEFS Sorting Test Performance." *Journal of Clinical Experimental Neuropsychology* 31 (2009): 624-631. DOI: 10.1080/13803390802419017

Føllesdal, Dagfinn. "Hermeneutics and the Hypothetico-Deductive Method." *Dialectica* 33, nos. 3–4 (1979): 319–36. DOI: 10.1111/j.1746-8361.1979.tb00759.x.

Fortes, Meyer and Edward E. Evans-Pritchard. *African Political Systems.* Oxford: Oxford University Press, 1940.

Foucault, Michel. *The History of Sexuality: An Introduction.* New York: Vintage, 1990 [1978].

Fortun, Kim. "Ethnography in Late Industrialism." *Cultural Anthropology.* 27(2012): 446–464.

Friedman, Kajsa and Jonathan Friedman. *The Anthropology of Global Systems: Historical Transformations.* New York: Altamira, 2008.

Frandy, Tim. "Review: *Beyond Nature and Culture. Journal of Folklore Research.* (1988). URL: http://www.jfr.indiana.edu/review.php?id=1639. Accessed May 16, 2016.

Friedman, Michael. *Reconsidering Logical Positivism.* Cambridge: Cambridge University Press, 1999.

Gaukroger, Stephen. *Objectivity: A Very Short Introduction.* Oxford: Oxford. 2012.

Geertz, Clifford. *Works and Lives: The Anthropologist as Author.* Stanford: Stanford University Press, 1988.

Goffman, Erving. *Frame Analysis: An Essay on the Organization of Experience.* Boston: Northeastern University Press, 1974.

Goodenough, Ward. *Culture, Language and Society.* Menlo Park: Benjamin/Cummings, 1981 [1971].

Harding, Sandra. *The Science Question in Feminism.* Ithaca: Cornell University Press, 1993.

Haraway, Donna. "Situated Knowledges: The Science Question in Feminism and the Privilege of Partial Perspective." *Feminist Studies* 14, no. 3 (1988): 575–99.

Heidegger, Martin. *Being and Time.* Translated by Joan Stambaugh. Albany: State University of New York Press, 1996 [1927].

Hempel, Carl. *Aspects of Scientific Explanation.* New York: Free Press, 1965.

Herzfeld, Michael. *Anthropology: Theoretical Practice in Culture and Society.* Oxford: Wiley-Blackwell, 2001.

Horstmann, Frank. *Leviathan und die Erpumper. Erinnerungen an Thomas Hobbes in der Luftpumpe.* Berlin: Mackensen, 2012.

Humboldt, Alexander von. *Views of Nature.* Edited by Stephen Jackson and Laura Walls. Chicago: University of Chicago Press, 2014.

Hunt, Shelby. "Theory Status, Inductive Realism, and Approximate Truth: No Miracles, No Charades." *International Studies in the Philosophy of Science* 25 (2011): 159–178.

Kant, Immanuel. *Perpetual Peace: A Philosophical Essay.* London: George Allen and Unwin, 1917 [1790].

———. *Critique of Pure Reason.* Dent: London, 1991 [1781].

———. "An Answer to the Question: What is Enlightenment." In *From Modernism to Postmodernism: An Anthology,* edited by Lawrence Cahoone 51–57. Oxford: Blackwell 1996 [1784].

Kaplan, Abraham. *The Conduct of Inquiry: Methodology for Behavioral Science.* San Francisco: Chandler, 1964.

Keller, Evelyn Fox. *Reflections on Gender and Science,* 10th anniversary ed. New Haven: Yale University Press, 1995.

Kitcher, Philip. *The Advancement of Science.* Oxford: Oxford University Press, 1993.

Kitcher, Philip and Wesley Salmon, eds. *Scientific Explanation.* Minneapolis: University of Minnesota Press, 1989.

Koertge, Noretta. *A House Built on Sand: Exposing Postmodern Myths about Science.* Oxford, Oxford University Press, 1998.

Kuhn, Thomas. *The Structure of Scientific Revolutions,* 2nd ed. Chicago: University of Chicago Press, 1970.

Kuznets, Simon. "Economic Growth and Income Inequality." *American Economic Review* 45, no. 1 (1955): 1–28.

Lakatos, Imre. "Falsification and the Methodology of Scientific Research Programmes." In *Criticism and the Growth of Knowledge,* edited by Imre Lakatos and Alan Musgrave, 205–59. Cambridge: Cambridge University Press, 1970.

Lapinski, Voytek. "Review of Philippe Descola's Beyond Nature and Culture." Accessed June 12, 2016.https://www.academia.edu/7084554/ Review_of_Philippe_Descolas_Beyond_Nature_and_Culture.

Latour, Bruno. "One More Turn after the Social Turn: Easing Science Studies into the Non-Modern World." In *The Social Dimensions of Science,* edited by Ernan McMullin, 272–92. South Bend: Notre Dame University Press, 1992.

———. *The Pasteurization of France.* Cambridge, MA: Harvard University Press, 1993.

———. "Why Has Critique Run out of Steam? From Matters of Fact to Matters of Concern." *Critical Inquiry* 30, no. 2 (2004): 225–48. DOI: 10.1086/421123.

Leplin, Jarrett. *A Novel Defense of Scientific Realism.* New York: Oxford University Press, 1997.

Lévi-Strauss, Claude. *The Elementary Structures of Kinship.* Boston: Beacon. 1969 [1949].

———. *The Raw and the Cooked; Introduction to a Science of Mythology.* New York: Harper and Row, 1975[1964].

Longino, Helen. *Science as Social Knowledge.* Princeton: Princeton University Press, 1990.

Lukes, Steven. *Emile Durkheim: His Life and Work, A Historical and Critical Study.* Stanford: Stanford University Press, 1973.

Lyotard, Jean-François. *The Postmodern Condition: A Report on Knowledge.* Minneapolis: University of Minnesota Press, 1984 [1979].

Marcus, George. "Experimental Forms for the Expression of Norms in the Ethnography of the Contemporary." *Hau* 3 (2013): 197-217. DOI: http://dx.doi.org/10.14318/hau3.2.011.

McGee, R. Jon and Richard Warms. *Anthropological Theory: An Introduction.* Houston: Mayfield, 2000.

McMillen, Liz. "The Science Wars Flare at the Institute for Advanced Study." *The Chronicle of Higher Education,* 16 May 1997, accessed 12 July 2015. http://chronicle.com/article/The-Science-Wars-Flare-at-the/76437.

Medwar, Peter. *Induction and Intuition in Scientific Thought.* Philadelphia: American Philosophical Society, 1969.

Megill, Alan. *Rethinking Objectivity.* Durham: Duke. 1994.

Miller, Earl K. and Jonathan D. Cohen. "An Integrative Theory of Prefrontal Cortex Function." *Annual Review of Neuroscience,* no. 24 (2001): 167–202. DOI: 10.1146/annurev.neuro.24.1.167.

Moore, Henrietta and Todd Sanders. *Anthropology in Theory: Issues in Epistemology.* Oxford: Blackwell Publishing, 2006.

Murdock, George. *Social Structure.* New York: Macmillan, 1949.

Niiniluoto, Ilkka. *Truthlikeness.* Dordrecht: Reidel, 1987.

Ortner, Sherry. *Anthropology and Social Theory: Culture, Power, and the Acting Subject.* Durham: Duke University Press, 2006.

Osbeck, Lisa and Barbara Held, eds. *Rational Intuition: Philosophical Roots, Scientific Investigations.* Cambridge, UK: Cambridge University Press, 2014.

Outhwaite, William. *Concept Formation in Social Science.* London; Routledge, 2011.

Piketty, Thomas. *Capital in the Twenty-First Century.* Cambridge, MA: Harvard University Press, 2014.

Plato. *The Republic.* Mineola: Dover, 2000.

Principe, Lawrence. *The Aspiring Adept: Robert Boyle and His Alchemical Quest.* Princeton: Princeton University Press, 1998.

Psillos, Stanthis. *Scientific Realism: How Science Tracks Truth.* London: Routledge, 1999.

Rabinow, Paul. "Representations are Social Facts; Modernity and Post-Modernity in Anthropology. In *Writing Culture,* edited by James Clifford and George E. Marcus, 234–261. Los Angeles: University of California Press, 1986.

Radcliffe-Brown, Alfred R. and Daryll Forde. *African Systems of Kinship and Marriage.* Oxford: Oxford University Press, 1950.

Resnik, David B. "Convergent Realism and Approximate Truth." In *PSA: Proceedings of the Biennial Meeting of the Philosophy of Science Association,* no. 1 (1992): 421–34.

Reyna, Stephen. "Literary Anthropology and the Case Against Science." *Man* 29, no. 3 (1994): 555–81.

———. "Theory Counts: (Discounting) Discourse to the Contrary by Adopting a Confrontational Stance." *Anthropological Theory* 1, no. 1 (2001): 9–31.

———. "Hard Truth and Validation: What Zeus Understood." Working Paper no. 65. Halle/Saale: Max Planck Institute for Social Anthropology, 2004.

———. "Hard Truths: Addressing the 'Crisis' in Anthropology." In *Beyond Writing Culture: Current Intersections of Epistemologies and Practices of Representation,* edited by Olaf Zenker and Karsten Kumoll, 163–86. New York: Berghahn, 2010.

Rorty, Richard. *Philosophy and the Mirror of Nature.* Princeton: Princeton University Press, 1979.

Russell, Bertrand. *The Problems of Philosophy.* Oxford: Oxford University Press, 1995 [1959].

Salmon, Wesley. *Four Decades of Scientific Explanation.* Pittsburgh: University of Pittsburgh Press, 2006.

Sanjek, Roger. *Fieldnotes: The Makings of Anthropology.* Ithaca: Cornell University Press, 1990.

Sargent, Rose-Mary. *The Diffident Naturalist: Robert Boyle and the Philosophy of Experiment.* Chicago: University of Chicago Press, 1995.

Schensul, Stephen, Jean Schensul, and Margaret Le Compte. *Essential Ethnographic Methods: Observations, Interviews, and Questionnaires.* Walnut Creek: Altamira, 1999.

Schlick, Moritz. *Das Wesen der Wahrheit nach der modernen Logik.* Vierteljahrsschrift für wissenschaftliche Philosophie und Soziologie, Jg. 34, 1910, p. 386–477.

Shapin, Steven and Simon Schaffer. *Leviathan and the Air-Pump: Hobbes, Boyle, and the Experimental Life.* Princeton: Princeton University Press, 1985.

Smaling, Adri. "Varieties of Methodological Intersubjectivity—the Relations with Qualitative and Quantitative Research, and with Objectivity." *Quality and Quantity,* 26, no. 2 (1985): 169–80. DOI: 10.1007/BF02273552.

Snow, C.P. *The Two Cultures.* Cambridge: Cambridge University Press, 2001 [1959].

Sokal, Alan. *Beyond the Hoax: Science, Philosophy and Culture.* Oxford: Oxford University Press, 2008.

Tyler, Steven. "Post-modern Ethnography: From Document of the Occult to Occult Document." In *Writing Culture,* edited by James Clifford and George E. Marcus, 122–41. Los Angeles: University of California Press, 1986.

University of Manitoba, Department of Anthropology. "Ethnographic Methods." Module 1 in *Method and Theory in Cultural Anthropology,* accessed 21 July 2015. https://www.umanitoba.ca/faculties/arts/anthropology/courses/122/module1/methods.html.

Volz, Kirsten G. and D. Yves von Cramon. "What Neuroscience Can Tell about Intuitive Processes in the Context of Perceptual Discovery." *Journal of Cognitive Neuroscience* 18, no. 12 (2006): 2077–87. DOI:10.1162/jocn.2006.18.12.2077.

Wallace, Walter. *The Logic of Science in Sociology.* Chicago: Aldine, 1971.

Weinberg, Steven. *Facing Up: Science and Its Cultural Adversaries.* Cambridge, MA: Harvard University Press, 2001.

Weinberger, David. *Too Big to Know: Rethinking Knowledge Now That the Facts Aren't the Facts, Experts Are Everywhere, and the Smartest Person in the Room Is the Room.* New York: Basic Books, 2014.

Weston, Thomas. "Approximate Truth and Scientific Realism." *Philosophy of Science* 59, no. 1 (1992): 53–74.

PART II
 Ontology

chapter three

Dialectics of Force

Contradiction, Logics, and
Conservation of *Délires*

> *Social change: the difference between the current and antecedent*
> *condition of any selected aspect of social organization or structure.*
> David Jary and Julia Jary, *Collins Dictionary of Sociology*

T his essay's goal is to formulate a critical structural realist approach to dialectics that seeks to explain two forms— iterational and transformational—of change that produce "difference between current and antecedent" social forms. It does so by formulating a position, termed "dialectics of force," that employs elements of Marxist and non-Marxist philosophers of force and power. The work needed to achieve this goal involves critiquing Hegelian dialectics, which analysis when performed provides clues as to how to construct a dialectics of force approach. There are three sections in the essay.

The first tells a ghost story in the haunted house of Hegelian dialectics. The next two sections take certain understandings made in the haunted house and employs them to, first, rethink the concept of contradiction and, then, offer a theory of how, under certain circumstances, change is realized in response to contradictions. The second section reconceptualizes contradiction. It broadens a structural Marxist view of contradiction based upon a synthesis of the views of Hobbes, Hume, Nietzsche, and Godelier. The third section presents a theory of realization that explains how actors realize solutions to the vulnerabilities due to contradictions, where the iterational and transformational changes in social forms are choreographed according to a principle of the conservation of *délires*. Finally, in the conclusion it is argued that change in human being is dominated by contradiction between logics of disorder versus those of order. Attention turns to a discussion of Hegelian dialectics, argued to have emerged out of the philosopher's theological disposition.

Ghost Story

Love him or loath him, Hegel has always attracted enormous debate organized in what might be termed a love/loathing dialectic. Loathing him, Schopenhauer in the nineteenth century labeled Hegel "a flat-headed, insipid, nauseating, illiterate charlatan" (1847 [1974]: 1). Continuing the hate in the mid-twentieth century, Marvin Harris opined that dialectics were a "Hegelian monkey" (1968: 230). Loving Hegel, Marx in the nineteenth century called him a "mighty thinker" (1867: 25), while Lenin at the beginning of the twentieth century spoke of "the great Hegelian dialectics" (1966 [1904]: 7).[1] Consider what is at issue when eliminating dialectics.

Marx had based his explanation of change on his version of Hegel's dialectics, which meant that Marxist dialectics tended to be swept away along with those of Hegel. Karl Popper (1945), for example, authored a famous dismissal of Marxian dialectics, in part because of its borrowing from Hegel. Anthony Giddens chided Marx for his "cavalier use of terminology" when discussing contradiction (1979: 137). The *Penguin Dictionary of Politics* (Robertson 1988) possesses no entry for dialectics, presumably because it deems it unworthy of definition. Jon Elster analyzed Marx's different usages of the dialectic and concluded Marx dealt with the subject in "vapid terms" (1985: 37).

In the 1960s, when Harris (1968) wrote, a person with a "monkey on their back" was someone "wasted" due to heroin addiction. Harris never explained why Hegel's monkey was so enervated by the heroin of dialectics. Of course, dialectics were at the heart of Marxist theories of change. So in declaring them a Hegelian monkey, Harris was denouncing them as the addled musings of a simian junky, leaving Marxist theory changeless, which Harris, and legions of liberals, were delighted to do. My goal in what follows is neither to glorify nor to deprecate Hegel but, rather, to winnow what is useful in him from what is not.

However, before proceeding to this winnowing, a curiosity might be noted. Independent of whatever is thought about Hegel, the concept of contradiction has had its own life. Man Ray, the surrealist artist at the turn of the twentieth century, confessed, "I like contradictions" (2015). Max Weber, famous for proposing an alternative to Marxian class analysis, was nevertheless comfortable working with a concept of "organizational contradiction" (1968). More recently, Barron Youngsmith, no Marxist he, when talking about the Soviet collapse in 1989, noted that, of course, it was due to "internal contradictions" (2010: 6). Daniel Bell, a card-carrying non-Marxist, insisted there are "contradictions within society" (1976: 10). Giddens, explicitly skeptical of Marx, worked with a concept of contradiction, one featuring a "dialectic of control" (1979: 149).

Elster, who believed Marx's dialectics to be "vapid," thought that social contradiction could be "an important tool for the theory of social change" (1985: 37). Recently, David Harvey (2014), in an expository tour de force, explicated much of the contemporary world in seventeen contradictions. The curiosity, then, is that even though dialectics have their detractors, contradictions from surrealists to liberals to leftists have been more affectionately treated. This oddity, then, offers something of a warrant for later employing contradiction in service of a reconceptualized dialectic. Now readers, thrill to the excitement of a (Hegelian) ghost story.

"Theologian of the Spirit"

> We can with some justification, then, speak of Hegel as a "theologican"— but why a "theologian of the spirit?" The answer is that "spirit" identifies for Hegel the distinctive ontological quality of God.
> —Hodgson, G.W.F. Hegel: Theologian of the Spirit

Louis Althusser, on the loathing side of the love/loathing dialectic, called Hegel a "specter" (2014). Specters are ghosts. I am in sympathy with his view, as is explained next. Idealism is commonly opined to be the core of Hegel's philosophy. Idealism was certainly there, but I believe Hegel's heart was with God. Hegel's "generations" were Lutheran pastors (Pinkard 2001: 3). The youthful Hegel began his intellectual life at the theological seminary at Tubingen— nicknamed "the Old Man" because of his serious, studious ways. Among other subjects in Tubingen, he "imbibed deeply of German and Swabian mystics" (Hodgson 1997: 1), and, as a mature philosopher, he championed a view that "philosophy is *theology*" (ibid.: 5, emphasis in the original). Specifically, according to the theologian Karl Barth, Hegel made "the dialectical method of logic the essential nature of God" (2002: 420).

However, his "theology" might be thought of as a modern one, caught up in a secularizing post-Enlightenment intellectual milieu.[2] So, for example, he rejected the dualistic Christian orthodoxy authored by St. Augustine (c. AD 415) that there were two cities—an earthly city and one of God. For Augustine, writing just after the Vandals' sack of Rome in AD 410, the earthly city, a metaphor for the state, was a place of corruption and evil. For Hegel, writing during the rising of Prussian nationalism, the state and God were conjoined. Hegel was crystalline on this topic, insisting in *The Philosophy of Right*: "The State is the Divine Idea as it exists on earth ... We must worship the State as the manifestation of the Divine on earth ... The State is the march of God through the world" (qtd. in Popper 1945: 29).[3] Let us explore Hegel's God marching through the world of the Prussian state. To make this exploration, attention is focused upon his views on spirit and history.

Hegel, in his *Encyclopaedia of the Philosophical Sciences* (1830), published the year prior to his death, asserted, "For these thousands of years the same Architect has directed the work: and that Architect is the one living Mind whose nature is to think" (1830). Readers may query: Who is the Architect whose Mind directs? The question was answered in *The Philosophy of History*, published posthumously, in which Hegel specified, "God governs the World, the Actual workings of his government … is the History of the World" (1899: 41). He is blunt: the Architect is God and "God governs." Furthermore, in the same work, he articulated his project, stating, "The phenomenon we investigate" is "Universal History" (ibid.: 19).[4] Hegel could not be clearer. He seeks understanding of Universal History, that is, world history, which he believes has an Architect—God—who "governs." Such a project is theological but involves a theology that reaches back before Christian times.

In the Spirit of Things

Knowing that the God-Architect is "Mind," raises the question: What is this Mind? Answering this question leads us to a central concept in Hegelian thought, Spirit, which had been fundamental since *Phenomenology of the Spirit* (1807). In the same sentence in which Hegel informed us that his object of study was Universal History, he further confided that this was the "realm of the Spirit" (1899: 19). The German term for Spirit is *geist*, translated in English as "soul," "mind," and often "ghost." I shall translate *geist* as ghost, which means that when Hegel is talking about *geist*, he is telling a ghost story.

Spirit is an old notion, with a palimpsest of meanings. In pre-Christian religion, *geist* was related to animistic conceptions and is the anima, spirit, or ghosts of animals or things (Murphy 2010). In animistic religions there is no scientific account of how the anima or spirit acts. It just does.[5] Christian theology appropriated the concept and made it the Holy Ghost, in German the *Heiligen Geist*. There is a large and varied Christian Holy Ghost theology called pneumatology, one aspect of which is that it is divine essence, godliness, that enters things, especially Christian believers, and directs them. By the Middle Ages, ordinary folk and thinkers alike in Germany and elsewhere in Christendom were thoroughly familiar with the Christian ghost story. It was hegemonic and explained how God governed.

In Germany, following the Middle Ages, *geist* was "adapted from religious discourse" and began a process of secularization (Boyer 2005: 55). The Romantics were important in this process, especially the two Johanns—Johann Fichte (1762–1814) and Johann Gottfried von Herder (1744–1803)—among whom the notion of *geist* "continued to index the pietistic calling of the infinite spirit at work in the individual" (ibid.: 56). Herder developed the notion of *volksgeist* (literally, "people's spirit"), which was a nation's language, aesthetic creations, institutions, and practices.[6]

Hegel, then, would have been thoroughly familiar with *geist*, both from his religious heritage and from its adoption by the Romantics. *Geist* ultimately for Hegel was a rational, self-conscious, purposive means of thinking. It was autonomous, undetermined by the world around it. In fact, when the Ghost made up its Mind it made the world, which was why Hegel was an idealist. Hegel developed a notion of the *weltgeist* (World Spirit) to explain Universal History. Particular nations had their *volkgeist*, but Universal History—the history of all nations—exhibited the telos of the *weltgeist*. What was *weltgeist*?

Hegel stated in *Elements of the Philosophy of Right*, "Each stage of world history is a necessary moment in the Idea of the World Spirit" (1821), which prompts the question: What was Hegel's Idea? Hegel links the Idea with God, insisting, "God and the nature of his will . . ., these we call, philosophically, the Idea" (1953: 21). Further, he links it with reason, stating, the "Idea or Reason is the True, the Eternal, the Absolute Power … that … manifests itself in the world" (ibid.: 11). God, the Holy Ghost, is the Idea. History is moments "in the Idea of the World Spirit," the "development" of "the moments of reason." Further, realization of the Idea leads to Freedom. This is Hegel's Ghost story. This leads us to what might be termed "Hegel's realization problem."

The Realization Problem

A realization problem is the need to present an adequate explanation of how something occurs, that is, how it is realized. It is known, for example, that smoking causes lung cancer. The problem is how does this occur. The explanation of lung cancer, then, suffers from a realization problem. Just as smoking provokes lung cancer, so Ghost produces history, and Hegel's realization problem is his need to explain how Ghost is realized in historical realities.

He begins his solution to this problem, in a section of his *Reason in History* titled "The Means of Realization," by insisting, "The Idea has within itself the determination of its self-consciousness, of activity" (1953: 21). In his *The Philosophy of World History* he states that there are "means the World-Spirit uses of realizing its Idea" (Hegel 1899: 20). These means are individual persons, carriers of subjective spirit, who realize the Idea. Their "vast congeries of volitions, interests and activities, constitute the instruments and means of World Spirit for attaining its Object; bringing it to consciousness, and realizing it" (ibid.: 29). However, not all persons are equal when it comes to realizing the Idea. The more important actors are World Historical Persons, whose own particular aims are deeply and powerfully infused with those of the Ghost and who turn out to be largely military types like Alexander, Caesar, and Napoleon. The question remains: How is the ghostly Idea brought to consciousness? Answering this question leads to Hegel's dialectic.

He discusses the dialectic in *The Philosophy of History* when explaining history's trajectory:

> Universal history—as already demonstrated—shows the development of the consciousness of Freedom on the part of Spirit, and of the consequent *realisation* of that Freedom. This development implies a gradation—a series of increasingly adequate expressions or manifestations of Freedom, which result from its Idea. The logical, and—as still more prominent—the *dialectical* nature of the Idea in general, viz. that it is self-determined—that it assumes successive forms which it successively transcends; and by this very process of transcending its earlier stages, gains an affirmative, and, in fact, a richer and more concrete shape. *(1899: ch. 72)*

History is the "realization" of Freedom that results from the Ghost's Idea that has a "dialectical nature." Hegel's Ghost is a Dialectical Ghost, and at this juncture we enter into debates between Hegel scholars over the nature of the dialectic.

Different views prevail in these debates, of which two are important: that Hegel's dialectics do not take the form many believe of them, and/or the dialectics need the addition of a non-Hegelian element in them to be useful. For example, concerning the first view, many have been taught that Hegel believed reason unfolds through thesis, which becomes an antithesis, which is resolved with a synthesis. However, according to Walter Kaufman:

> Fichte introduced into German philosophy the three-step of thesis, antithesis, and synthesis, using these three terms. Schelling took up this terminology. Hegel did not. He never once used these three terms together to designate three stages in an argument or account in any of his books. And they do not help us understand his Phenomenology, his Logic, or his philosophy of history. (1966: 166)

What, then, was the Hegelian dialectic. Michael Inwood has offered what might be termed the "standard" of the non–thesis–antithesis–synthesis understanding:

> Hegel's dialectic involves three steps: (1) One or more concepts or categories are taken as fixed … This is the stage of UNDERSTANDING. (2) When we reflect on such categories, one or more contradictions emerge in them. This is the stage of dialectic proper, or negative REASON. (3) The result of dialectic is a new, higher category, which embraces the earlier categories and resolves the contradiction in them. This is the stage of SPECULATION or positive reason. (1992: 81–82)

Thus, for Kaufman, what people thought to be Hegel's dialectic was not. Inwood seems to be offering the thesis–antithesis–synthesis view of contradiction in other terms.

Regarding the second set of views about Hegel's dialectic, consider that of the philosopher Charles Peirce, who wrote in his *Fixation of Belief* that

Hegel "himself calls his method *dialectics*, meaning that frank discussion of the difficulties to which any opinion spontaneously gives rise will lead to modification after modification until a tenable position is attained" (1893: 17). What Peirce was saying was that Hegel's dialectic was "frank discussion" of "difficulties" leading to "modification after modification" until a "tenable" view was reached.

Quite recently Slavoj Žižek has bet upon another interpretation of the Hegelian dialectic, confiding that Žižek's "wager was (and is) that, through their interaction (reading Hegel through Lacan and vice versa), psychoanalysis and Hegelian dialectics mutually redeem themselves, shedding their accustomed skin, and emerging in a new unexpected shape" (2012: 18). The metaphor here is confusing. The "shedding" of skin referred to in the preceding quotation is that of snakes, with it asserted that by shedding their snake skins psychoanalysis and Hegelian dialectics will "mutually redeem themselves."

Žižek seems to be saying that a proper dialectics is Lacanian. Findlay has gone further than any of the preceding views, explicitly denying that there was any dialectical method at all in Hegel (1958: 353). To appropriate Žižek's metaphor, let us imagine each version of the Hegelian dialectic as a snake. Consequently, the Dialectical Ghost is something of a tangle of competing snakes, implying knowledge of it is a jumble of disputing serpents, which means that it is difficult to know which of the hissing serpents is *the* Hegelian dialectic.

Regardless of the difficulties with the dialectic, there remains this question: How is the Dialectical Ghost realized in the world? Hegel responds to this question by answering, "This element of abstract action is to be regarded as the bond, the middle term, between the abstract Idea, which reposes in the inner recesses of Spirit, and the external world" (1953: 34). How does this "middle term" operate? Hegel teaches us that:

> Purposes, principles, and the like, are at first inner thoughts, our inner intention. They are not yet in reality ... A second element must be added for it to become reality, namely, activity, actualization ... It is only through this activity that the concept and its implicit ("being-in-themselves") can be actualized. (1953: 27-28)

The question here is: What is "actualization?" Hegel tells readers it is "activity." However, what is actualized is activity, which leads to the unsatisfying, circular conclusion that activity leads to activity. We shall return to the implications of the preceding for the realization problem, following a summary of Hegel's ghostly project.

The project asserts six principles:

1. Universal History progresses in one direction; it is teleological.
2. Each stage of Universal History is the "necessary moment" of the World Ghost (*weltgeist*) "for attaining its Object."

3. The World Ghost is the Idea, which is reason that works according to a dialectic that strives for "the realization of its Ideal being."
4. The means of the World Ghost are individuals—some important World Historical Figures, others ordinary folk—within whom the Ghost is potent and acts according to the "determination" of the Idea's "actualization."
5. This ghostly teleology is toward the Prussian state.
6. Because "God governs," the state must be worshipped "as the manifestation of the Divine on earth."

This is a theory of change strung out over a ghostly telos. Two complaints can be leveled against it that will help orient the approach later argued in the essay.

Complaints

A first complaint has to do with whether the basic concept, Ghost, in Hegel's theory suffers haecceity glitches. *Istheit,* it will be recalled from the introduction is "being itself."[7] The more a concept either lacks any actuality that "is," or the more that it lacks sensational hooks that make it possible to observe the "is" of a concept, the more the term is a conceptual blur exhibiting haecceity glitches—and the less its usefulness in securing empirical knowledge.[8] For example, phlogiston in early modern chemistry was a combustible substance supposed to provoke burning. It was never found. *Istheit* challenged, it was discarded. Haecceity-glitched concepts are blurry phantasms of realities not there or not knowable to be there. What is the *istheit* of the Dialectical Ghost?

Recall that the Ghost is Mind and Idea. It is individuals' "immediate substance" and is immanent in them. It is their "volitions." It is brought "to consciousness." So there is an "is" that is Ghost—individuals' "immediate substance." But what is this stuff? Every person is supposed to have it within them. It produces "will," presumably as a result of being brought "to consciousness." Descartes, whose notion of soul bore a resemblance to Hegel's *geist,* located the soul in the pineal gland. However, Hegel never detailed what sensations would be reports of the *geist*'s "immediate substance." Further, Hegel linked Ghost with God, and one wonders just where God was located in the "immediate substance" and what sensational hooks would allow observation of Her.[9] The Hegelian Ghost at worst is another phlogiston and at best suffers a haecceity glitch due to observational problems.

There is another complaint. Whatever the Ghost is, it "strives for realization of its Ideal being." This was Hegel's solution to the earlier outlined realization problem. One way that the Ghost realized its Idea was through the functioning of dialectical reason, with the dialectic raising the Spirit's Idea to consciousness. However, it was previously argued that his dialectics were problematic, because it was simply not clear what they were. There was an Inwood version, a Peirce version, a Žižek version, and a Findlay version, and it was indeterminate which dialectic was *the* Hegelian dialectic, and if it was unclear what dialectical reason might be, it was blurred how the Ghost became realized.

Moreover, Ghost becomes realized in the "external world" through "actualization," presumably guided by dialectical reason. "Actualization," as will be recalled, is "activity." But what sort of activity? Here Hegel is silent. Consequently, it is unclear what dialectical reason and actualization might be; there is no resolution of the realization problem. Rather, he takes an old animist concept, Ghost, keeps it and its operations conceptually blurred and (w)rapt in obscuring divinity, and makes it the "architect" of history. As a theory of change, it is an animistic Ghost story. At which point, Wittgenstein's axiom in the *Tractatus* (1961) seems relevant: "Whereof one cannot speak, thereof one must remain silent."

Given the preceding, how is one to proceed in the search for an explanation of change? One way is for Hegelians to continue to formulate their views, perhaps by removing haecceity glitches. Nonetheless, it is equally sensible to encourage alternative approaches. I take the latter approach and say good-bye to the Hegelian monkey–chasing animistic ghosts through the moments of history. But two lessons have been learned from our visit with Hegel. First, if one is to have a defendable dialectic it should be based upon an ontology with a notion of contradiction that is empirically analyzable, and, second, the realization problem needs to be addressed. Now let's turn to a critical structural realist alternative to the Old Man's dialectics.

Contradiction

> And do you know what "the world" is to me ? ... a play of forces and
> waves of forces, at the same time one and many ... a sea of forces,
> flowing and rushing together ... out of the play of contradictions.
> —Nietzsche, *Will to Power*

The dialectic formulated below has a strong Nietzschean element in that it understands contradiction in terms of "opposed forces ... flowing and rushing together."[10] However, before offering this view of contradiction, it is important to suggest an ontological alternative to Hegel's ghostly metaphysics. This will involve the views of Hobbes and Hume, as well as those of Nietzsche and Althusser, for it is by their views that critical structural realism's ontology as well as a revised understanding of contradiction are formulated.

Ontology: Structure, Force and Power

The structural Marxists had a view about the nature of being. Louis Althusser put it this way, "*The real*: it is structured" (1970: 36), in the sense that being, including human being, exhibits parts in some relationship to some other parts, which parts and relationships are knowable. The objects of study in such an ontology are the observed actualities of different sorts of structures. The structures I am interested in are not those imagined by the 1940s–1960s French structuralists, which, with the exception of the structural Marxists, ultimately concerned structures of the mind.

Rather, critical structural realism studies the organization of "human being." What is such being? Consider the following event that recently occurred in the American West but that could have happened anywhere. An older couple, who had been married for more than a half century, pulled out of a store's parking lot onto a heavily traveled highway. The husband, the driver, did not see the onrushing traffic. There was a terrible collision. When help arrived at the scene, they found the old couple dying, holding hands. In all places, in all times, in different ways, that is what humans do—hold hands—which is a trope for making connections. "Connections" in this optic are doing things together, even if, as was the case with the older couple, it is the last thing they do.

Human being is a space and time of reality, that of humanity, with humans reaching out to connect with others. Structures are connected parts. They may be small and intimate, a dying couple reaching out to hold each other's hand, or vast and impersonal, transnational corporations thrusting their hands into multitudes of pockets throughout the globe. What is distinctive about this standpoint is that it understands that human being has force within it with the power to make connection. Force and power are often not analytically differentiated.[11] Moreover, force generally has the bad connotation of being thuggish violence. In critical structural realism they are distinguished, with there being an especial emphasis on force. The two terms are discussed at length below but, for the moment, understand "reaching out" as the force that has the effect, the power, of making connections.

"Reaching out" occurs within a number of structural domains of human and nonhuman being. Human being is based upon structures found in "E-space," which is composed of social forms *external* to persons connected with other structures in "I-space," which includes biological forms *internal* to individuals, importantly the nervous system (Reyna 2002). E- and I-space are spaces both of place and of time. Structures operate in places; their operation occurs over time. E- and I-space are two spatiotemporal places but they are equally something of a monad, because your brain is in your body and your body is out and about in the external world of social forms.

The connections between E- and I-space are conditions for the existence of each other. I-space, through its structures that allow thinking, feeling, and muscle movement, make it possible for actors to act in E-space. E-space, through its structures that provide nutrients to biological structures, especially those of the brain, make it possible for these structures to operate in I-space. Importantly, as originally stressed by cultural ecologists (Steward 1955; Rappaport 1968), human being is articulated with nonhuman structures in the biological and physical environments in which it is found.

E-space structures are termed "social forms" and include practices, institutions, systems, and social beings. Persons using their force to do things in some sequence will be termed "actors," with the things they do, the powers they create. Actors, to use the trope of Lego construction toys, are the bricks of social forms. Actors, in binding with other actors, doing things, achieving particular forces and powers, will be understood to construct "practices" (as in surgical or dental practices), "institutions," cooccurring, interrelated practices (as in the institution of medicine), "systems," institutions connected with other institutions (as in political or economic systems), and "social beings," the most complex forms of human being, with the connections between these due to strings of force/power dyads, which strings exhibit logics. (Force/power dyads, strings, and logics are discussed at greater length in the section on power.)

Social forms in human being are generally "open" in that in some way and at certain times they interact with other structural units in human being, as well as animate and inanimate structures beyond it. They are also generally "autopoietic" in the sense that there is no external force—for example, Hegel's God—playing with the actor bricks. Rather, the actors themselves are capable—not forever, but for considerable periods of time—of reproducing and altering social being. Finally, social forms are autopoietic because they are "reflexive" in that they are capable of reflecting upon events and altering actions and practices in accord with the information provided by reflection to effect reproduction.[12]

There is a major difference between Lego constructions and social forms besides the latter's reflexivity and autopoiesis. Lego constructions, once built, pretty much just stand there. Social forms, in contrast, are terribly busy, buzzing with activity, always doing things—things that have their telos, which tend to keep them the same, or things that tend to change them. This is because immanent in social forms are their aforementioned force and power. It is time to consider these more fully.

Thomas Hobbes back in the seventeenth century helped to explain the singular theoretical significance of force and power (Reyna 2001, 2003). He said about the two: "*correspondent to* cause *and* effect, *are* power *and* act" (qtd. in Champlain 1651 [1971]: 68, italics in the original). Power for Hobbes was the flow of causality in reality, with causes being forces having the capacity to produce effects, powers. David Hume, a century later, accepted Hobbes's position, announcing, "It is universally allowed that matter, in all its operations, is actuated by a necessary force, and that every natural effect is so precisely determined by the energy of its cause that no other effect, in such particular circumstances, could possibly have resulted from it" (Hume, 1737). Force and power in this view are important because they are cause and effect, and cause and effect are what makes what happens in being.

This view has had its critics. An important category of criticism, especially among some postmodernists, is to reject causality (see Rosenau 2006: 201). However, postmodernists offer no compelling refutations of the existence of causality, nor do they hazard any guess as to what it might be in the place of causality that produces connections between phenomena. Consequently, it seems credible to accept the existence of causality and, in fact, I support Wesley Salmon's (1998) conceptualization of it, in which causal strings "are the means by which structure and order are propagated ... from one space–time region ... to other times and places" (1998: 298).

The structures that critical structural realism is interested in are those of force and power, with the parts in these structures being organizations whose operations in one space–time place make connections with other space–time places, with the power of effecting those later organizations' operations. Marx in *Capital*, volume 1, when discussing the working day remarked, "Between equal rights force decides" (1867: 259). Generalizing from Marx's consideration of the working day, it might be said that force is important because it "decides" what powers there will be. Below we see how this is the case.

Force

Critically, it is important to grasp that the term "force" is employed differently than its common usage, where it is understood to be physical coercion or violence. Force is causes, and there are many things besides physical coercion that operate as causes. Nonviolent causes are equally included as forces.[13] "Force resources" are what cause effects. Utilizations of force resources are "exercises of force."

There are five varieties of resources. The first of these involves "instruments"—tools, monies (capital), technologies, and so on—things that individuals have devised that, when used, make things happen. The second force resource is "land," raw materials that people use when they make things happen. A third force resource is "actors," individuals performing practical or discursive action. "Discursive" action is the use of the body to write or speak. "Practical" action is the use of the body, usually with tools, to get something done. Labor, of course, has been a particularly important sort of practical action in economic groups. Actors using instruments on land can make things happen, if they have the fourth and fifth force resources.

"Culture," a fourth force resource, involves signs learned and shared by people, with signs being representations of being, or representations of representations that may, or may not, be about being. A distinction can be made between technical, ideological, and worldview forms of culture. "Technical" culture refers to procedural messages: how to do things; a barber's knowledge of how to cut hair and a surgeon's of how to cuts bodies are examples of technical culture. "Ideological" culture involves representations favored by particular social positions in a population, advocating particular views that they desire to be widely accepted.

Some elites favor nationalist ideologies, in which the emphasis is upon "my country, right or wrong," so the adherents of such an ideology desire to support a country no matter what it does. "Worldview" (or what some might term "cultural hegemony") features cultural representations of the broadest scope. Their messages are widely shared by groups in different social positions. They may specify procedural detail, but they are very much about perceptual features of being, especially understanding of the nature of that being. The sociologist C. Wright Mills, for example, speaking of the 1950s, insisted there was a "military metaphysic," a "cast of mind that defines international reality as basically military" (1956: 222), which was, and is, a widespread and cherished American worldview.

A distinction (Reyna 2002) has been made between "neuronal" (I-space) and "discursive" (E-space) culture, with the former "enculturated" (some now prefer "embodied"), that is, learned and stored in cortical memory networks, and the later externalized, contained in speech or writing. Further, a distinction is made between "perceptual" and "procedural" forms of neuronal and discursive culture, with the former being messages about *what is* and the latter information about *what to do about it*. These messages result from actors' cultural neurohermeneutic systems that identify the nature of events, how they feel, and how to proceed vis-à-vis them.

In part, a brain makes an interpretation by employing a "hermeneutic." This notion is a novel one, and its rationale requires reflection upon the recent history of hermeneutics. Weber had defined sociology as the science of the "interpretive understanding of social action" at the beginning of the twentieth century (1968: 4). Schutz in the early part of the twentieth century critiqued Weber for not explaining how actors constituted meaning (1932 [1967]). A hermeneutic is information from technical culture, ideology, or worldview or—as will be introduced later—a public *délire* stored in neural memory networks involving a "perceptual/procedural pair." Perceptual/procedural pairs inform actors "what is" and "what to do about it," thereby constituting knowledge needed for any action, including the choreographing of force resources in space and time.

For example, it was reported by Maurice Godelier that the Baruya, who live in the highlands of New Guinea, call men "sweet potatoes" if they lack "exceptional qualities" (because cultivating their gardens, which include sweet potatoes, is what such males do). Men perceived to be great warriors are called *aoulatta* (qtd. in Feil 1984: 101, 102). How does a Baruya treat a sweet potato? Just like an ordinary person, while great warriors are, among other things, "respected" and "eulogized" (ibid.: 102). Here, then, are two hermeneutics choreographing male gender. The perceptual/procedural pair for ordinary men is perceive a sweet potato, proceed to treat him in an ordinary manner. The perceptual/procedural pair for a great warrior is perceive a *aoulatta,* proceed to treat him with respect.

Culture is a force resource because hermeneutics enable choreographing of other force resources. Choreographing organizes the operation of force resources because it specifies who the actors are, what their tools are, and how to use them in particular exercises of force. A Chadian Arab sees a *fil* approaching. He yells to a bunch of children, "Fil fi! Jara, jara" ("There is an elephant! Run, run!"). *Fil* is the perceptual culture (an elephant), *jara* the procedure (run). Communication of the Arab's message, "Fil fi! Jara, jara," choreographs the children's action, giving the man the power of making the children run. This example may help to distinguish between the choreography and exercising of force. Transmission of the cultural message is the choreographing of force. The Arab, his choreographing, and the children running from one place at an earlier time to another place at a later time are the exercise of force.

"Authoritative" force resources are the fifth type of force resource, being the right, in some way institutionally granted, to choreograph specific force resources in specific perceived situations. For example, Henry VIII (1491–1547), the sort of monarch who fired the imagination of Hobbes's absolutist heart, noticed that the monasteries were corrupt (a perceptual cultural judgment). This posed a puzzle. What should be done about the monasteries? Henry authorized their "dissolution" (because as king one of his authoritative resources was the right to terminate institutions). This authorization choreographed a string of events that Thomas Cromwell, Henry's vicar-general, implemented, which removed the monasteries from the ownership of church properties and gave them to private individuals.[14]

Finally, Francis Bacon famously supposed that "scientia potential est"— "knowledge itself is power." A view others have enthusiastically championed. Wrong! It is a generalization that oversimplifies the complexity of exercising force. Power does not spring from a single force resource. Without cultural or authoritative force the other force resources cannot be used. But, without the other force resources, cultural force is just babbling in the wind. Knowledge is certainly a condition of choreographing the other force resources, but these other resources are equally necessary to generate powers. Knowledge, then, is one among a number of necessary force resources, but it is the organized exercise of the different force resources that is necessary and sufficient for the attainment of power. Marx said, "Force decides." Now, let's consider what is decided.

Power

Power is *any* effects or outcomes of exercises of force, which means what force decides is what power occurs. The emphasis upon *any* in the previous sentence is deliberate. Certain renderings of power, famously Parsons (1963), emphasize goal attainment. Mann adopted such an understanding when he said, "Power is the ability to pursue and attain goals" (1986: 6). It is certainly true that actors exercise force intending to do something (i.e., attain goals). However, sometimes the something attained was unintended, and to ignore these somethings is to condemn a whole category of powers to analytic oblivion. "Intended" powers are effects that were premeditated by actors choreographing the forces that brought on the effects. "Unintended" powers are effects that were unplanned by the actors exercising the forces that brought on the effects. Scipio's victory at Zama (202 BC) ending the Second Punic War was an intended power, Hannibal's defeat was bitterly unintended and a waste of eighty good elephants.

It is useful to distinguish between the theoretically possible power that social forms may possess and the actual powers they achieve when exercising force. The "potential power" of a social form is the total powers it is hypothetically capable of, given the total amount of force resources it possesses. The "kinetic power" of this social form is the intended powers it achieves when it actually exercises certain of its force resources. Clearly, the United States has enormous potential powers; Finland has less. The relationship between potential and kinetic power is not invariably positive. A social being may have great potential power but not be especially good at exercising forces resources to acquire great kinetic power. For example, in a comparative evaluation of the quality of educations systems, the US educational system was judged to be "stagnant" (Layton 2013) since the turn of the century and rather mediocre, ranking seventeenth among developed countries, while Finland ranked first (*Huffington Post* 2012).

The United States' kinetic powers in education seem less than would be expected given its overall potential power. It is the exercise of force causing certain powers that gives social forms their temporal motion in certain directions—in the case of US education, a motion in the direction of stagnation. Temporal motion may be conceptualized in terms of strings and logics.

Strings and logics are chronologies in time and placements in space of connected kinetic powers. So understood, strings and logics are history. History at the empirical level is the discovery of strings. At the theoretical level it is the logics of these strings. A "string" is a series of events in space and time in which cultural messages choreograph force resources to choreograph a series of events. An "event" is a force/power dyad in which a particular exercise of force produces a particular power. Strings are connected force/power dyads. Humans, then, possess not only the power to make events but the still greater power of linking events together in strings.

The Kula ring, for example, reported on by Malinowski (1922: 82–104) for the people living in the western Pacific on the Trobriand and neighboring islands, involved strings. Malinowski said that the Kula ring was "fixed and regulated" by "rules and conventions" (1982). These "rules and regulations" in CSR terms are perceptual and procedural cultural messages. The ring was a string of events involving travel to different islands to give away certain valuables (*vaygu'a*). One of these was a particular type of necklace that was perceptually culturally understood to be a *soulava*.

The other valuable was an armband that was perceptually culturally understood to be a *mwali*. The procedural cultural messages for what to do with the necklaces and armbands were simple: *soulava* were exchanged for *mwali* of roughly equal value and vice versa. Exchange of these valuables was not haphazard. Rather, it was between partners, who might live close by or be hundreds of miles away and could only be reached by long sailing trips. Hence, a partner perceived a *soulava* and proceeded to give it away to a copartner for a *mwali*, while the copartner perceived a *mwali* and proceeded to give it away for a *soulava*. A valuable received could not be hoarded. It had to be given away. A valuable given had to be returned with one of equal value. These perceptual and procedural messages were the perceptual/procedural pairs of what might be called the *kula* hermeneutic.

This Kula hermeneutic choreographed force resources in the sense that it organized islanders with armbands or necklaces and put them in canoes with paddles, sails, and so on to get them to other islanders with valuables, so they could give each other valuables, which was the creation of a particular power, an exchange. Each organizing people, so that they gave and received, was a force/power dyad. If the islands in this area of the Pacific are recognized to be arrayed in a roughly circular fashion, then the Kula hermeneutic choreographed strings composed of force/power dyads of gift givings involving movement of necklaces going in a roughly clockwise direction in exchange for necklaces going in a counterclockwise direction. Logics in this optic are vectors of force, that is, exercise of force going in a certain direction with a certain magnitude. The example just given is of an exchange logic whose telos is that of continual circulation of equal valuables.

Given the preceding, a critical structural realist ontology is one in which the "is" of the universe is no ghostly Spirit but causality: "plays of force" and their powers in space and across time. Human being in this ontology is the exercise of the force resources—land, instruments, actors, culture, and authority—that cause the effects of intended and unintended kinetic powers, whose spatiotemporal occurrences are strings and logics found in social forms. What, then, is contradiction?

Contradiction: Logics of (Limited) Disorder

Structural Marxists, responding to criticisms of the dialectic like that of Harris, developed a view of contradiction that they believed coincided with "advanced scientific practice" (Godelier 1972: 90). Their "advanced ... practice" placed contradictions in E-space social forms. Explicitly, Godelier believed, "What causes a contradiction to appear is the appearance of a limit, a threshold, to the conditions in which a structure does not change. Beyond this limit a change of structure must occur" (1972: 90).[15] What is novel in this view of contradiction is the explicit introduction of the notion of limit. The concept of limit employed here denotes some point, edge, or boundary beyond which an action, practice, institution, system, or social being exercising force cannot exceed. Limits are discovered through observation.

The temperature of 212 degrees is the limit beyond which water ceases to be a liquid. Heating water on a stove is the force with the power to push its limit as a liquid. A family's total income is the limit beyond which its spending cannot go. Acquisition of food, lodging, health care, and so on are forces driving families toward their spending limits. Specifically, "contradictions" are logics whose component strings are social forms exercising force moving themselves or other social forms toward their "limit of functional compatibility" (Friedman 1994: 48).

The notion of a "limit of compatibility" refers to the existence of conditions in a structure of force resources in which parts that formerly interacted in exercises of force to produce powers are less and less able to achieve their former power. The parts in a social being are its force resources—land, action, instruments, and various forms of cultural and authoritative choreography—distributed to its component social forms. Parts become "incompatible" when those formally present disappear, when they become too few or too much, or when they are altered in some way that makes them defective.

At the point of the limit, structures tend toward disorder and are obliged to transform. Marx, writing in *Theories of Surplus Value* (1905–1910), insisted, "crises exist because ... contradictions exist" (qtd. in Selsam, Goldway, and Martel 1983). Crisis exists because as social forms approach their limits their parts become incompatible, obliging either disorder or transformation.[16] Here, then, is a Nietzschean element in contradictions because it is "plays of force" (with "plays" understood as exercises of force) that propel social forms to their limits and crises.

Consider, for example, the amount of CO_2 in the atmosphere. In August of 2014 there were 397 parts per million of CO_2 in the atmosphere as measured at the Mauna Loa observatory in Hawaii (Scripps 2014). The amount of CO_2 in the atmosphere is due to a "land/capital" contradiction. This is because exercise of the forces of capitalism in order to accumulate capital depends upon operations that consume land, especially in the form of fossil energy. These operations directly or indirectly release CO_2 into the atmosphere. Unfortunately, the more CO_2 in the atmosphere, the more vulnerable the earth becomes to the deleterious consequences of global warming. The more capital use of land energy resources, the more those land resources are injurious to human survivability. It is believed that 350 parts per million of CO_2 is the limit beyond which the injurious consequences of global warming begin. This limit was reached in 1988. In 2012 it was estimated that global warming cost an estimated $1.2 trillion per year and was responsible for 400,000 deaths annually (Hertsgaard 2012), which is something of a crisis.

Marx's own analyses of contradictions emphasized emerging incompatibilities and limits during the exercise of forces within and between the productive forces and relations of capitalist systems. Mao Tse Tung (1937) and Althusser (1977) broadened the location of contradictions, extending them into political systems. So, two important types of contradictions can be distinguished. First, there are those arising within, and between, political systems, called "political." Intrapolity contradictions can occur between the central government and different regions or between opposing institutional groups.

The former contradiction existed in the United States prior to 1860, when relations between Washington and the South became irreconcilable, provoking the crisis that resulted in the Civil War (1860–1865). The latter contradictions exist today in the Unite States between groups like the Tea Party, which favors policies that eliminate government intervention, and liberals, who support policies involving intervention. Interpolity contradictions have very often existed between competing empires when the operations in one empire are incompatible with those in other empires. For example, the Norman Empire's aspiration to land in the Anglo-Saxon Empire in the eleventh century was incompatible with the English desire for the same land. A second variety of contradiction, called "economic," includes those that exist within or between economic systems. Two sorts of economic contradictions exist in capitalist systems: "cyclical" ones, in which the contradiction produces alternation between growth and decline, and "systemic" ones, in which the contradiction is such that its intensification threatens the ability of an economic system to reproduce.

When contradictions worsen, moving toward their limits, they "intensify." They may also worsen because they "coalesce," which refers to an increasing cooccurrence of contradictions.[17] Coalescence increases incompatibilities by having more strings in more places that hamper each other's operation in different parts of the social being. Such coalescence may be so extensive that social being–wide incompatibilities emerge. For example, a conundrum of Marxist thought has been to explain why the 1917 revolution against capitalism came in Czarist Russia, the least capitalist of European states.

One answer to this puzzle was that Russia was a site of an increasing coalescence of contradictions. There were contradictions pertaining to feudalism (between lords and serfs), capitalism (between capital and labor), and colonialism (between the imperial core and its colonies; see Althusser 1977). Different social beings at roughly the same times may exhibit different collections of contradictions. Equally, the same social being at different times may have different collections of contradictions. The set of contradictions and their degree of intensification at any moment in a social being may be said to be its "concatenation."

In sum, contradictions are incompatible plays of force—whose logic moves them towards limits and the contradictory crises provoked by these limits. This leads us to the realization problem. The following section specifies the nature of this problem and formulates a theory of how it is addressed.

Realization Theory

The realization problem for Hegel was how the Ghost realized its Idea, and I have argued that it went unsolved. In the approach under formulation, the realization problem concerns how actors realize solutions to the vulnerabilities posed by contradictions intensifying toward crisis. The following four sections assemble the understandings necessary for a critical structural realist theory of realization. These show that actors, especially elite ones, institute logics of order, using hermeneutic politics involving public *délires,* which over time tend to follow a principle of the conservation of *délires.* A fifth section synthesizes the insights of the four preceding sections into an explicit theory of realization. This analysis begins with clarification of what it is precisely that contradictions threaten.

Reproductive Vulnerabilities and Fixes

Contradictory crises are threats to order because they challenge the reproduction of social forms. Reproduction is, generally, re-creation of form, any form. Social reproduction, the type of reproduction considered in this text, is the re-creation of social forms. Human reproduction, as earlier noted, is autopoietic. Certain social forms, or parts of social forms, exist to reproduce the larger social whole. Marx, in volume 1 of *Capital*, talking about capitalist systems, distinguished between "simple" and "extended" reproduction (1906: chs. 23 and 24), with the former being operations that refabricated order, but without growing that order, and the latter being operations that grow the order. I understand simple and extended reproduction more generally as situations in which there is either no growth or growth in *any* social form. Both types of reproduction are threatened by contradictions, so it is in the realm of reproduction that solutions to the reproduction problem will be found. What links contradiction to reproduction?

There is a single-word answer to this question: sensation, that is, brain operations that detect happenings in E-space and I-space. The sensing of E-space is done through the sensory organs—eyes, ears, and so on—sending neural signals to the "primary sensory areas" in the sensory cortex. These include the visual cortex in the occipital lobe, the auditory cortex in the temporal lobe, and the somatosensory cortex in the parietal lobe (Bear, Connors, and Paradiso 2001: 210). Together these areas detect being. "Sensation" is the detection of the "is" happening both in E- and I-space (Wolfe, Kluender, and Levi 2011).

Sensation should be distinguished from "perception," which is brain operations that identify what it "is" that has been sensed. Perception involves assigning neuronal cultural and emotional status to sensation. This may happen almost immediately. A Chadian Arab sees a slithering thing moving along the ground and instantly reaches into her neuronal culture and knows it's a *dabib* (snake). Perception is required before any procedures can be taken to address what to do about the sensation of what "is." The Arab knowing the slithering thing is a *dabib* yells out, *hafad dabib* (take care, a snake). Without sensation there is no detecting of "is." Without perception there can be no procedures for addressing what to do about what "is."

Actors participating in being, caught in contradictory perturbations, sense something, perceive it is disturbing, and, fearing disturbance, form a desire to proceed to fixing it. "Reproductive vulnerability" denotes the perception of a contradiction. "Reproductive fix" indicates procedures to relax a contradiction. Actors insensitive to reproductive vulnerability are "hermeneutically blind." Those sensitive to vulnerability are aware of a hermeneutic puzzle.

A "hermeneutic puzzle," generally, is any vulnerability that actors apprehend needs procedures to fix. Hermeneutic puzzles are in I-space and are in the realm of consciousness.[18] Actors facing hermeneutic puzzles do not interpret them in terms of intensifying contradictions. Rather they understand them in terms of the thoughts and feelings in their neuronal cultural memory that bear upon the sensed vulnerabilities. Andrew Carnegie, the late nineteenth-century capitalist ruffian, may not have known that the Homestead Strike in 1892 was a manifestation of capitalist/proletariat contradiction, but he "sure as shootin'" knew that a "strike" was on in one of his factories, it threatened him, and he was puzzled as to how to end it fast.

A current example shows that certain Americans with conservative cultural ideologies have tucked away in their neuronal culture the view that the "47 percent" (the percentage of US workers too poor to pay income tax) in the capitalist/proletariat contradiction are "lazy cunts," while many of these workers have stored in their neuronal culture that capitalists are "rich assholes." Consequently, as a recession deepens, capitalists are likely to treat workers as "lazy cunts," and workers to view capitalists as "rich assholes."[19] This leads to a key question: how do actors respond to reproductive vulnerabilities and create fixes? The answer is that they get reflexive.

Getting Reflexive, Creating Fixes

"Getting reflexive" concerns two sorts of reflexivities—individual, involving the operation of an individual actor's cultural neurohermeneutic system, and social, involving several actors in hermeneutic politics.

Individual Reflexivity and the Cultural Neurohermeneutic System

Individual reflexivity involves an actor reflecting upon—that is, perceiving and thinking about procedures for addressing—sensations of reality bearing upon hermeneutic puzzles. When actors get reflexive they give social beings the possibility of autopoiesis. "Reflecting" reality is done by a cultural neurohermeneutic system (Reyna 2002). It is the brain sensing being, perceiving "it," and deciding what to do about "it." The way actors do this in terms of their neuronal culture, what is already remembered in their neural tissues concerning what to think and feel about being, and what the already existing interpretations of it are. Reproductive fixes are choreographies resulting from actors connecting sensations of contradictory being with hermeneutics stored in their neuronal culture that offer possibilities for organizing force resources to resolve vulnerabilities.

Connection occurs through the retrieval of hermeneutics into actors' working memories. "Working memory" includes brain subsystems that store and manipulate visual images or verbal information as well as a central executive that coordinates the subsystems.[20] The visual images are sensations. The verbal information is the perception of what the sensations are. The central executive includes parts of the brain that think about what to do about the perceptions. "Retrieval" is bringing into working memory the sensation and perceptions about which the central executive judges how to proceed.

To illustrate, consider an example from everyday economics. I.P. Standin, CEO of Pretty Urinals Incorporated (P.U. Inc.) smells (i.e., senses) that something bad has happened. His working memory connects this sensory unease with the perception of high labor costs resulting in "poor profits," which poses the hermeneutic puzzle of what to do. His central executive retrieves the memory of what all his competitors are doing and notes, "One way of addressing profit loss is to initiate offshore outsourcing." I.P. Standin outsources P.U. Inc. to Vietnam. He has solved his vulnerability by connecting his lowered profit circumstances with a particular perceptual/procedural pair in his business hermeneutics. Specifically, the perceptual/procedural pair is if perceptually a sensation indicates poor profits, then procedurally commence offshore outsourcing.

Social Reflexivity and Public Délires

In situations involving larger, more complex social forms, the fixes arising from individual reflexivity do not immediately become reproductive fixes. This is because different individual interpretations of hermeneutic puzzles pertaining to a reproductive vulnerability emerge for a number of reasons: differences in actors' social positions, differences in actors' individual experiences, or differences in their technical, ideological, or worldview cultures. For example, two US elites—one a general in the Joint Chiefs of Staff and the other a deputy treasury secretary coming from Wall Street—are likely to have different interpretations of the puzzle of how to control adversaries. The general might opt for a military fix, while his treasury counterpart proposes a financial fix. These different interpretations are resolved through social reflexivity, which involves the institutionalization of public *délires* involving hermeneutic politics.

Hermeneutic politics are plays of force used to achieve the power of determining how vulnerabilities will be fixed in situations of competing possible fixes. Of course, reality is shambolic. Lots of things happen and it is not clear what to concentrate on and when. Moreover, humans confront cluttered reality with a noisy, clamor of differing individual experiences, social positions, and technological, ideological, and worldviews. Public *délires* are "means of interpretation" in a messy world assisting actors to know what to do about what is, so, as such, they might be imagined as "focus" prompters.[21] Public *délires* focus attention on a selected number of perceptions and procedures.[22] Such *délires* are not the desires of anybody; anybody does not count. Rather, they are the desires of elites, those allocated the force resource of authorizing institutionalization of policies, programs, laws, administrative pronouncements, and imperial orders.[23]

Consider, to illustrate, the current situation of severe droughts in the US Southwest brought on by global warming, a consequence of a land/capital contradiction. Drought makes different people in different social positions vulnerable. Ranchers need water for their livestock. Farmers need it for their crops. Homeowners want it for their lawns and swimming pools. This leads to different fixes for water use, with homeowners preferring provision of water for residential use, while ranchers and farmers favor it for animals and plants. Usually the hermeneutic politics concerning water use during drought pit these three groups, and their preferred fix, against each other.

The politics occurs in town councils, with council members voting for different fixes in the form of different ordinances. Often the ranchers and farmers predominate, and when they do, these ordinances limit the public's watering their lawns, punishing them with fines if they do. Such ordinances are public *délires*. Their hermeneutic is perceptual, if unlawful water use is perceived, then procedurally fines are imposed on ordinance violators. The voting of the ordinance is the institution of the *délire;* sending police to monitor citizens' water use is its implementation. Should global warming–related droughts intensify, making it impossible even to water plants and animals, a new round of hermeneutic politics seeking new public *délires* would occur.

"Hermeneutic politics," then, may be formally defined as elite actors mobilizing force resources to achieve the power of having their fix selected as a public *délire* to solve a hermeneutic puzzle. What force resources might be needed to prevail in such a politics varies with the nature of the political process determining how to win a political debate. Winning may involve getting desired public *délires* in the form of laws voted in by legislatures, administrative decrees from top management in business, executive branch orders, dictators' dictates, the Pope's speaking ex cathedra, or Islamic clerics declaring fatwas. If political debates are resolved by a vote, the resources needed are those designed to win a vote. If these debates are resolved by administrative decrees, dictators' dictates, and the like, the resources needed are those necessary to "get the ear" of the boss with the authority to make a decision vis-à-vis a hermeneutic puzzle.

Hermeneutic politics tends to hermetically seal actors on opposing sides into particular interpretations. The notion of hermetic seal (similar to groupthink) helps account for why collections of actors think and act alike. Specifically, "hermetic seal" is the operation of strings of events choreographed to enter actors' I-space to make them think and feel X, in conjunction with the operation of strings of events choreographed to make them ignore not-X. In conservative Republican families in America, children are taught naughty and nice: wicked is a Democrat; good is a Republican.

Consequently, the hermeneutic puzzle of what to be politically for these children is solved, with them sealed into being nice Republicans. Global warming, as we know, presents a serious reproductive vulnerability. The puzzle of how to resolve this has led to a hermeneutic politics dominated by nice Republicans hermetically sealed into market solutions to global warming, on one side, versus naughty Democrats hermetically sealed into government fixes, on the other. Sometimes fixes only partially work or fail. The next section discusses what happens when this is the case

Creating Fixes When a Fix Didn't Fix It

In situations of problematic fixes, actors tend to become involved in "try-and-try-again" hermeneutic politics based on reflecting-and-reflecting-again upon sensations of contradictory vulnerability. Long ago Lewis Henry Morgan (1877) observed that societies solved their needs by attempting and reattempting ways of addressing them. The information gained from repeated attempts he called "experimental knowledge" (1985 [1878]: 258). President Franklin Roosevelt was certainly aware of this when he said in 1932, as the United States suffered the reproductive vulnerabilities of the Great Depression, "The country needs, and unless I mistake its temper, the country demands bold, persistent experimentation … It is common sense to take a method and try it. If it fails, admit it frankly and try another" (1932).

Situational and Experimental Fixation

Morgan's experimental knowledge might be rethought of in terms of situational and experimental fixation. Certain situations occur and reoccur, and reoccur again. When this occurs, the situations tend to cause people to reflect upon them. Reflection upon reoccurring events may be said to be "situational fixation." For example, if you get a toothache that lasts for ten minutes and then goes away, you do not think much of it. However, if that toothache continues on for several days, then it is something you fixate upon and want to do something about. Generally, the more pleasing or painful a reoccurring situation, the more you fixate upon it.

"Experimental fixation" is an exercise of force to fix something upon which actors are situationally fixated. For example, the US military became situationally fixated upon its vulnerabilities in the Vietnam War and experimented with numerous fixes to the puzzle of winning. Generally, the greater vulnerability revealed in situational fixation, the more likely the occurrence of experimental fixation. Different procedures to fix the same vulnerability will be said to be different "iterations," with actors involved in such events said to be "fixated."

US military elites during the Vietnam War fixated on the bitter vulnerability of losing to their opponents, who they disparaged as primitive "gooks." Different security elites tried iteration after iteration to win. There were free-fire zones, places where everyone including civilians were killed; napalm campaigns, which involved barbequing entire villages; search and destroy missions, where villages were attacked by air cavalry; defoliation campaigns, where the forest cover in whole regions was destroyed by Agent Orange, which also killed wildlife and people; overt strategic bombing in North Vietnam; and covert strategic bombing in Cambodia.

Getting reflexive may not work no matter how often actors reflect upon the vulnerability they experience because of either hermeneutic deception or blindness. "Hermeneutic deception" refers to interpretations of situations that are *intentionally* partial or completely incorrect, so that actors have trouble fixing problems associated with the situations because the understanding of them is erroneous. For example, during the Vietnam War some US governmental elites intentionally deceived others about the success of their operations, knowing full well they were unsuccessful. "Hermeneutic blindness" refers to interpretations that are *unintentionally* incorrect, which also causes actors to have difficulties fixing what they do not understand. For example, bleeding was for a long time the reproductive fix for many illnesses. It was a case of hermeneutic blindness, because its practitioners were blind to the causes of the illnesses. How much hermeneutic deception and blindness hamper solving hermeneutic puzzles is unclear and, consequently, worthy of further research.

In sum, actors sensing contradiction become autopoietic. Autopoiesis, based upon individual and social reflexivity, is a logic of order. Individual reflexivity is about actors' engaging sensations of contradiction, with their cultural neurohermeneutic systems putting into their working memories perceptual and procedural cultural memories forming hermeneutics about the "is" of the sensation and what to do about it. What should be done is implementation of fixes. Social reflexivity throws different individual fixes into arenas of hermeneutic politics in which a particular fix ultimately prevails, hopefully to snatch order from contradictory disorder. Logics of order will be further discussed when the realization theory is fully presented. They will be found to have three moments.

Two more general points: First, in individual reflexivity, when actors perceive vulnerabilities and, consequently, hermeneutic puzzles needing solutions, it is the real world, full of contradiction, out in E-space, that initiates operations of the cultural neurohermeneutic system in I-space to solve the puzzles. The cultural neurohermeneutic system is no Hegelian Spirit. Rather, it is a structure—a complex, material, neural structure, accessible to scientific analysis—for fixing what is happening outside of itself. Second, social reflexivity with its public *délire* producing hermeneutic politics that tests, and retests, different iterations is an E-space structure involving social forms operating to select particular fixes.

Marshall Sahlins once wrote that "categorical distinctions" are "vulnerable to a pragmatic revaluation" (2001: 51). Such "distinctions" involve the meaning of things, and what Sahlins appears to be saying is that what things mean depends on their pragmatics, that is, how well they do, or do not, work. Sahlins's recognition of the pragmatics of meaning has implications for the hermeneutics involved in social reflexivity, because this reflexivity involves a "pragmatic revaluation." Individual reflexivity may yield all sorts of fixes, which are composed of messages with meanings that choreograph these fixes. Some of these fixes may be unworkable, others workable. The meanings that endure are those that choreograph fixes that pragmatically work or are perceived as working. Such a hermeneutics, then, is only interested in the meaning of things insofar as those meanings work in the conduct of human being. It is a "pragmatic hermeneutics."

Clearly not all actors are equal with regard to the power they command in hermeneutic politics. Let us contemplate privileged actors with more force resources at their disposal, which leads to a discussion of elites.

Elites as Puzzle Masters and the Conservation of *Délires*

C. Wright Mills observed, "The history of modern society may be readily understood as the story of the enlargement and the centralization of the means of power—in economic, in political and in military institutions" (1963: 25). Mills's "means of power" is our "force resources." What might the persons authorized to determine operations of forces resources in important institutions be called? Mills understood elites to be actors "whose positions enable them to transcend the ordinary environments of ordinary men and women; they are in positions to make decisions having major consequences" (1956: 3–4). While comfortable with this definition, consistent with critical structural realism's emphasis on force and power, it seems helpful to elaborate upon how it is that elites come to have "major consequences."

In this optic, "elites" are actors who occupy positions authorized to choreograph the operation of large amounts of force resources, including those resources constituting fixes to reproductive vulnerabilities. So, in a sense, elites, because they disproportionately control force resources, are puzzle masters, allowing them to confront major hermeneutic puzzles.

The Puzzle Masters and Their Foes

Elites should be understood as class actors, though the notion of class employed here is broader than in classical Marxism, where it was applied only to economic actors. "Class" relations in the present perspective are those between actors due to their differences in the regulation of force resources (not just productive ones). Upper classes are those who control the greatest amount of force resources and who use these, among other things, to have the power of directing to themselves, and their kind, as much value as possible. Elites are those members of the upper class in positions with authority over the largest amount of force resources. Lower classes are those with the least control over these resources, struggling for as much value as possible with their lesser force resources. Consequently, classes are in contradiction, and "elites," controlling vast amounts of force, are the upper classes' champions in class conflict.[24]

Upper classes in contemporary social beings are capitalist elites (CEOs, CFOs, UFOs, vice-presidents, etc.) regulating economic institutions; official elites (presidents, dictators, ministers, parliamentarians, senior bureaucrats) regulating political institutions; educational elites (chancellors, vice-chancellors, senior professors) regulating various institutions of schooling; cultural elites (religious, museum, and media heads) regulating cultural institutions; and bluntly, but accurately, killing elites (generals, admirals, chiefs of police) regulating military and police institutions. Elites with authority or influence over the killing elites control enormous force to inflict violence and will be called "security elites."

Hermeneuts are an important type of elite in contemporary social beings. Hermes was the Greek god who, on winged feet, brought messages from gods to mortals. "Hermeneuts" are specialized educational or cultural elites who bring messages on the winged feet of media from the godlike highest elites to illuminate the I-space of others. Hermeneuts are masters of hermeneutic deception. Their messages are credible because they are the specialists in producing persuasive communications. Their credibility results from rhetoric or science. A preacher like Jerry Falwell was for the most part a hermeneut to the middling or poorer sort, whose ability to illuminate derived from his mastery of "unifying interpretive conventions" governing fundamentalist rhetoric (Harding 2000: xi). A military analyst like Albert Wohlstetter was a hermeneut to security experts, whose ability was to illuminate the science of devising "more effective ways" of "using" violent force (Bacevich 2005: 154).

Class warfare is often treated, by apologists for the wealthy, as something restricted to the revolting, meaner masses. Yet, it is the upper classes, occupying positions controlling most of the forces resources, with the most weapons to wage class war. With this in mind, "class war" is understood to involve elites exercising force, fixing reproductive vulnerabilities in manners congenial to themselves—especially regarding the copious movement of value to them, with ordinary people eventually coming to resist such predations.

The strings of class warfare are empirical manifestations of an elite/non-elite contradiction. The more elite hermeneutic politics institutes iterations of public *délires* gratifying their specific desires, and not those of ordinary people, the less likely it is that nonelite desires are satisfied. These are moments rife with hermeneutic deception. Hermeneuts—Rush Limbaugh, Sarah Palin—spread the word that ordinary folks' problems are not authored by elites but by themselves, the iron laws of the economy, alien Others, fate, or God. Nonelites facing stagnant or declining wealth and insecurity sense anger and misery.

Their individual reflexivity becomes active, imagining all sorts of fixes for their vulnerabilities. However, problems arise for nonelites at the level of social reflexivity because, by and large, they lack authority and control over forces resources. Revolutionary situations occur when elites lose force resources and when nonelites devise fixes that allow them to seize control of existing, or develop new, force resources to create public *délires* that gratify their desires.[25] It is time to introduce situations exhibiting the conservation of *délires* and what happens when such conservation efforts are doomed.

Conservation of Délires *and Iterational and Transformational Change*

Public *délires* arising out of elite puzzle masters' hermeneutic politics tend to generate a conservation of *délires*. Recall that social reflexivity, operating as part of the logic of order, produces public *délires*, which choreograph the exercise of force to reproduce. So long as the desires of the elite remain constant, the public *délires* instituted to ensure their reproduction will remain similar, or, to use the term introduced earlier, they will be iterations of each other. "Conservation of *délires*," then, is a principle that social change moves iteration by iteration to attain public *délires*, with "iterational change" understood as situations in which current fixes are only incrementally different from antecedent ones as a means of addressing contradictory vulnerability. For example, the different tactics of US security elites during the Vietnam War were different iterations of a single public *délire*, that of winning the conflict.[26]

It happens that sometimes elites have seemingly tried every fix without achieving the power to stop the march toward contradictory limits. The conservation of *délires* has failed in such situations. Transformational change is likely, because nothing else worked. The closer social forms approach their limits, the more reproductive fixes have been fixless, the nearer crises of disorder loom. Then, if order is to be saved, significant changes are needed. "Transformational change" is expected when iterational change has run out of iterations and in situations where current fixes qualitatively differ from antecedent ones. Transformational change is a rare occurrence. It is the change from Romanoff Imperial Russia to Lenin's Bolshevik state. With the preceding, all the elements needed for a theory of realization have been introduced. It is time to explicitly state that theory.

Theory of Realization

Social change is the explanation of the dynamics of social forms. Logics are abstract and general accounts of strings, that is, the movements of social forms. The different times of these movements are logics' moments. The theory of realization consists of twelve statements explaining what happens during four moments, constituting a logic of order responding to intensifying and coalescing contradictions. The first moment is of the recognition of reproductive vulnerability, the second is that of creating fixes, the third is reiterating fixes when the initial fixes do not work, and the fourth moment is the transformation of fixes. The theory is as follows:

Moment 1: Recognition

1. Logics of disorder, involving intensification and coalescing of contradictions, occur in social forms, leading to their reproductive vulnerability.
2. Recognition of vulnerability results from sensation of contradiction, which sensation produces hermeneutic puzzles.
3. Hermeneutic puzzles provoke the search for their fixes based upon the hermeneutics in the neuronal culture of actors who have sensed the contradiction.

Moment 2: Fixing

4. Actors sensing contradiction become autopoietic, creating fixes based upon individual and social reflexivity.
5. Individual reproductive fixes are choreographies resulting from actors' brain operations in the cultural neurohermeneutic system involving retrievals that bring to consciousness hermeneutics derived from neuronal culture, which offer possibilities of organizing force resources to moderate vulnerabilities.
6. When there are competing individual fixes in social systems, the competition is solved through the operation of hermeneutic politics.
7. Hermeneutic politics involving elites results in the institution and implementation of public *délires*.

Moment 3: Fixing Fixes

8. Failed fixes lead to situational and experimental fixation.
9. Experimental fixation causes different iterations of public *délires*.
10. Because elite participants in hermeneutic politics tend to have similar *délires*, the different iterations of public tend to resemble each other, exhibiting a principle of the conservation of *délires*.

Moment 4: Transforming

11. When the iterations constituting a conservation of *délires* fail, elites' individual and social reflexivity, guided by a pragmatic hermeneutics to fix fix-

less fixes, will devise involving greatly different types and choreographies of force, thereby transforming the public *délires* used to combat logics of disorder.

12. Taken together the four moments realize logics of order that mitigate logics of disorder resulting from contradictions.

It is time to offer a conclusion to the arguments presented in the essay and, in so doing, make explicit what is meant by a dialectics of force and the understanding of transformational change it suggests.

Conclusion

This essay has examined two approaches to dialectical change, those of Hegel and of critical structural realism. In the Hegelian dialectic, Ghost is minding the store of human being in the sense that what happens in history is the result of the realization of Ghost's Idea. The Idea is progress toward Freedom, with history being the dialectical realization of the Idea of Freedom, which has a whiff of an animistic divinity about it. We said good-bye to all that, agreeing with Professor Harris that it was a monkey on the back of understanding change for three reasons: (1) the approach was *istheit*—challenged due to an inability to observe Ghost, (2) it was not possible to know precisely what exactly Hegel's dialectics were, and (3) it was not possible to know how Ghost realized its effects.

The dialectics of force approach just presented, is a concatenation of Nietzsche's assertion of the importance of force (argued earlier by Hobbes and Hume) in social beings with the structural Marxists', especially Godelier's, recognition of imperfection in the operation of force due to the existence of structural limits in social beings. In this dialectics, change—differences between subsequent and antecedent human being—is the product of a continual play of forces. The first play is that of a logic of disorder, marching according to the dictates of contradiction. The second play is that of a logic of order, countermarching to the strictures of the theory of realization. This means that force dialectics are out of mind. They are the operation in E-space of a general contradiction that operates in numerous particular instances in struggles between logics of order against those of disorder.

What does the preceding imply for transformational change? The conservation of *délires* means that social beings, especially great and complex ones like the twenty-first–century United States, change course slowly, like giant aircraft carriers, gliding through seas of space and time. There is no necessary zigzagging advancement from the heights of synthesis to still higher synthesis. Rather, they keep doing the same thing in different ways. Human being is the space of social beings inching along, making new iterations, seeking to achieve old public *délires* to solve their contradictory vulnerabilities.

Such change is conservational, not transformational, because actors make different iterations in order to maintain course toward the North Star of their public *délires*. Hegel himself seems to have recognized the existence of iterational change when he observed that "inventions, appropriate arrangements, accompanied by long intellectual struggles in order to find out what is appropriate" occur in states (1953: 30). Hegel's "inventions" and "arrangements" are our iterations, while his "intellectual struggles" are our hermeneutic politics to find the inventions or arrangements that, in Hegel's terms, are "appropriate." It may seem daft for a leftist argument to take the position that much change is iterational and, hence, conservational. Daft or not, it is the way much change appears to work in human being.

There appear to have been relatively few transformational changes in history. Rather, what seems to have been the case is the emergence of a certain sort of transformational change, followed by iteration after iteration to reproduce it. For example, certain stateless social forms were transformed into imperial systems in the third millennium BC, which allowed elites to accumulate vast amounts of value. Since, then, for millennia upon millennia, as empires battled their contradictions, there have been different public *délires* producing different imperial iterations, from those of the Assyrians to that of the North Americans. Similarly, economic systems were transformed when capitalism emerged in early modern times from agrarian systems, providing capitalists with an extremely lucrative way of accumulating value. Since then there have been iterations upon iterations of capitalism, most recently starting in the last half of the twentieth century, those based upon Keynesianism and those based upon neoliberalism.

Transformational change occurs rarely, but it brings major benefits. Iterational change occurs more commonly to reproduce the benefits of the original transformation, against the contradictions which threaten it. How, then, does transformational change occur?

One way certainly seems to be due to failure to fix the vulnerabilities posed by contradictions. Public *délires*, even if attained, may not fix contradictory vulnerabilities due to hermeneutic deception or blindness. Worse, attainment of public *délires* may further intensify contradictions, as is the case of the neoliberal public *délires*, which even as they enrich elites, exacerbate the land/capital contradiction. The preceding suggests the following generalization:

Concentration and Intensification of Contradictions	→	Decrease of Ability to Find Iterative Fixes	→	Greater Likelihood of Transformative Change

Bluntly put, when logics of order are having trouble formulating fixes that relax the logic of disorder, their telos is toward the black hole of contradictory
disorder. When the choice is between transformation and disorder, the times
are propitious for transformational change.

Mao, in his essay "On Contradiction," appears to support the importance
of iterational and transformational change in human being, when he states:

> There are two states of motion in all things, that of relative rest and that of con-
> spicuous change. Both are caused by the struggle between the two contradictory
> elements contained in a thing. When the thing is in the first state of motion, it is
> undergoing only quantitative and not qualitative change and consequently pre-
> sents the outward appearance of being at rest. When the thing is in the second state
> of motion, the quantitative change of the first state has already reached a culminat-
> ing point and gives rise to the dissolution of the thing as an entity and thereupon
> a qualitative change ensues, hence the appearance of a conspicuous change. (1937)

Mao's first and second "states of motion" correspond to iterational and transformation change.

Finally, what can be said of the current moment? It is one in which different iterations of public *délires* have failed, the hermeneutic politics of social
reflexivity have been impotent, and reproductive fixes have been fixless. The
land/capital contradiction intensifies and coalesces with the labor/capital contradiction as CO_2 mounts in the atmosphere and the precariat burgeons on
earth. Be very clear: if not relaxed, huge portions of humanity will perish in
the black hole of disorder. Moreover, hermeneutic blindness is significant. It
is unclear what energy source can replace that spewing CO_2. Consequently,
a conclusion of the dialectics of force approach just crafted is that there are
two possibilities—transform or die (in large numbers). Equally understand,
powerful capitalist elites and their hermeneut myrmidons choreograph hermeneutic deceptions to hinder reproductive fixes to the contradictory crisis
which means. Time to organize a revolution!

Notes

1. Blunden (2014) provides access to sixty critics of Hegel from the nineteenth through
   the twenty-first centuries. Marx both praised Hegel as a "mighty thinker" and rejected
   the idealist aspects of his dialectics as a "mystical shell" (1906: 25). Eduard Bernstein,
   in the late nineteenth century, established a revisionist Marxism that argued change
   could not be explained by a Hegelian dialectic, because cooperation was the driving
   force of change (Bernstein 1898–1899). During World War I, in part in response to
   Bernstein, there was something of a revival of Hegelian thought, especially in Lenin's
   (1976) and Lukác's (1923) work. Enthusiasm for Hegel continued in what came to be
   termed "Western Marxism" (Anderson 1976). Hegel was strong among some of the
   Frankfurter school's critical theorists. Marcuse (1941) argued for Hegel's centrality in
   the rise of *all* social theory. Adorno (1966) was more circumspect, like Marx finding

certain elements of Hegel useful and others useless. Althusser had little use for Hegelian dialectics, asserting that Marx's work was so different from Hegel's that between
the two there was a "rupture" (1971: 93). Concerning contemporary times, Bertell Ollman notes, "Recent years have witnessed a modest renaissance of interest in dialectics"
(2003). There has been a dialectical critical realism (Roy Bhasker 1993) and a systematic dialectic "focused on Hegel's Logic and how this fits the method of Marx's Capital"
(Arthur 2011: 1, see also 2004). Recently, Žižek has championed a "new foundation"
for dialectical materialism based upon integration of Hegel and Lacan's thought (2012,
2014)

2. Walter Kaufman, Hegel's defender, said "that Hegel was . . . a philosopher who consid-
    ered himself Christian and tried to do from a Protestant point of view what Aquinas
    had attempted six hundred years earlier." (1959). Aquinas had tried to reconcile nat-
    ural reason with speculative theology. Hegel might be said to have tried to reconcile
    the Christian notion of spirit with dialectical reason. The role of religion in Hegel's
    thought is controversial. Dickey (1987) emphasizes it. Pinkard (2001) does not, pre-
    ferring to depict Hegel as laboring to understand the modern condition.

3. Some have thought Hegel "has been badly misunderstood" on the state and that he was
    not referring to actually existing states but to their "ideal" (Hartman 1953: xxvii, xxviii
    Popper (1945) was appalled by Hegel's insistence upon state reverence and thought it
    led to German totalitarianism.

4. Much of the slant upon Hegel's thought presented in the text comes from *The Philos-
    ophy of History,* first published in 1837, which has a long and complicated publishing
    history, in part because the text was compiled from notes. I have used two versions.
    The first text was an 1899 translation by J. Sibree. The second was a 1953 translation by
    R. Hartman, given a different title than the 1899 translation, *Reason in History: A Gen-
    eral Introduction to the Philosophy of History.* The Hartman version interpolates some
    material from other editions and, thus, has slightly more material than the translation.

5. Tylor (1871) first drew attention to the importance of animism in anthropology, argu-
    ing it to be the first religion that originated in "primitive" peoples' failed attempts to
    explain natural events like dreams. Tylor's views have been contested.

6. Later in US anthropology, under the guidance of Franz Boas, *volksgeist* would morph
    into the notion of a people's culture (Stocking 1968).

7. Hereafter, when referring to a something that is supposed to be, it will be put in quo-
    tation marks

8. Concepts like zero do have *istheit* because they do refer to something that "is," though
    what it "is" is not there. For example, two oranges take away two oranges leaves zero
    oranges. The "is" that zero stands for here is the absent oranges.

9. Neuroscientific research reveals that volition and consciousness are produced by brain
    operations (Dehaene 2014). The presupplementary motor area, the anterior prefrontal
    cortex, and the parietal cortex are all involved in producing human volition (Haggard
    2008). Are they Hegel's "immediate substance?" Is God in the left or right parietal
    cortex?

10. David Harvey recently asserted that contradictions arise "when two seemingly op-
    posed forces are simultaneously present within a particular situation, an entity, a
    process or an event" (2014: 1). Harvey sounds Nietzschean when he speaks of contra-
    dictions being about "opposed forces." He seems less Nietzschean when those opposed
    forces are only "seemingly" so.

11. For example, in German a single word, *kraft*, can mean both force and power (Inwood 1992: 10).
12. The terms "open," "autopoietic," and "reflexivity" come from systems theory (see Luhmann 1995). Maturana and Varela (1973) introduced the notion of autopoiesis. The reflection involved in reflexivity involves brain operations that input information from external reality, which is then processed emotively and cognitively.
13. The forces analyzed in the text always involve humans. As such they are social as opposed to inanimate force. When readers read "force" on a page it really means social force.
14. Authoritative resources are unequally distributed in contemporary populations. Many individuals possess few authoritative resources. A few possess an enormous amount of such resources. The term "window of authority" denotes the amount of force resources to be exercised in the number of situations allocated to an actor. Those with lots of authoritative resources possess large windows. Those with little authority possess small windows. Clearly, the larger an actors' window of authority, the greater is their agency.
15. The concept of limit is important in calculus, where a limit is some value that a function, or sequence, approaches (Steward 2008). Limits had become important in economic theory by the 1950s. Economics at that time was considered the most advanced social science. So by appropriating the concept for use in defining contradictions, Godelier (1972) could believe he was making the concept part of "advanced scientific practice."
16. Contradictions will be named after the incompatible structural parts. So, for example, a major contradiction in Marx's thought was the labor/capital contradiction.
17. The notion of the coalescence of contradictions owes something to Althusser, who, following Lenin, spoke of the "fusion" of an "accumulation" of contradictions producing revolution (1977: 99). It is observed that contradictions often cooccur, when they do they accumulate, which means that problems provoked by each contradiction are added to those of every other cooccurring contradiction, i.e., they are fused together. This is coalescence, which produces a variety of instabilities that may include revolution.
18. The term "consciousness" goes undefined because while it is known that consciousness is the result of brain operations these are not well understood (Searle 2005). However, the conscious brain produces sensation and perception, with these having both cognitive and emotional aspects (Dehaene, 2014).
19. In passing, it might be noted that US capital and labor tend to share a worldview that categorizes bad people in terms of sexual and anal orifices.
20. The concept of working memory owes much to Alan Baddeley (2007). There is debate over the nature of working memory, especially concerning its physiological components. Baddeley has reviewed these debates (2002). Recall is sometimes used as an alternative for retrieval. While it is clear that retrieval occurs, it is unclear how this is so (Schacter, Gilbert, and Wegner 2011). The central executive appears to be located in the frontal cortex, primarily in the dorsolateral prefrontal cortex, the anterior cingulate cortex, and the orbitofrontal cortex. Hermeneutics in the sense of the perceptions and procedures bearing upon sensations appear to be retrieved mostly from posterior portions of the cortex, near where sensations are stored.
21. Symbolic interactionists might observe that public desires and *délires* "frame" situations. I agree but emphasize that this framing process takes place as part of a political struggle to control interpretation.

22. The notions of public desires and *délires* resemble Goffman's notion of frames, which are "the definitions of a situation" (1974: 10). Public desires and *délires* do define, in the sense of interpreting, situations. However, Goffman's frames tend to be located in "subjective" realms (ibid.). Public desires and *délires,* though they may have been created in I-space, exist in E-space as discourse and behavior-containing understandings.

23. Elites' public *délires* vary in their scope, ambiguity, and degree of compulsion. A *délire* is low in scope and ambiguity if its perceptual/procedural pair refers to small amounts of social being and does so without vagueness. A *délire* is high in scope and ambiguity if its perceptual/procedural pair refers to large amounts of social being in ways that are perceptually and/or procedurally unclear. The degree of compulsion of a public *délire* is the extent to which elites whose windows of responsibility open on the social being covered by it are obliged to implement its procedures. A law specifying that a stretch of road will have a speed limit of thirty kilometers per hour is a public *délire* of low scope and ambiguity. *The Monroe Doctrine* (1823), announced during a State of the Union address of President James Monroe, forbade European attempts to colonize land or in other ways to interfere with states in North and South America and further warned that such interference would be perceived as aggression that the United States would eliminate. Clearly, the scope of the Monroe Doctrine is vast—European meddling in the Western Hemisphere, equally clearly, it contains ambiguity: what constitutes "interference" in the New World? Ambiguity allows US governmental elites some freedom as to whether to proceed to eliminate European meddling. For example, the United Kingdom heavily invested in certain South American countries in the nineteenth century, an intervention to which American authorities turned a blind eye.

24. Classic Marxist thought insisted upon a complex relationship between class, consciousness, and action, specifically, class position produced class consciousness, which in turn was responsible for class action. My understanding of the relationship between class and consciousness might be said to be a "sense and sensibility" perspective and is based upon the judgment of a former CIA chief. George Tenet, CIA director in the Clinton and second Bush administrations, once quipped, "Where you stand on issues is normally determined by where you sit" (2007: xxi). "Consciousness" in a critical structural realist perspective is an actor's sensations interpreted by her or his cultural neurohermeneutic system, forming her or his sensibility. Those sitting in the same position sense similar actualities leading to similar sensibilities. This is Tenet's Tenet: where you sit leads to common sense, which leads to common sensibility.

25. The current US moment (2015) of class warfare is as follows: elites have instituted different iterations of neoliberal public *délires,* generating rising wealth for themselves and stagnant or declining wealth for everybody else (Duménil and Levy 2011). This has led to a *precariat* among nonelites (Bourdieu 1998), an appellation that evokes a common sensation experienced by nonelites of everyday in every way instability. Emergence of the *precariat* has provoked "stirrings," "protests," "outpourings," and "days of rage" (Standing 2011: vii). US elites, nervous about such incivilities, have countered by increasing their surveillance of nonelites, as directed by the Patriot Act in 2001 (Tye 2014) and changed the law with the John Warner National Defense Act of 2007 to allow the military to quell civil unrest (see US Army 2014 for a discussion of how they plan to do it).

26. *Deadly Contradictions* (Reyna 2016) documents a global domination public *délire* instituted in 1950 to fix vulnerabilities introduced by an imperial contradiction between

the United States and the Union of Soviet Socialist Republics that characterized the Cold War period.

References

Adorno, Theodor. *Negative Dialectics*. Oxford: Polity, 2008 [1966].
Althusser, Louis. *Reading Capital*. Edited by Louis Althusser and Étienne Balibar. London: New Left Books, 1970.
———. *The Spectre of Hegel: Early Writings*. London: Verso, 2014.
Anderson, Perry. *Considerations on Western Marxism*. London: Verso, 1976.
Arthur, Christopher J. *The New Dialectic and Marx's Capital*. Leiden: Brill, 2004.
———. "Towards a Systematic Dialectic of Capital." chrisarthur.net, accessed 3 April 2016. http://chrisarthur.net/wp-content/uploads/2016/02/towards-a-systematic-dialectic-of-capital.pdf.
Augustine, Saint. *The City of God*. Peabody: Hendrickson, 2008 [c. AD 415].
Bacevich, Andrew. *The New American Militarism: How Americans Are Seduced by War*. Oxford: Oxford University Press, 2005.
Baddeley, Alan D. "Is Working Memory Still Working?" *European Psychologist* 7, no. 2 (2002): 85–97. DOI.org/10.1027//1016-9040.7.2.85.
———. *Working Memory, Thought, and Action*. Oxford: Oxford University Press, 2007.
Barth, Karl. *Protestant Theology in the Nineteenth Century*. Grand Rapids: Eerdmans, 2002 [1947].
Bear, Mark, Barry Connors, and Michael Paradiso. *Neuroscience: Exploring the Brain*. Philadelphia: Lippincott, Williams and Wilkins, 2001.
Bell, Daniel. *The Coming of Post Industrial Society*. New York: Basic Books, 1976.
Bernstein, Eduard. "Dialektik und Entwicklung." *Die Neue Zeit* 17, no. 2 (1898): 327–35; 17, no. 2 (1899): 228–33.
Bird-David, Nurit. "'Animism' Revisited: Personhood, Environment, and Relational Epistemology." *Current Anthropology* 40, no. S1 (1999): S67–S91. DOI: 10.1086/200061.
Bhaskar, Roy A. *Dialectic: The Pulse of Freedom*. London: Verso, 1993.
Blunden, Andy. "Hegel's Critics." *Hegel by Hyper Text*, accessed 3 April 2016. https://www.marxists.org/reference/archive/hegel/pg_other.htm.
Bourdieu, Pierre. "La Précarité Est Aujourdhui Partout." In *Contre-feux*, vol. 2. Paris: Raisons d'agir, 1998.
Boyer, Dominic. *Spirit and System: Media, Intellectuals, and the Dialectic in Modern German Culture*. Chicago: University of Chicago Press, 2005.
Champlain, John. *Power*. New York: Atherton Press, 1971.
Dehaene, Stanislas. *Consciousness and the Brain: Deciphering How the Brain Codes Our Thoughts*. New York: Viking, 2014.
DeNys, Martin. *Hegel and Theology*. New York: T&T Clark International, 2009.
Dickey, Laurence. *Hegel: Religion, Economics and the Politics of Spirit*. Cambridge, UK: Cambridge University Press, 1987.
Duménil, Gérard and Dominique Lévy. *The Crisis of Neoliberalism*. Cambridge, MA: Harvard University Press, 2011.
Elster, Jon. *Making Sense of Marx*. Cambridge, UK: Cambridge University Press, 1985.

Feil, Daryl. *The Evolution of Highland New Guinea Societies.* Cambridge, UK: Cambridge University Press, 1984.

Findlay, John N. *Hegel: A Re-examination.* New York: Macmillan, 1958.

Friedman, Jonathan. *Cultural Identity and Global Process.* London: Sage, 1994.

Gay, Peter. *The Dilemma of Democratic Socialism: Eduard Bernstein's Challenge to Marx.* New York: Columbia University Press, 1952.

Giddens, Anthony. *Central Problems in Social Theory: Action, Structure and Contradiction in Social Analysis.* Los Angeles: University of California Press, 1979.

Godelier, Maurice. *Rationality and Irrationality in Economics.* London: Monthly Review Press, 1972.

Goffman, Irving. *Frame Analysis.* New York: Harper and Row, 1974.

Haggard, Patrick. "Human Volition: Toward a Neuroscience of Will." *Nature Reviews Neuroscience* 9, no. 12 (2008): 934–46. DOI:10.1038/nrn2497.

Harding, Susan F. *The Book of Jerry Fallwell: Fundamentalist Language and Politics.* Princeton: Princeton University Press, 2000.

Harris, Marvin. *The Rise of Anthropological Theory.* New York: Crowell, 1968.

Harvey, David. *Seventeen Contradictions and the End of Capitalism.* London: Profile Books, 2014.

Hegel, Georg W.F. *The Philosophy of History.* Translated by John Sibree. New York: Colonial Press, 1899 [1857].

———. *Reason in History: A General Introduction to the Philosophy of History.* Translated by Robert S. Hartman. Indianapolis: Bobbs-Merrill, 1953 [1837].

———. *Encyclopaedia of the Philosophical Sciences.* Translated by William Wallace. Oxford: Clarendon, 1971 [1873].

———. *Phenomenology of Spirit.* Translated by Arnold V. Miller. Oxford: Oxford University Press, 1977 [1807].

———. *Elements of a Philosophy of Right.* Translated by H.B. Nisbet. Cambridge, UK: Cambridge University Press, 1991 [1821].

Hertsgaard, Mark. "Climate Change Kills 400,000 a Year, New Report Reveals." *The Daily Beast,* 9 September 2012, accessed 16 June 2015. http://www.thedailybeast.com/arti cles/2012/09/27/climate-change-kills-400-000-a-year-new-report-reveals.html.

Hodgson, Peter. Introduction. In *G.W.F. Hegel: Theologian of the Spirit,* 1–38. Minneapolis: Fortress, 1997.

Hornborg, Alf. "Animism, Fetishism, and Objectivism as Strategies for Knowing (or Not Knowing) the World." *Ethnos* 71, no. 1 (2006): 22–24.DOI:10.1080/00141840600603129.

Huffington Post. "Best Education in the World. Finland, South Korea Top Country Rankings, U.S. Rated Average." *Huffington Post,* 11 November 2012, accessed 16 June 2015. http://www.huffingtonpost.com/2012/11/27/best-education-in-the-wor_n_2199795 .html.

Hume, David. *A Treatise on Human Nature.* Project Gutenberg eBook #4705, 2012, accessed 17 June 2015. http://www.gutenberg.org/ebooks/4705?msg=welcome_stranger.

Ingold, Tim. "Totemism, Animism and the Depiction of Animals." In *The Perception of the Environment: Essays on Livelihood, Dwelling and Skill,* 111–31. London: Routledge, 2000.

Inwood, Michael. *A Hegel Dictionary.* Oxford: Wiley-Blackwell, 1992.

Jary, David and Julia Jary. *Collins Dictionary of Sociology.* Glasgow: HarperCollins, 1995.

Kaufman, Walter. *From Shakespeare to Existentialism: Studies in Poetry, Religion, and Philosophy.* Boston: Beacon Press, 1959.
———. *Hegel: A Reinterpretation.* New York: Anchor, 1966.
Kojève, Alexandre. *Introduction to the Reading of Hegel: Lectures on the Phenomenology of the Spirit.* Ithaca: Cornell University Press, 1980 [1947].
Korsch, Karl. *Marxism and Philosophy.* New York: Monthly Review Press, 1970 [1923].
Layton, Lyndsey. "U.S. Students Lag around Average on International Science, Math and Reading Test." *Washington Post,* 2 December 2013, accessed 10 August 2014. http://www.washingtonpost.com/local/education/us-students-lag-around-average-on-international-science-math-and-reading-test/2013/12/02/2e510f26-5b92-11e3-a49b-90a0e156254b_story.html.
Lenin, Vladimir I. *One Step Forward, Two Steps Back: The Crisis in our Party.* Moscow: Progress Publishers, 1969 [1904].
———. *Philosophic Notebooks. Vol. 38: Collected Works.* Moscow: Progress Publishers, 1976.
Luhmann, Niklas. *Social Systems.* Stanford: Stanford University Press, 1995.
Lukács, György. *History and Class Consciousness: Studies in Marxist Dialectics.* Cambridge, MA: MIT Press, 2000 [1923].
Magee, Glenn. *Hegel Dictionary.* London: Continuum, 2010.
Malinowski, Bronislav. *Argonauts of the Western Pacific.* London: George Routledge and Sons, 1922.
Mann, Michael. *The Sources of Social Power,* vol. 1. Cambridge, UK: Cambridge University Press, 1986.
Mao, Tse-Tung. "On Contradiction." *Selected Works of Mao-Tse-Tung,* accessed 3 April 2016. https://www.marxists.org/reference/archive/mao/selected-works/volume-1/mswv1_17.htm.
Marcuse, Herbert. *Reason and Revolution: Hegel and the Rise of Social Theory.* Boston: Beacon Press, 1970 [1941].
Marx, Karl. *Capital: A Critique of Political Economy.* New York: Modern Library, 1906 [1867].
Maturana, Humberto and Francisco Varela. "Autopoiesis and Cognition: The Realization of the Living." In *Boston Studies in the Philosophy of Science,* vol. 42, edited by Robert S. Cohen and Marx W. Wartofsky, 63–135. Dordecht: Reidel, 1980 [1973].
Mills, C. Wright. *Power, Politics, and People: The Collected Essays of C Wright Mills.* New York: Oxford University Press, 1963.
———. *The Power Elite.* New York: Oxford University Press, 2000 [1956].
Morgan, Lewis Henry. *Ancient Society.* Tucson: University of Arizona Press, 1985 [1877].
Murphy, Tim. *The Politics of Spirit: Phenomenology, Genealogy, Religion.* Albany: State University of New York Press, 2010.
Nietzsche, Friedrich. *Will to Power.* Kindle eBook 2012 [1901]
Ollman, Bertell. *Dance of the Dialectic: Steps in Marx's Method.* Champaign: University of Illinois Press, 2003, accessed 26 July 2014. https://www.nyu.edu/projects/ollman/docs/dd_ch00_content.php.
Parson, Talcott. "On the Concept of Political Power." *Proceedings of the American Philosophical Society* 107, no. 3 (1963): 232–62. Accessed 10 January 2015. http://www.jstor.org/stable/985582.
Peirce, Charles. "Fixation of Belief." In *Philosophical Writings of Peirce,* edited by Justus Buchler, 5–22. New York: Dover, 1955 [1893].

Pinkard, Terry. *Hegel: A Biography.* Cambridge, UK: Cambridge University Press, 2001.

Popper, Karl. *The Open Society and Its Enemies,* vols. 1 and 2. Princeton: Princeton University Press, 1966 [1945].

ProOxygen. 2014. "Atmospheric CO_2—Weekly Data." *CO_2.Earth.Org,* accessed 11 September 2014. http://co2now.org/current-co2/co2-now/.

Rappaport, Roy. *Pigs for the Ancestors.* New Haven: Yale University Press, 1968.

Ray, Man. "Quotes about Contradiction." *Goodreads,* accessed 9 June 2015. http://www .goodreads.com/quotes/tag/contradiction?page=1.

Reyna, Stephen. "Force, Power, and *String Being?*" *Max Planck Institute for Social Anthropology Working Papers,* working paper no. 20 (2001): 1–31.

———. *Connections: Brain, Mind and Culture in a Social Anthropology.* London: Routledge, 2002.

———. "Force, Power, and the Problem of Order: An Anthropological Approach." *Sociologus* 3, no. 2 (2003): 199–223.

———. *Deadly Contradictions: The New American Empire and Its Global Warring.* New York: Berghahn, 2016.

Robertson, David. *Penguin Dictionary of Politics.* London: Penguin, 1988.

Roosevelt, Franklin Delano. "Address at Oglethorpe University in Atlanta, Georgia, May 22, 1932." *The American Presidency Project,* accessed 21 August 2014. http://www.presid ency.ucsb.edu/ws/?pid=88410.

Rosenau, Pauline Marie. *Post-Modernism and the Social Sciences: Insights, Inroads, and Intrusions.* Princeton: Princeton University Press, 1992.

Sahlins, Marshall. "Historical Metaphors and Mythical Realities." In *The New Social Theory Reader,* edited by Steven Seidman and Jeffrey C. Alexander, 47–55. New York: Routledge, 2001.

Salmon, Wesley. *Causality and Explanation.* New York: Oxford, 1998.

Schacter, Daniel, Daniel Gilbert, and Daniel M. Wegner. "Retrieval: Bringing Memories to Mind." In *Introducing Psychology,* 137–40. 2nd ed. New York: Worth Publishers, 2011.

Schopenhauer, Arthur. *On the Fourfold Root of Sufficient Reason.* Chicago: Open Court Publishing, 1974 [1847].

Schutz, Alfred. *The Phenomenology of the Social World.* Evanston: Northwestern University Press, 1967 [1932].

Scripps. "CO2.earth". *Scripps Hourly and Daily CO2.* Accessed 3 December 2016. https:// www.co2.earth/daily-co2

Searle, John. "Consciousness: What We Still Don't Know." *New York Review of Books,* 13 January 2005, accessed 3 April 2016. http://www.nybooks.com/articles/2005/01/13/ consciousness-what-we-still-dont-know/.

Selsam, Howard, David Goldway, and Harry Martel. *Dynamics of Social Change: A Reader in Marxist Social Science.* New York: International Publishers, 1983.

Stalin, Josef V. "Dialectical and Historical Materialism." In *Problems of Leninism,* 835–73. Peking: Foreign Languages Press, 1976 [1938].

Standing, Guy. *The Precariat: The New Dangerous Class.* London: Bloomsbury, 2011.

Steward, Julian. *Theory of Culture Change.* Urbana: University of Illinois Press, 1955.

Stewart, James. *Calculus: Early Transcendentals.* Belmont: Thompson, 2008.

Stocking, George. *Race, Culture, and Evolution: Essays in the History of Anthropology.* New York: Free Press, 1968.

Tenet, George. *At the Center of the Storm: The CIA during America's Time of Crisis.* New York: Harper Perenniel, 2007.

Tye, John. "Meet Executive Order 12333: The Reagan Rule That Lets the NSA Spy on Americans." *Washington Post,* 18 July 2014, accessed 12 September 2014. http://www .washingtonpost.com/opinions/meet-executive-order-12333-the-reagan-rule-that-lets-the-nsa-spy-on-americans/2014/07/18/93d2ac22-0b93-11e4-b8e5-d0de80767fc2 _story.html.

Tylor, Edward B. *Primitive Culture,* vol. II. New York: Harper Torch Books, 1958 [1871].

US Army. "U.S. Army Techniques Publication 3–39.33: Civil Disturbances." *Public Intelligence,* 15 August 2014, accessed 12 June 2015. https://publicintelligence.net/usarmy-civil-disturbances/.

Weber, Max. *Economy and Society: An Outline of Interpretive Sociology,* vol. 1. New York: Bedminster Press, 1968.

Wilde, Lawrence. "Logic: Dialectic and Contradiction." In *The Cambridge Companion to Marx,* edited by Terrell Carver, 275–95. Cambridge, UK: Cambridge University Press, 1991.

Wittgensrein, Ludwig. *Tractus Logico-Philosophicus.* New York: Humanitirs Press, 1961.

Wolfe Jeremy, Keith Kluender, and Dennis Levi. *Sensation & Perception,* 3rd ed. Sunderland: Sinauer Associates, 2011.

Youngsmith, Barron. "Warriors, Hot and Cold." *The New Republic,* 2 September 2010, accessed 28 April 2014. http://www.newrepublic.com/book/review/hawk-and-dove-nicholas-thompson-nitze-kennan-cold-war-soviets.

Žižek, Slavoj. *Less Than Nothing: Hegel and the Shadow of Dialectical Materialism.* London: Verso, 2012.

———. *Absolute Recoil: Toward a New Foundation of Dialectical Materialism.* London: Verso, 2014.

PART III

Critical Science

chapter four

Right and Might
Of Approximate Truths
and Moral Judgments

I must remind the reader of the obvious; namely, that this whole global,
yet American, postmodern culture is the ... expression of a whole new wave
of American military and economic domination throughout the world.
—Jameson, *Postmodernism*

Unfortunately, or fortunately, depending upon where one's loyalties lie ...
this radical contrast, inherited from the ancients, between "knowledge"
(episteme) and "opinion" (doxa) has been breaking down.
—Geertz, "A Lab of One's Own"

This essay is a contribution to a larger project that seeks to analyze postmodernism as an expression of the current state of late capitalism (see Jameson 1991; Harvey 1989). Specifically, however, I am concerned with moral judgment. The moral philosopher Jeffrey Reiman, writing of postmodern times, contends that the "current sorry state" is one in which "we are unable to identify the difference between right and might" (1990: 1). This prompts two questions: how is it that we have reached such a "sorry state," and how does one better apprehend morality? These are our topics.

Before proceeding, however, a word is in order about the use of the term "mighty." These are persons in distributions of power who command larger amounts of force and who, thus, have grander powers. Over the centuries, the tendency has been to eulogize such folk as the highest of the high, the most serene of the serene, and on and on. Clearly, regardless of how their praises are sung, those with more force are those with greater power, which makes them those with a greater ability to do more wrong. Now I should reveal a personal concern. The current batch of the mighty, capitalists and high officials, have had more power than those who preceded them. This power was used throughout the twentieth century to produce the greatest slaughters of peoples recorded in history. The reality of this butchery means that any discipline that rigorously seeks to apprehend social life and moral truth must pay special attention to the mighty. This essay gives them the attention that they have so richly earned.

The argument develops over three sections. The first section shows how Geertz used his variant of postmodernism, termed "conjectural hermeneutics," to help construct an interpretation that supported the Indonesian and US government's legitimation of the former's mass killings of Communists and their allies in the mid-1960s. This judgment was that the Indonesian Army, and those working for it, were morally right to kill on the order of 800,000 persons in 1965 and 1966.[1] The end of the first section leaves readers in suspense. Did the mighty really have the right to kill so many?

The second section offers a way of answering this question. It begins by introducing a notion of moral apprehensibility and an appreciation of how the mighty can diminish such apprehension when they direct what Michel Foucault (1996) termed "regimes of truth." Then *causal moral analysis* is formulated as a method for apprehending the approximate truth of moral judgments. The third section explores the virtues of causal moral analysis by applying it to the killings. It suggests that the mighty did not have it even approximately right with regard to their justification of the massacres. The article concludes with a consideration of Geertz's (1990) observation that the contrast between episteme and doxa is "breaking down" and of the relevance of this decay for postmodernism and intellectual responsibility.

Conjectural Hermeneutics

Below, I argue that Geertz (1973, 1983) formulated an interpretive anthropology—termed "conjectural hermeneutics," for reasons made explicit below—which he used in his *After the Fact* (1995, hereafter *ATF*) to craft a narrative concerning the Indonesian killings. This narrative represents the killings in a manner that supports US and Indonesian governmental claims that the killings were justified.

Geertz's hermeneutics emphasizes three assertions and five rejections. The first of the assertions has to do with how Geertz understands social and cultural realities, about which he says, "It is Heraclitus cubed and worse" (1995: 2). "Time" is "larger and smaller streams twisting, and turning and now and then crossing, running together for a while, and separating again" (ibid.). There are no histories or biographies, "but a confusion of histories, a swarm of biographies" (ibid.). There are only "swirls, confluxions, and inconstant connections." (ibid.). The first avowal is that social and cultural realities are extraordinarily "inconstant."

How does one represent reality in such an ontology? To this question Geertz responds, "Whatever reality is, besides existent, our sense of it … comes inevitably out of the way we talk about it" (1995: 18). This is a second assertion, one to the effect that saying it is so forms our sense that it is so. It prompts another question: when studying humans, what should the anthropologist actually do so that she or he may talk about reality? Here, of course, the famous answer is that what the anthropologist does is "thick description," and such description directs the anthropologist to interpret peoples' meanings as if they were "trying to read (in the sense of 'construct a reading of') a manuscript" (Geertz 1973: 10). However, Geertz regards the anthropological vocation to be "in important respects a literary one" (1988: 142), which means that a text-building strategy (ibid.: 69), a rhetoric, is important when an anthropologist presents her or his thick description. This, then, is the third of Geertz's assertions: one should do thick description and write it up with rhetorical panache.

There are five rejections. The first of these is that Geertz decided that he "never really bought" science (Handler 1991: 608). The first rejection, then, is of science itself. The other four rejections follow from the first. Geertz rejects the search for generalization because, he asserts, "There is no general story" (1995: 2). He dismisses causality because he believes it is "not possible … to isolate the Y's from X's." (1973: 23).[2] He refuses the validation of interpretation because he believes, "You either grasp an interpretation or you do not, see a point or you do not" (1973: 24). Finally, uninterested in causality, indifferent to validation, Geertz shows little concern for truth: "I have always thought that understanding social life entails not an advance toward an omega point, 'truth.'" (1995: 117). This, of course, makes sense when reality is "inconstant" because it means that there is simply nothing that holds still to which truth might correspond.

Now it is time to specify why the preceding may be termed a "conjectural hermeneutics." Given Geertz's five rejections, his interpretations are made in the absence of "specifiable evidence" (Crapanzano 1992: 67), so that his attributions of meaning are pretty much, as Cohen has put it, "conjectural, unverifiable" (1974: 5). The four rejections reveal a strong antiscience bias. Such skepticism toward science is a hallmark of postmodern thought (Lyotard 1984). Geertz certainly shares this skepticism, so it is in this sense that conjectural hermeneutics is a postmodern project.

In 1995, three decades after the events, Geertz applied his hermeneutic to the 1965–1966 Indonesian killings. On pages 6–10 of his text he works in quintessential Geertzian fashion, suggesting to readers that they were getting the interpretation of reality of the killings directly from those who were there. He says that, with the passage of time, the killings "hardly seemed a memory at all" (1995: 10) to the villagers in a village where they occurred. This is a claim about what has occurred in reality, and what is claimed is that the villagers have pretty much forgotten about the killings. This assertion could easily be validated by observing whether villagers do or do not actually have strong memories of the killings. Faithful, however, to the canons of his hermeneutics, Geertz makes no such validation. This means that readers must judge the assertion "the killings are pretty much forgotten" to be "true."

One suspects, however, that it is actually untrue, because Geertz reports on villagers with haunting memories of the killings. For example, he has a member of the local elite speak—a former Nationalist party leader who had been given to "patrician maneuvering" (1995: 8). This man reports that a head was "hung on the footbridge in front of his house with a cigarette stuck between his teeth. There were legs and arms and torsos every morning in the irrigation canals. Penises were nailed to telephone poles" (ibid.: 9). Geertz goes on, having caught his readers' attention with visions of mutilated genitalia, to establish a moral judgment concerning the massacres by allowing the old Nationalist to issue a moral decree. He says, "In the beginning, things could have gone either way. Each side was trying to kill the other side first" (ibid.: 10). This is Geertz's interpretation of a native's interpretation of the killings, which was offered in the form of a moral judgment.

A crucial question arises: is it also Geertz's judgment? Nowhere in *ATF* does Geertz say that he finds a government's killing of huge numbers of its citizens ethically repugnant. This implies that he judges such actions to be good under certain circumstances and that one of these is in which a government kills in its self-defense. Does Geertz actually believe this? Here the text is equivocal. It states, in a paragraph matter of factly listing what happened in the town following a 1955 election, that prior to the massacres, "An 'it's us or them' frenzy had descended on the town" (1995: 6). Geertz presents this statement without any qualification that it is an interpretation of those in the town. Rather, it is submitted as a statement of what actually happened, though characteristically without observations that support that what was asserted to happen actually happened. This means that its approximate truth is unvalidated, so that it is merely "true."

Now, on page 10 Geertz has the old Nationalist say it was kill or be killed and on page 6 he asserts a kill or be killed "frenzy" actually "descended." This leaves the impression that Geertz accepts the old Nationalist's moral judgment. Ambiguity exists, however, because Geertz never explicitly states that he personally believes the killings happened in a kill or be killed situation. Thus it is uncertain what Geertz believes. It is, however, certain that on page 6 he represents the killings as occurring out of self-defense and on page 10 he represents the old Nationalist as interpreting them in this manner.

This brings us directly to the question of just whose moral judgment concerning the killings is Geertz actually representing. Geertz believes that Hughes (1967) has provided the "best general survey" of the killings (Geertz

1995: 172). The Indonesian Army's justification for the slaughter, according to Hughes, was "It was the Communists or us. If we hadn't killed them they would have killed us" (1967: 189). This view was supported by the CIA, who insisted that the coup "was in every respect the planning of the PKI" (CIA 1968: 226). The PKI was the Indonesian Communist party, which means that the CIA agreed with the Indonesian Army. It was self-defense. Thus the moral judgment that Geertz represents both as the way natives saw things and as the way things were was actually that of the mighty in the Indonesian military and the CIA. So the killings were right for the mighty because they were self-defense.

Geertz's readers in *ATF* are intellectuals in the social sciences and humanities—respected people whose opinions count. Now, nowhere in *ATF* does Geertz warn his readers that what he is representing as the moral truth of the killings is in actuality the propaganda "truth" of the Indonesian Army and the CIA. Intellectuals might be skeptical of what they regarded as government propaganda, so by using a text-building strategy that withholds the fact that he is representing government views, he strengthens his ability to convince his readers. But, by so doing, Geertz is participating in US and Indonesian regimes of truth. He is using conjectural hermeneutics to take these governments' moral justification of the killings and sow them among influential folk who might otherwise be skeptical of this "truth." Consider the point at which we have arrived in our argument: the stage is littered with legs, heads, torsos, and penises—800,000 or so real people hacked apart. Is Geertz telling the "truth" or the truth about their deaths?

Causal Moral Analysis

It is important to specify precisely how I propose to answer this question. *Moral situations* are fields of individual action and social practice about which investigators wish to formulate moral opinions. *Moral judgment* is attributing moral qualities to actions and practices found in such situations. The problem of formulating moral judgments is one of achieving moral apprehensibility. Such *apprehensibility* is knowledge that accurately distinguishes between good and bad actions and practices.

Moralizing within philosophy generally has involved three mutually supporting lines of study. It has been concerned with the practical problems of what are right actions or practices (with morality proper), it has been interested in deciding which ethical canons are right and which are wrong (ethics proper), and, lastly, it has analyzed the theoretical foundations of ethical systems (metaethics; Engel 1981: 147). Moral apprehensibility is not concerned with the rationales underlying ethical systems. Nor does it provide grounds for preference between different ethics. Readers, then, will not learn below what is right and wrong and why. Rather, they will learn a method for apprehending whether actions or practices are right or wrong given a particular ethics justified by a particular metaethics.

The attainment of moral apprehensibility, then, is a bit like solving some mystery. It is the acquisition of knowledge of what actually happened—who did what to whom—so that one can judge whether these actions and practices are right. Such knowledge depends to a considerable degree upon the ability to distinguish "truth" from truth. This raises the question: what is the difference between a truth that must stand between quotation marks and one that stands alone? Foucault can be helpful in answering this question. In "Two Lectures," as part of an exposition of his genealogical method, Foucault claimed that genealogies should be understood to be "anti-sciences" (1994: 204).

Having asserted this, he was concerned to specify exactly what he objected to in science. So he stated that he was not "opposed … to the contents, methods, or concepts of a science, but to the effects of the centralizing powers which are linked to the institution and functioning of an organized scientific discourse within a society" (Foucault: 204). Foucault had, thus, distinguished "contents, methods, and concepts" of sciences themselves from the "centralizing powers" that institutionalized them.

Elsewhere Foucault said that such institutionalizations were parts of "regimes of truth." These were a society's "general politics" of what "it accepts and makes function as true" (1996: 379). In contemporary society, the knowledge that functions as true is often expressed in "the form of scientific discourse" and "is produced and transmitted under the control, dominant if not exclusive, 'of a few great political and economic apparatuses (university, army, writing, media)'" (ibid.). There is an important distinction here between "science itself" and "regimes of scientific truth." Foucault is not opposed to science itself. He is troubled by regimes of truth in which the mighty in powerful institutions make science, like a trained parrot, mouthing "truths." (Hereafter, such "truths" will be distinguished from those of science by placing them in quotation marks.)

Certain specifics of modern "regimes of truth" as they pertain to exploitation, class, and moral apprehensibility need to be clarified in order to suggest why we might be in Reiman's "sorry state." Foucault had said, echoing Nietzsche, "that the relations of power that function in a society such as ours essentially rest upon a definite relation of forces" (1994: 213). *Force* is that which creates capacities to do things, and *power* is those capacities that get realized. *Resources,* which get utilized when doing things, form the basis of force. *Economic force* is based upon economic resources. *Violent force* involves military resources. *Coercive force* depends upon coercive resources (e.g., prisons). *Authoritative force* rests upon authoritative resources: official and legal entitlements to regulate others' actions. *Cultural force* involves interpretive and normative resources, that is, knowledge of what is and of what should be done and what is.

Exploitation and class may be defined in terms of the organization of force. *Class* refers to interrelated persons whose relationships result from the type of control they exert over different forces. Following Wright (1976), one can distinguish three forms of control: that over the allocation and investment of force, that over the physical apparatus involved in the production of force, and that over the labor power used to produce force. There are three major modern classes: agents, their subordinates, and the workers. *Agents* are those who have force made for them and who subsequently control this force's allocation and investment, the physical apparatus involved in its production and reproduction, and the labor power that uses this apparatus.

Subordinates are those to whom agents have delegated authoritative force, which gives the subordinates control over the physical apparatus and the labor power that produces or exercises force. *Workers* are persons who possess none of the three forms of control and whose labor is used to operate the physical apparatus to produce or exercise force. Classes relate to each other in regimes. A *regime* is an institution, or an organization of institutions, in which subordinates and workers make force for agents. The term "exploitation" is reserved for relationships in which certain classes produce, and reproduce, force for other classes. Workers and the subordinates are exploited because what they do is make force for their agents, who, consequently, become mighty.

Regimes of truth in advanced capitalist states involve organizations of institutions (radio, television, funding agencies, universities, private foundations, publishers, etc.) in which subordinates and workers produce cultural force for agents of capital and the state. The force they produce is knowledge of what "truly" is and of what should "truly" be done with what is. These last "truths," of course, concern moral judgments. Now, because there has been a mammoth accumulation of cultural resources in the hands of agents, and because the mighty rather insist on being right, there has been an enormous production of moral "truths." It is difficult to distinguish right from might because the mighty, through their regimes of truth, invade human consciousness, ordaining what is "truly" right. This is, perhaps, one reason we are in Reiman's "sorry state." I shall be in a position to suggest another reason by the chapter's end.

I shall argue below, respecting Foucault's distinction between science itself and science as a part of a regime of truth, that science itself can be applied in causal moral analyses to facilitate knowing whether the mighty are mouthing "truths" or truths. Validation will turn out to be the key to acquiring this knowledge. Science is a way of representing reality.[3] It is theoretical because its representations are of a particular type of knowledge, theory. Actually theory involves a double knowledge, for it is both a comprehension of how and why reality is the way it is and an evaluation of how well it is known that reality is as it is. *Explanation* is knowledge of how and why things are the way they are. *Validation* is knowledge of the reliability and validity of explanations, that is, information concerning how well they are known. Ultimately this is what truth is all about.

Explanation involves the creating of a special type of knowledge, that of generalizations. These are verbal (qualitative) or numerical (quantitative) concepts that represent realities and their connections. *Theories* are generalizations whose component concepts are generally high in scope and abstraction. *Empirical generalizations* and *hypotheses* are generalizations that are lower in scope and abstract. What it means to say that generalizations represent "connections" between realities needs clarification. If an event regularly occurs in any way with other events, then the cooccurring events may be said to be connected by association.

If an event regularly occurs in some place before or after the other events, then it may be said to be connected in some sort of spaciotemporal order. If certain antecedent events bring about, in the sense of "help to make occur," subsequent events in a spaciotemporal order, then the antecedent events may be said to be causes, the subsequent events effects, and the connection between the events causal. Smoking, an antecedent event, brings about cancer, a subsequent event.[4] Generalizations that represent such relationships are *causal explanations.*[5]

Systems of validation are practices that help scientists to distinguish between more and less true generalizations (Kaplan 1964). Validation is about the accuracy of a generalization. *Accuracy* concerns how well it is known that there is a fit between what a generalization represents to happen and what is observed to happen. A generalization asserts that a sequence of events occurs in the world, and the greater the number of times beings behave the way they are represented to behave, the greater the fit. But it must be acknowledged that there are events that go unobserved in the past and in the future.

Typically they went unobserved in the past just because they escaped observers. As for the future, because it has not yet occurred, it is impossible to observe it. This means that there are invariably events of relevance to a generalization that go unobserved. So, the knowledge of reality proposed by generalizations may be validated by existing observations but cannot be confirmed or verified in any absolute sense. Validation, then, is a process of coming to know how many times what is observed to be is as it is represented. Now, the more reality is observed to be as an explanation represents it to be, the more accurately it is known that a generalization approximates being true. It is in this sense that there are *approximate truths.*[6]

There are two manners of assessing the approximate truth of generalizations. The first concerns a generalization itself, and the second compares a
generalization to other generalizations. *Evidence* (or data) is the facts. *Facts* are
measurements based upon observations made of realities represented by generalizations. If the facts agree with the theory for only one set of observations,
then it has been validated and, for that set of observations, it is true. The more
observations there are supporting a generalization, the greater its approximate
truth. This is the first manner in which a generalization can be approximately
true. A second way is to compare different generalizations dealing with the
same realities to see which fits more facts. The preceding implies that there
may be different truths for the same reality. Newtonian and quantum mechan-
ics are both exhaustively validated representations of the solar system. However, quantum physics correctly represents more of the universe than does its
Newtonian alternative, so that it is an approximately truer theory.

Now it should be clear what the difference is between approximate truths
and "truths." The latter must function as "true" and need only to give the appearance of "truth." They do not have to be validated. Approximate truths must
be validated. The critical distinction here is that discussions of truth always
concern validation, while those of "truth" concern the management of appear-
ances. Let us now bring this understanding of how to distinguish "truth" from
truth to the task of strengthening moral apprehensibility.

Greater moral apprehension can be achieved if moral judgments have
been rigorously validated. An ethical canon, like a generalization, makes a representation of the way situations should be. Validation here is the observation
of whether the actual social situation fits with the way the ethical canon says
it should be. If, for example, one accepts the moral precept that "It is good not
to lie" and observes that George Washington lied about his home life, then it
might be suspected to be approximately true that Washington was bad because
he lied.

Crucially, the greater the validation of the fit between different situations
and the ethical canons bearing upon those situations, the greater the approximate truth of one's moral judgments. For example, if it was further found that
Washington lied about his finances, land dealings, war record, and gambling
debts, then one might have more confidence in the judgment that the first
president was bad because he lied. Here, then, are two clear rules for increasing
the apprehensibility of moral judgments. First, demand to see the validation
of the moral judgment. If there is none, reject the judgment. Second, if there
are competing moral judgments, the moral judgment supported by the most
extensive validation is to be preferred as approximately truer.

It might be observed that ethical canons tend to represent two sorts of
situations. The first is that of a single state of affairs that the canon judges to be

right or wrong. The injunction "Do not lie" is such a canon. There are many canons, however, that pertain to situations involving a chain of related affairs in which agents provoke practices that cause further affairs. Here persons are judged to be right or wrong according to whether they did or did not cause a situation to occur. The formulation of a moral judgment in this second sort of situation must involve validation of causal generalizations. This validation may be said to be a causal moral analysis because what is confirmed by observation is whether a person caused something good or bad to occur. Did, at an antecedent time, A, person or persons, X, cause certain actions or practices that produced at a subsequent time, B, further events that can be classified according to an ethical canon as right or wrong? Such a form of analysis can help one to distinguish between whether the mighty have it "truly" or truly right. It is time now to return to Indonesia.

"Best News"?

On the evening of 30 September 1965 there was a coup attempt in the capital of Jakarta, called Gestapu by the military, against the army general staff. Major-General Suharto, head of the Army Strategic Reserve (KOSTRAD), crushed Gestapu, and over the following months exterminated the PKI and their suspected followers. Gone was President Sukarno. In was the army with a New Order—army control over state power. Agents and subalterns in the regimes of truth of advanced capitalist states were delighted. *Time* crowed that the slaughters were "the West's best news for years in Asia" (1966: 26). Perhaps this was the "best news" for capitalist states, but was it also good news?

Causal moral analysis can be used to answer this question by recasting the moral judgment of the Indonesian/US governmental regime of truth as a causal generalization. This was one stating that armed uprisings of the PKI and their allies at a time, A, produced at time B defensive military responses on the part of the army and its allies. Because the army's responses came only as a defensive measure, they can be classified as self-defense and judged to be good. Validation of the truth of this generalization depends upon observation of the occurrence of three sets of events.

The first of these is that at an antecedent time there was a PKI uprising. The term "PKI uprising" refers to an organized insurrection of PKI members led by PKI leaders involving coordination across regions. The second set of events required for validation is that the army's military actions were, indeed, defensive. The final evidence needed for validation is observation that these uprisings actually produced the army's response, with the term "produce" here interpreted to mean brought about defensive military action on the part of the army. Below, I document the buildup of PKI and army forces in the years between independence and the attempted coup. Then I, respectively, inquire into allegations of PKI uprisings, into the nature of the army response, and finally into what produced this response.

"No Significant Capability"

The period 1945–1949, which the Indonesians recall as revolutionary, was one of armed struggle against the Dutch for independence. When sovereignty was finally achieved and Sukarno became the first president in 1949, a new constitution was adopted (1950) based upon a Dutch multiparty proportional representational system (Ghoshal 1982: 2).[7] There followed a period, between 1950 and 1957, when "Political power ... was mainly the ability to mobilize voters to win seats in Parliament" (Hindley 1966: 239–40). The problems confronting the central government in the 1950s—those of economic development; administrative reform, especially devolution of authority to regional and local levels; modernization of the armed forces; and internal security—went largely unsolved, and Sukarno became convinced that the party system was a "barrier to the realization of the kind of society for which the Revolution had been fought" (Liddle 1970: 69).

Accordingly, in November of 1956, he sought the "burial" of political parties and their replacement by a "Guided Democracy" (Sukarno qtd. in Palmier 1973: 174). Sukarno had his way. A period known as that of Guided Democracy began in 1957 and lasted until the killings. During this time, recruitment to office was not by election, parties were diminished, and parliament was unimportant. Those occupying central governmental offices "were to be chosen by the President himself" (ibid.: 177).[8] Political rivalry was for the favor of Sukarno. Those vying for this were largely, though by no means entirely, the army and the PKI. A problem with such a system of political recruitment was that the rules of political struggle were ambiguous—especially as there was no provision for what would happen after Sukarno.

The PKI and the army followed different trajectories in the accumulation of force in this situation of ambiguous political conflict. The PKI's case is considered first. It was officially founded in 1920 and initiated a revolt in 1926 that was decisively routed in two weeks, putting "an effective end to Communist activity ... for the rest of the period of Dutch rule" (McVey 1961: 677).[9] In 1948, a revitalized party again led a rebellion centered on the town of Madiun. This revolt was against the army and nationalists. The Madiun Affair, as it came to be known, had disastrous results.[10] It was quickly routed but resulted in large sections of the army adopting a "lastingly hostile attitude towards anything leftist" (Sundhaussen 1982: 40). Two years later, in mid-1951, the PKI, in a now fully independent Indonesia, was again involved in insurrections. These were again suppressed by the army. Three times the PKI had used violent force to acquire different powers. Three times they failed.

In 1951, Stalin reversed an earlier policy and ordered that Communist movements in countries like Indonesia switch from confrontation to collaboration with bourgeois nationalism. In Indonesia this meant collaboration with Sukarno. D.N. Aidit had emerged as the secretary general of the PKI, and early in 1952 he unveiled a new, "united national front" strategy of cooperation with the government. The PKI's chief goal under Aidit was to transform itself from a small, elite cadre-style party into a mass movement. The rationale for setting such a goal "was the assumption that power was attainable through the democratic process" (Palmier 1973: 159). Explicit in this policy was the renunciation of violence, at which the PKI had been incompetent anyway.

This building of a mass party achieved striking success. There were only about 8,000 PKI members in 1952. Thirteen years later there were over 3 million party members. Furthermore, various organizations associated with the PKI had also grown immensely. The Trade Union Congress (SOBSI) had 3 and a half million members, the Indonesian Peasant Front (BTI) had 9 million adherents, the Women's Organization (GERWANI) had 3 million members, as did the Youth Organization (PEMUDA RAKJAT), while the Cultural Association (LEKRA) and the Student Movement (CGMI) had, respectively, 500,000 and 70,000 members (Brackman 1969: 29).

Thus by 1965 roughly 21,570,000 persons belonged to organizations over which the PKI exercised some authority, an authority that allowed the party to mobilize its members in a number of activities, basically those of voting for the party's candidates and of agitating for party policies. So changes in the PKI's strategy of political struggle caused increases in its authoritative force. However, there were no increases in PKI violent force. It is time now to explore the case of the army.

The army had grown during the revolutionary period to roughly 200,000 soldiers (Sundhaussen 1982: 25). It had been during this time a loose amalgam of lightly armed, locally or regionally based guerilla forces. The transformation of this hodgepodge of guerilla bands into a tightly centralized command structure began in 1950, guided by A.H. Nasution, the chief of staff. Such a program was costly. However, the Indonesian government handsomely funded military budgets. According to one source, some 70 percent of the national budget was spent upon defense in the late 1950s and early 1960s (Kennedy 1965: 99).

Additionally, there was considerable support for the armed forces from the advanced capitalist and socialist camps. Holland, the United States, England, West Germany, the Soviet Union, and China provided military funding between 1950 and 1965. The two most significant of these donors were the Soviet Union and the United States. However, in 1957–1958 the CIA infiltrated arms and personnel for antigovernment rebellions.[11] Sukarno tilted leftward, perhaps influenced by this CIA adventurism. By the 1960s the USSR was committed to a total of about 1,000 million dollars of military aid to Indonesia (Hindley 1963: 113).

The United States remained a significant contributor to Indonesia's military buildup. This was because the US National Security Council had adopted a policy document calling for "appropriate action … to prevent Communist control of Indonesia" as early as 1953 (Scott 1985: 245), and it was believed that military assistance was the key to preventing this control. The United States channeled its aid directly to the military, bypassing the central government, and emphasized matters of training, command, and control. This was done, according to a 1958 US Joint Chiefs of Staff memorandum, to provide "encouragement" to Nasution to "carry out his 'plan' for the control of Communism" (ibid.: 246). Resources went to the founding of the Indonesian Army Staff and Command School (SESKOAD), which after 1958 became a focal point of Pentagon, CIA, RAND Corporation, and even Ford Foundation "attention" (ibid.: 248).

SESKOAD, led by General Suwarto, was the key to army modernization, which involved acquisition of new military technologies, especially those in the areas of communication and transportation, so that the army high command could actually talk to, supply, and move units widely stationed throughout Indonesia. The Kennedy administration set up a Military Training Advisory Group (MILITAG) in 1961 to implement what it called a "civic action" and what SESKOAD called a "civic mission" program. MILITAG' s training and aid helped establish or extend military authority over "the civil administration, religious and cultural organizations, youth groups, veterans, trade unions, peasant organizations, political parties and groups at regional and local levels" (Sundhaussen 1982: 141). It was precisely these "civilian groups" that later "provided the structures [i.e., the groups that did the actual killings] for the ruthless suppression of the PKI in 1965" (Scott 1985: 249).

Indonesian armed forces experienced considerable combat throughout the 1950s and early 1960s, eliminating warlords in the provinces, suppressing secessionist rebellions, halting Islamic revolts, and invading western New Guinea (Maynard 1986). These campaigns were successful, which is to say that the Indonesian Army perfected its killing skills by killing.

By the mid-1960s the Indonesian Army totaled 300,000 people, one third again as large as it had been in 1946. More importantly it possessed modern armaments and means of transportation. It was backed by 120,000 police. MILITAG and SESKOAD had created an effective centralized command and control structure and a counterinsurgency strategy aimed largely at the PKI. Thus the army accumulated a very considerable amount of violent force between 1945 and 1965. The army was also acquiring a cultural force that increasingly targeted who the enemy was and when to act. In a time of protracted military reverses during the revolutionary period, major officials in the independent government, including Sukarno, seemingly gave up and allowed themselves to be captured by the Dutch.

This "infuriated the officers" who "even considered kidnapping Sukarno and forcing him to come with the army" (Sundhaussen 1982: 41). These officers perceived the politicians' surrender to be a betrayal, which prompted the belief among them, as one general expressed it, that "Whether our Republic will perish or continue ... depends upon whether the Republic still lives in the hearts of the officers, non-commissioned officers, and soldiers of the Indonesian National Army" (ibid.: 31). This belief was a normative sense that the army should be the ultimate governmental arbiter because politicians were untrustworthy. At roughly the same time, because of the previously observed Madiun Affair, "large sections of the army hitherto indifferent to communism ... were to adopt a lasting hostile attitude toward anything leftist" (ibid.: 40).

Then in the late 1950s, working through SESKOAD a new, strategic doctrine, called "territorial warfare," in part formulated by US military strategists, redefined the military's chief goal to be that of suppressing insurgency. A central tenet of territorial warfare was that the army should concentrate upon liquidating internal enemies. This meant that the army's idée fixe in strategy, tactics, and training was Communist suppression, because the PKI was the only formidable, internal foe. The US government strengthened this obsession by making "repeated assurances to the Indonesian military of the US support in the event of a blow against the PKI." (Brands 1989: 805). In effect what the Indonesian Army knew was that they would be rewarded (i.e., get "support") if they attacked the PKI.

There was also an indoctrination campaign aimed at the Indonesian Army that appeared to derive from US civil society. Certain US academics in 1958 with ties to either the CIA or the US military, "began pressuring their contacts in the Indonesian military ... to seize power and liquidate the PKI opposition" (Scott 1985: 247). Guy Pauker of the University of California and the RAND Corporation was prominent among these. He brought General Suwarto to the RAND Corporation in 1962, apparently urging him to take a hard line against the communists (ibid.). Suwarto was the head of SESKOAD and the architect of both military centralization and the counterinsurgency program. General Suharto was Suwarto's protégé. The preceding suggests that, nurtured by contacts with public and private US agents and subalterns, there arose a particular type of cultural force: normative knowledge that it was good for the army to interfere in all sectors of the government and, especially, to oppose the PKI.

This normative knowledge, of course, implied an interpretive scheme, one in which the army "read" its social world, searching for opportunities to fulfill its prime directive: to get the PKI. Thus the army by 1964 had accumulated enormous amounts of violent force. The PKI responded to this in the following manner. The PKI created the Special Bureau for clandestine activities in November of 1964, which was headed by an aid to Aidit named Sjam. Sjam's goal was to infiltrate the military so that officers would support the PKI (in effect recognizing its authority). The Special Bureau appears to have been largely unsuccessful: only a "tiny proportion" of officers were "fully committed" to the PKI by the middle of 1965 (Crouch 1978: 83).

Aidit proposed to Sukarno in January, 1965 that the government arm workers and peasants. The Chinese offered to equip this militia, which they called a Fifth Force, with 100,000 small arms. Sukarno supported this proposal, presumably to counter the army's huge accumulation of force. Soon he and Aidit were pressing the case for a Fifth Force in speeches to the National Defense Institute. The PKI had begun paramilitary training in its youth organizations by July, anticipating the formal approval of the Fifth Force. The army, as might be expected, was "infuriated" (Brackman 1969: 49). However, PKI acquisition of military resources had gone nowhere by the time of the coup attempt. The CIA, no friend of communists, concluded that the PKI had "brought" no weapons into the country prior to the coup attempt (CIA 1968:173). Thus, though the PKI certainly planned to arm itself, it "was in no position to defend itself." by 30 September 1965 (Crouch 1978: 135).

Consider Indonesia during the summer of 1965. The Communists menaced the army with their mass authoritative force. Their Special Bureau worked, though apparently ineffectively, to infiltrate the military. Plans to develop a Fifth Force raised the prospect of a PKI that might someday meet violence with violence. Equally, the army's enormous accumulation of violent force, in conjunction with its acquisition of cultural forces targeted at the Communists, posed an inordinate threat to the PKI. This was a politics, to appropriate an image from Geertz, of two cocks warily circling. There was, however, a critical disparity between these animals. One, and only one, the army, had razors attached to its legs! After all, the CIA concluded that in 1965 the PKI "had no significant capability of its own for armed action" (CIA 1968: 175). Then on 4 August, Sukarno fell ill. The Chinese doctors who examined him diagnosed signs of a cerebral hemorrhage and warned that another attack might be fatal. Two months later the extermination of the PKI would be in progress.

"I Heard about the Coup from the Radio"

The army never denied that it was responsible for the killings. It insisted, however, that it had acted as a result of a coup attempt that culminated in the murder of six high generals by the "30 September Movement," a faction within the army consisting of middle-level, progressive officers led by Colonel Untung. The 30 September Movement believed that a council of generals was planning its own coup for 5 October against the ailing Sukarno. So their coup sought to hand state power to a revolutionary council that would govern in support of Sukarno. The Untung coup was crushed less than twenty-four hours after its onset. The anti-PKI killings were in full swing by the end of October. Thus the period between 30 September and 30 October is the antecedent time that needs to be investigated for evidence of a PKI uprising. It is the attempted coup and its sequel that would constitute this uprising.

There has been lively controversy concerning who was responsible for the Untung coup attempt. Over the years there has been an increasing tendency to place responsibility upon the army while not completely excluding the PKI.[12] The case against the army is that "by inducing, or at a minimum helping to induce" the Untung coup attempt "the right in the Indonesian Army eliminated its rivals," thus paving the way to a long-planned elimination of the civilian left and, eventually, to a military dictatorship" (Scott 1985: 239–40). Evidence supporting this view turns on the fact that "the same battalions that supplied the 'rebellious' companies were also used to put the rebellion down" (ibid.: 242–43). Further, these were units commanded by officers with connections to Suharto.

Elements of the army under Suharto's command sought from the very first days after the coup attempt to identify the PKI as the *dalang* (puppet master). Aidit was immediately captured by the army. He lived long enough to confess, "I alone bear major responsibility" (Sejarah 1991: 165) and was then summarily executed. The army's brief against the PKI was based upon the alleged role of Sjam. Crouch explains the army's position as follows:

> When Sukarno suddenly fell ill on August 1965, Aidit feared that he might die or become incapacitated, in which case the army leadership could be expected to move to consolidate its position at the expense of the PKI. To forestall such a possibility, Aidit ordered Sjam to mobilize PKI's supporters in the armed forces to take action against the army leadership. (1978: 104)

There are problems with this interpretation. First, much of it comes from Sjam during trials subsequent to his capture, when Suharto controlled the state (Crouch 1978: 104). Presumably to help himself, Sjam would have said what Suharto wanted. Additionally, Sjam did not work only for Aidit. He was, according to the CIA, a "double agent" who worked as an "informer for the Djakarta Military Command" (CIA 1968: 107).

Wertheim has discovered that Suharto had personal ties with Untung and other officers involved in the coup attempt (Wertheim 1970) as well as with Sjam (Wertheim 1979). Wertheim thus believes that these officers and Sjam were manipulated by Suharto and his followers to trick the PKI into participation in the coup attempt. Two points are salient, whatever the communist's role in the Untung coup attempt may have been. First, the "overt participants" in operations came "mainly from the army" and, second, no PKI members were "associated with the leadership of the coup attempt" (Crouch 1988: 107).

The major evidence of PKI involvement in the planning and implementation of the coup attempt comes from PKI leaders at their trial in 1966, following the killings and Suharto's assumption of state power. The picture that emerges from the leaders' testimony is of a PKI that was extremely worried about Sukarno's health and that believed in the existence of a council of generals, whose takeover would be disastrous for the PKI, and so became involved as secondary players in what Crouch characterizes as an "almost defensive" move (1988: 108). This evidence was coerced at a show trial, and so may not be correct. However, the point to be taken here is that even at army-controlled trials the worst case that could be made against the PKI was that they acted in a "defensive" manner.

How is one to evaluate these claims and counterclaims? My judgment is that none of the evidence points to the Untung coup attempt as a PKI uprising, regardless of who turns out to be the puppet master. The leaders of the attempt, Untung, and his conspirators were not PKI. Operations involved in it were conducted by units associated with Suharto and put down by those same units. No one has ever said either that Suharto was PKI or that the troops were PKI. How can one have an uprising if one's leaders do not lead it and one's soldiers do not fight it?

An argument might, however, be made that the coup attempt was only a part of what was occurring in Indonesia in late 1965 and that elsewhere there were armed PKI revolts timed to be coordinated with the events in Jakarta. Here the evidence is unequivocal. There were no PKI interregionally coordinated insurrections. Nothing happened! Hefner has documented the sequence of events in the east Javan area around Pasuruan between the night of the coup attempt and the onset of the killings. He states that "the Pasuruan PKI" was caught "by surprise" by the coup attempt (Hefner 1990: 209). Then, a few weeks afterward, Muslim youth organizations targeted the PKI, "destroying whole families" in attacks that "involved widespread mutilation and torture" (Ibid.: 210). Finally, two months after the attempted coup, the army arrived and the remaining PKI were exterminated (ibid.: 212). Absent from this sequence of events is a communist uprising.

This situation repeated itself in Kediri, also in East Java. The local PKI did nothing immediately after the coup attempt. Then, two weeks later, anti-PKI groups heard "of widespread unchecked violence against the communists ... and of swift actions of the RPKAD, an elite paratrooper unit, against the communists" (Young 1991: 79). This news strengthens the resolve of the anticommunists to act. An ANSOR (Muslim youth group) demonstration was held outside of the PKI headquarters on 13 October. The demonstration became an ANSOR attack on the headquarters, whose defenders were "surprisingly ill-prepared" and so were "beaten and hacked to death" (ibid.: 80). Thereafter, a vicious slaughter of the PKI spread throughout the Kediri region. Again missing in this account is a PKI uprising, which makes sense because the communists were "ill-prepared."

There were, to be sure, incidents of communist violence between 30 September and 30 October. These were spontaneous, unorganized affairs. The Center for Village Studies, an agency biased in favor of the army's view, reported a break-in of a government office in Manisrenggo to steal three guns (Cribb 1991: 143–44). There was the killing of a single soldier by PKI youths, which set off the orgy of PKI killings in Bali (ibid.: 91). Such incidents, while violent, hardly qualify as a PKI uprising, and they are the only types of incidents of PKI violence reported.

Thus, there is no evidence of a PKI armed insurrection outside of Jakarta between the coup attempt and the killings. Rather, the PKI waited, and did so in what must have been mounting terror. The following quotation from an anonymous woman with high-level PKI ties catches the atmosphere, "My husband left for China on 21 September … and I heard about the Coup from the radio. Friends didn't come to visit any more …, so I didn't understand what was going on, what the problem was" (Lucas 1991: 229). One rather imagines that if you are in the business of staging an uprising you arrange it so that your operatives know what is happening and do not learn about it on the radio.

"On Display"

The evidence I seek in this section is that bearing on the degree to which army operations during the killings can be characterized as defensive. Cribb provides a general overview of the nature of these operations, reporting:

> When the opportunity arose, anticommunist units, especially KOSTRAD and the RPKAD, moved quickly to destroy the PKI, both by direct killing and by encouraging, arming and training civilian vigilantes who were sent out to do the job. In most cases, the killings did not begin until elite military units had arrived in a locality and had sanctioned violence by instruction or example (1991: 21).

The RPKAD, as previously noted, were elite paratroopers. Former US diplomats and intelligence officers confirm that US embassy and CIA officials provided a list of PKI members to facilitate KOSTRAD and the RPKAD's work. It is reported, "Embassy officials … checked off the people on the list as they were killed" (Cribb 1991: 7). These are offensive operations. Anticommunist units did not respond after attack. Rather, they took the offense and "move[d] quickly" against the PKI. This is a bit like dispatching the US Special Forces hither and thither to exterminate Republicans. There are numerous reports that PKI members went to their destruction with "meekness" (ibid.: 35).

Indeed, there is an account by Hughes of PKI personages in Bali calmly accepting their fate and walking peacefully with their killers to the killing grounds, dressed in white funeral robes (1967: 181). Some observers have suggested that such an action implied an acknowledgement of guilt. However, Cribb has argued, "Passivity is so frequently reported in the stories of the Indonesian massacres that it probably was indeed the typical response of victims, but the most plausible explanation is that victims were paralyzed by that combination of uncertainty and vague hope which makes acquiescence right" (1991: 35).

Hefner's account of the killings in Pasuruan amplifies Cribb's view. Remember that in this region the PKI had been "surprised" by the attempted coup, waited, and was then attacked by anticommunists. Then about two months after the coup attempt, "Muslim groups from the lowlands, armed and accompanied by a smaller number of army supervisors, arrived in the region to begin carrying out the blood purge. Three weeks before their arrival, village officials had been ordered to place local-level PKI members in detention, shaving their heads to identify them" (1990: 212). The round-up occurred and precipitated "a wave of collective possession" (ibid.). As screening teams moved from village to village, "whole communities were swept by incidents of spirit possession. Individuals were seized by ancestral guardian spirits … The spirits spoke through the possessed, vainly urging reconciliation and an end to violence" (ibid.: 214). But the spirits worked in vain.

The communists were duly collected, and as they were being led off to execution, a small crowd gathered in one village. Hefner describes the scene as the men slated for execution appeared:

> Someone in the crowd let out a low moan, and then someone else another. Soon a handful of villagers began sobbing, shaking, and crying out furiously, their bodies stiff with force of possessing spirits … There was no resistance, only the gasping voices of ancestral spirits calling for peace and the release of loved ones. (1990: 214)

It does not seem appropriate to characterize such nonresistance as the passivity of the guilty. Rather, it would seem to be a cultural expression of the horror of the weak at their inability to defend those they love against a superior, offensive force.

According to Cribb, "Although the elimination of the PKI was necessary for the establishment of army rule, the scale of the violence of 1965–66 seems gratuitous" (1991: 22). The nature of "gratuitous" in this instance was expressed by one spokesman for one group of killers, when he says that his men "just went wild against the Communists" (Hughes 1967: 159). "Going wild" meant that many people were not merely executed, they were butchered in ways that often involved torture and sadism. Consider, for example, the end of an important PKI leader in Bali. The man was corpulent. His death involved the slicing of the fat off his living body. Only afterward was he finished off with a bullet to the head (Cribb 1991: 30).

Cases involving sexual butchery, as was reported by Geertz, were especially commonly recounted. There is an important anonymous account from an Indonesian of the killings in East Java. The author proceeds by giving the place of the killing, the name or names of those killed, and the manner of death. Around Nglegok, "Japik … was killed along with her husband Djumadi … They had been married only thirty- five days. She was raped many times and her body was then slit open from her breasts to her vulva" (Anonymous 1991: 172). The same account notes that in the district of Banyuwangi the killings began on 20 November and ended on Christmas Day. "In many cases, women were killed by being stabbed through the vagina with long knives until their stomachs were pierced. Their heads and breasts were cut off and hung on display in the guard huts along the road" (ibid.: 175).

What is striking about such killings is their use of violent force to create a new cultural force, a normative knowledge of the way things would be in Suharto's New Order. Sexual body parts became essential icons in the business of constructing this new knowledge. What they reminded folk was that if you crossed the army some thug would shove a knife up your vagina into your belly, hack your breasts off, and nail them to a post. How did you know this? You saw the breasts on display. Given the preceding, suggestions that the army conducted defensive operations during the killings lack credence. Certainly, this is not the evidence that was on display.

A Clean Sweep

The question now arises with some urgency as to what was it that produced such savage killings. The following evidence suggests one answer. Hindley has reported that Sukarno, who liked to balance rivals against each other to counter growing PKI influence in the late 1950s, attempted "to meet the material needs of the armed forces" (1963: 114). This was done by allowing officers to run nationalized, often agricultural or extractive, enterprises, especially those expropriated from the Dutch in 1957 and thereafter from other countries ranging, from the British to the pro-Communist Chinese. A second way that officers acquired business holdings was to form partnerships with Chinese businessmen (Crouch 1988: 39). Consequently, officers in the army became an "economic elite" (ibid.: 22), one with capitalist proclivities, because their position depended upon the profits of their enterprises. Such officers were called "bureaucratic capitalists" because they were government officials who used public authority to further their private exploitation (Feith 1962: 398–99).

However, soon after the military had gone into the business of business, the business went bottom up. By the end of the 1950s "financial instability had increased, and economic development had been inhibited as a result of inflation, deficit financing, declining prices for imports, and the neglect of factors vital to the … productive capacity and the functioning of the infrastructure" (Mortimer 1974: 251). Military skimming of the profits of the enterprises that they managed exacerbated the economic problems.[13] By 1964 the economy was in a shambles and there appeared to be "little that the government" could do about it (Mackie 1967: 41). Urban workers "suffered a severe decline in real wages and standards of consumption." Rural peasants experienced "a general trend toward impoverishment" (Mortimer 1974: 273). The PKI and its affiliated institutions prospered during the economic turmoil of 1964–1965.

According to Dahm, "The chief reason why the Communist organizations gained ground while other parties stagnated … was the appalling economic situation, for which only the PKI claimed to offer a remedy" (1971: 218).[14] This remedy, which began to be administered at the end of 1963, involved the "unilateral action" (*aksi sepihak*) of seizing lands from larger landowners, without recourse to legal proceedings, usually by the PKI's peasant organization, the BTI. Such seizures continued through 1964 and 1965 and occasionally involved violence that pitted BTI cadres against local army units. For example, a group of BTI squatters on a large government-owned estate, called the "Betsy" plantation, beat an army officer to death in May 1965 (Brackman 1969: 46). Here was class conflict. The PKI, with the BTI, agitated to ameliorate agrarian exploitation in a time of extreme rural penury.

There is evidence that different agents in the army at this time interpreted the rise of unilateral actions as an indication that the PKI had gone too far, and this of course turned on their normative understanding that it was time for the army to do its duty and seize state power. As Mohammed Hatta, one of Indonesia's founding nationalists, remarked of the land seizures, "I felt their [the PKI] move in the rural area was a maneuver to raise the people against the Army" (Brackman 1969: 45). If the nationalists read the situation thus, imagine how the officers must have seen it. Cable traffic from the US Embassy in Jakarta to Washington discussing the state of military preparation against the PKI indicates an increasing state of army preparedness in 1964–1965.

In early March 1964, Mr. Howard Jones, the US ambassador to Indonesia, met Nasution. The cable describing this meeting, sent 6 March, said that Nasution "avoided like the plague any discussion of a possible military take-over, even though this hovered in the air throughout the talk" (qtd. in Brands 1989: 794). A few weeks later Jones pressed Nasution concerning how the army would deal with PKI attempts to capitalize upon "discontent among the Indonesian masses." According to the cable reporting the conversation, "Nasution replied that he did not think the PKI was prepared to make a bid for power. But if it did the Army would be ready" (ibid.). By January of 1965, Jones was reporting back that army officials were developing "specific plans for a takeover of government the moment Sukarno exited" (ibid.: 798). In March of 1964 the possibility of an army takeover "hovered in the air." Two weeks later the army was "ready." By January of 1965 there were "specific plans."

Somebody in the army was planning to seize state power. Further, the cable traffic makes it clear that this planning was prior to the attempted coup. Was there only a single set of conspiracies from a single location within the army? I do not know, but I suspect this to be unlikely, as the army had its factions. A more likely situation is one in which Untung and his followers had their plans and Suharto with his allies had their, ultimately more successful, plans for a New Order.

One aspect of Suharto's plans for seizing state power was revealed by military actions immediately after the coup attempt. The Untung conspirators had sought to capture Nasution. He escaped, though in the incident his daughter, Irma, was wounded and died. Hughes reports that at her funeral, six days after the coup attempt, the navy chief

> passed the word to anti-Communist Moslem student elders. As he brushed by them, from the corner of his mouth he spat out a single word, *sikat*. They had no difficulty in grasping his meaning. The word means "to wipe out." The message was to go out and clean up the Communists. (1967: 132)

Of course, the navy chief might just have been giving vent to his own private spleen. However, this does not appear to have been the case because "within a few days ... after the coup attempt ... army public relations units" were disseminating throughout Jakarta the "message [that] the events of 30 September had been a PKI planned attempt to seize power and ... the PKI had at last gone too far" (Cribb 1991: 29). Langenberg further specifies that "within days of the failure of the 30 September Movement, the commanders of ... KOSTRAD, and of the paracommando unit RPKAD, together with their allies embarked upon a deliberate campaign to promote a climate of fear and retribution" (1991: 47). Two points need to be grasped here. The first of these is that the Suharto plan was in implementation "within days" of the coup attempt. The second is that it involved, in Langenberg's terms, a "propaganda campaign" (ibid.). In our terms, such campaigns are but one type of a regime of truth.

US officials seem to have contributed to this regime of truth. Less than a week after the coup attempt, the new US ambassador, Mr. Marshall Green, sent a cable to Washington recommending covert efforts to "spread the story of the PKI's guilt, treachery, and brutality" (qtd. in Brands 1989: 802). The ambassador's recommendation appears to have been accepted, and the CIA is reported to have assisted in disseminating deception aimed at the PKI (McGehee 1981).

This propaganda campaign gained momentum in October and then began to diminish at the end of November 1965. Usually some agency of the army would reveal a "truth" about the PKI, and then the various media—especially the press and radio—would disseminate this "truth" throughout the country. Two big "truths" that the military public relations specialists sought to inculcate were that the PKI and its allies were the aggressors and that they were "devils" (*sétan*). (For a discussion of the October/November campaign, see Southwood and Flanagan 1983: 66–71). One crude way this was done was by implicating the PKI in the deaths of the generals killed during the coup attempt. The generals had been murdered at the Halim air force base near Jakarta. According to the army account as reported in Cribb:

> After the arrival of the captured generals at Halim, it was widely rumored, members of the left wing woman's organization GERWANI stripped and performed a lascivious "Dance of the Fragrant Flowers" before an audience of PKI cadres and air force officers, culminating in the ritual mutilation of the generals ... The frenzied women allegedly gouged out the eyes of their victims, cut off their genitals and, after dumping the remains down a nearby well, abandoned themselves to an orgy with the watching officers and cadres, Aidit himself awarding medals to the most depraved. (1991: 29)

When the devils handed out medals for their debauched aggression, then certainly the PKI needed to be crushed "with the urgency of 'kill or be killed'" (Langenberg 1991: 49). Of course autopsies later performed on the bodies of the generals revealed that the above accounts of their deaths were "fabrications" (Cribb 1991: 29).

In summary, there appears to have been an understanding among those elements of the military associated with Suharto that the coup attempt would start the "wiping out" of the PKI from Indonesia. This was done, in part, by putting into operation a regime of truth to produce "truths" that the PKI was the aggressor and monstrous to boot. "People were willing to believe" (Cribb 1991: 29) these "truths." So it may have been the "truths" that, in good measure, produced the "gratuitous" nature of the massacre. Certainly, the gratuity of the killings did produce a clean sweep of the PKI. Sufficient information has been collected to respond to the question of whether or not the killings were good news.

Let us summarize the findings of the causal moral analysis to make this judgment. Analysis showed that the PKI had no real military capability prior to 30 September 1965 and mounted no significant military operations between 30 September and 30 October 1965. There was no PKI uprising. Analysis further revealed that Suharto and his allies, starting in early October, initiated attacks upon the PKI and their supporters—attacks whose violence was so "gratuitous" as to result in frequent reports of sexually sadistic behavior on the part of the killers. The army struck offensively. Finally, analysis hinted that what may have produced army actions were understandings among many in the Indonesian military, perhaps provoked by the PKI's campaign against agrarian exploitation that the PKI had gone too far. These understandings, in turn, seem to have produced "specific plans." Plans that Suharto and his followers were to implement as a regime of truth whose two "truths" were that the PKI had started it and that they were devilish fiends who could thus be killed in fiendish ways.

These findings do not support the judgment that the killings were in self-defense. This is because the antecedent event (PKI uprisings), which had to occur for this judgment to be sustained, did not occur. Equally, the subsequent effect (army defensive operations), which also had to occur for the judgment of self-defense to be sustained, did not occur. There were no PKI uprisings and the army acted in anything but a defensive manner. Said plainly: something cannot cause something else if something and something else did not occur.

However, there are disturbing aspects of the situation that need to be made explicit. The Indonesian Army, through the intense propaganda campaign of October and November 1965, constructed the "truth" that the killings were in self-defense. Geertz probably got this "truth" from the old Nationalist, who would have heard it on the radio during the 1965 propaganda blitz. Then Geertz distributed this "truth" to his readers, not as that of the mighty but as the way things were and the way they were interpreted by those who were there. But it was a big lie. Those responsible for horrific butchery covered it up through a regime of "truth" that told horrible lies about those they butchered. So the approximate truth of the situation was that the killings were bad news, the work of deeply immoral mighty.

Conclusion

There remain a few loose ends whose tying up will serve by way of a conclusion. These include the discovery that a second reason for the difficulty in distinguishing right from might has to do with the deterioration of the difference between episteme and doxa and a contemplation of the relevance of this discovery for postmodernism and exploitation.

Readers will recall that the chapter began with a quotation from Geertz in which he said that the "contrast" between episteme and doxa was "breaking down." Geertz was being overly modest. He has been a champion of the obliteration of any distinction between the two. Consider that conjectural hermeneutics, because Geertz "never really bought" science and does not validate its understandings. Rather, each judgment is bestowed as a conjecture that you either "see … or you do not." Such judgments are beside the fact because what they represent as fact is not checked by observation to see if the representation fits the facts.

Doxa, as understood by Aristotle, is "opinion" in the sense of representations that are "things that are said" (Honderich 1995: 206). The "truths" loaded into peoples' consciousness by the mighty's regimes of truth are things that people are saying. People said in Indonesia, following the army's propaganda campaign, that the PKI were devils. Episteme, on the other hand, again as understood by Aristotle, is scientific knowledge (Audi 1995: 40). Such knowledge is validated. It is validation that distinguishes opinions that are doxa and merely "truthful" from those that are episteme and approximately true. Conjectural hermeneutics, by removing validation from the sociocultural thinker's tool kit, collapses episteme into doxa.

A second cause of the difficulty we have distinguishing right from might is that thinkers like Geertz conflate episteme with doxa, creating a situation in which it is not possible to distinguish between the "truth" and the approximate truth of situations. Geertz in *ATF*, following conjectural hermeneutical canon, did not bother to investigate whether the killings of the PKI had been in self-defense. Rather, he appears to have simply accepted the doxa of the old Nationalist and repeated it to his readers, and in so doing he parroted the "truth" of the Indonesian and US mighty. So Geertz never saw it. Thirty years after the fact it was still not clear to him that the butchering of 800,000 people might just be a moral outrage.

Postmodernism enters the conversation at this point. Conjectural hermeneutics is postmodern. Different variants of postmodernism, like conjectural hermeneutics, are skeptical of science. They largely accept Baudrillard's contention that "truth doesn't exist" (1986: 141). If you are antiscience and reject truth, then you have pretty much turned episteme into doxa. There will be no validation of whatever moral judgment you profess. This leads us back to Jameson and the quotation that began this article.

Jameson said that postmodernism was an "expression" of American domination. The findings of the article suggest a slightly differently interpretation. Postmodernism may well express domination, but it is equally an important means of that domination. First the mighty flood peoples' consciousness through regimes of truth, with moral judgments congenial to the mighty's exploitative desires. Then the postmodern antivalidation ethic ensures that the accuracy of these "truths" goes unchallenged. This allows the mighty to shape doxa in an unimpeded fashion with the "truths" they need for their various exploitations. Certainly, as the Indonesian Army propaganda campaign had it, the PKI were the aggressors. Certainly, they were monsters. Certainly, it would be self-defense to sweep them. Let the butchery begin!

But causal moral analysis, as a form of reason, can show whether the moral judgments of the mighty are anywhere near approximately right. Such an analysis, when applied to the 1965–1966 Indonesian massacres, revealed that the mighty's moral judgment was a grotesquely immoral posturing with no approximate truth. The analysis showed that the PKI were agitating against exploitation in a manner that threatened the army's continued exploitation, that the army operated a regime of truth to produce the "truth" of the PKI as aggressor monsters, and that Geertz, using his postmodern conjectural hermeneutics, represented the army line as "true." It is in such a manner that postmodern thought assists the mighty to get on with the business of maintaining exploitation. And reader, you would do well to remember what this nasty business has involved—castration, flaying alive, knives up vaginas into bellies.

What are the ethical responsibilities of intellectuals in such a universe? Two seem primordial. First, have the decency to let others know whose views you represent. Second, should you presume to issue a moral judgment, only do so on the basis of some form of analysis at least as rigorous as causal moral analysis.

Notes

1. The exact numbers killed is "contentious," though at least one CIA agent and Amnesty International concurred in suggesting a figure above 800,000 (Brands 1989: 786). *The Times* of London and the University of Indonesia estimated that over a million were liquidated (Brackman 1969: 114). The most complete compilation of different estimates of the numbers killed is in Cribb (1991: 12–13).
2. Geertz later acknowledged, "Social events do have causes … but it just may be that the road to discovering what we assert in asserting this lies … through noting expressions and inspecting them" (1983: 34). While Geertz went on to note "expressions," he never showed how they might be causal, perhaps because he still found it impossible to isolate the Ys and the Xs.
3. My understanding of science is derived from reading, among others, Carnap (1953), Hempel (1965), and Miller (1987).
4. There is an enormous body of literature discussing the nature of causality and suggesting methods to analyze it (see, for an introduction, Bunge 1957). Discussion of social causality can be found in Blalock (1961, 1971). There have been attempts in hermeneutics, starting with Weber (1968: 20), to develop methods of causal analysis; of interest in this regard is von Wright (1971).
5. The question as to whether all explanation is ultimately causal is debated; Miller (1987) argues in the affirmative.
6. The concept of *approximate truth* has been elaborated upon by Miller (1987).
7. The observations in this section, unless otherwise noted, are derived from Feith (1962) and Lev (1966).
8. Crouch (1978), Geertz (1968), and Anderson (1972) noted a similarity between Sukarno's rule during "guided democracy" and that of the Majapahit or Mataram sultans

of traditional Indonesian states. Like such rulers, Sukarno appointed courtiers (i.e., ministers) to administer affairs of state while he laid down the general lines of policy and secured his position by balancing the roles played by competing courtiers. This meant that recruitment to office in "guided democracy" became a competition for the sultan's (i.e., Sukarno's) ear.

9. Analysis of the communist rebellions of 1926–1927 can be found in McVey (1961, 1965) and Benda (1955). Description of the history of the PKI through the early 1950s can be found in Lubis (1954) and Kroef (1965: 44–53).

10. Analysis of how the PKI came to be revitalized at the end of the colonial period and of the 1948 revolt can be found in Kroef (1965: 21–43).

11. US and CIA involvement in the 1958–1961 rebellions are analyzed in Kahin and Kahin (1996).

12. Crouch provides a useful summary of the range of theories concerning the identities and intentions of the Untung coup plotters (1988: 101–34). There has been interest in a possible US role in the attempted coup. Scott argues this to have been considerable (1985). Brands believes there was "relative noninvolvement" (1989: 806).

13. Discussion of the Indonesian economy throughout the 1950s and early 1960s can be found in Feith (1962: 303–9, 373–78, 445–49, 570–72). Mackie (1967) is especially useful for understanding the causes of the hyperinflation that occurred in the first half of the 1960s.

14. Robinson (1996) documents a hardening of rural class lines and the rise of a political consciousness among land-hungry tenant farmers in Bali during the late 1950s and early 1960s.

References

Anderson, Benedict R. *Java in Time of Revolution.* Ithaca: Cornell University Press, 1972.

Anonymous. "Additional Data on Counter-Revolutionary Cruelty on Indonesia." In *The Indonesian Killings of 1965–1966,* edited by Robert Cribb, 169–76. Clayton: Centre of Southeast Asian Studies, Monash University, 1991.

Audi, Robert. *The Cambridge Dictionary of Philosophy.* New York: Cambridge University Press, 1995.

Baudrillard, Jean. "Forgetting Baudrillard." *Social Text* 15 (1986): 140–44.

Benda, Harry J. "The Communist Rebellions of 1926–27 in Indonesia." *Pacific Historical Review* 24, no. 2 (1955): 139–52. DOI: 10.2307/3634574.

Blalock, Hubert M. *Causal Inferences in Nonexperimental Research.* Chapel Hill: University of North Carolina Press, 1961.

———. *Causal Models in the Social Sciences.* Chicago: Aldine, 1971.

Brackman, Arnold C. *The Communist Collapse in Indonesia.* New York: Norton, 1969.

Brands, H.W. "The Limits of Manipulation: How the US Didn't Topple Sukarno." *Journal of American History* 76, no. 3 (1989): 785–809. DOI: 10.2307/2936421.

Bunge, Mario. *Causality, the Place of the Causal Principle in Modern Science.* Cambridge, MA: Harvard University Press, 1957.

Carnap, Rudolph. "Testability and Meaning." In *Readings in the Philosophy of Science,* edited by Herbert Feigl and May Brodbeck, 47–93. New York: Appleton-Century-Crofts, 1953.

CIA, 1968. *Indonesia—1965: The Coup that Backfired.* Accessed December 2, 2016, https://www.cia.gov/library/readingroom/docs/esau-40.pdf.

Cohen, Abner. *Two-dimensional Man: An Essay on the Anthropology of Power and Symbolism in Complex Society.* Los Angeles: University of California Press, 1974.

Crapanzano, Vincent. *Hermes' Dilemma and Hamlet's Revenge: On the Epistemology of Interpretation.* Cambridge, MA: Harvard University Press, 1992.

Cribb, Robert. "Problems in the Historiography of the Killings in Indonesia." In *The Indonesian Killings of 1965–1966,* edited by Robert Cribb, 1–44. Clayton: Centre of Southeast Asian Studies, Monash University, 1991.

Crouch, Harold. *The Army and Politics in Indonesia.* Ithaca: Cornell University Press, 1978.

Dahm, Bernhard. *History of Indonesia in the Twentieth Century.* New York: Praeger, 1971.

Engel, S. Morris. *The Study of Philosophy.* New York: Holt, Rinehart & Winston, 1981.

Feith, Herbert. *The Decline of Constitutional Democracy in Indonesia.* Ithaca: Cornell University Press, 1962.

Foucault, Michel. "Two Lectures." In *A Reader in Contemporary Social Theory,* edited by Nicholas B. Dirks, Geoff Eley, and Sherry B. Ortner, 201–21. Princeton: Princeton University Press, 1994.

———. "From 'Truth and Power.'" In *From Modernism to Postmodernism: An Anthology,* edited by Lawrence E. Cahoone, 379–83. Oxford: Blackwell, 1996.

Geertz, Clifford. *Islam Observed.* New Haven: Yale University Press, 1968.

———. *The Interpretation of Cultures.* New York: Basic Books, 1973.

———. *Local Knowledge.* New York: Basic Books, 1983.

———. *Works and Lives.* Stanford: Stanford University Press, 1988.

———. "A Lab of One's Own." *New York Review of Books* 37 (8 November 1990): 19–22. Accessed December 8, 2016. http://www.nybooks.com/articles/1990/11/08/a-lab-of-ones-own/.

———. *After the Fact.* Cambridge, MA: Harvard University Press, 1995.

Ghoshal, Baladas. *Indonesian Politics, 1955–1959.* Calcutta: K.P. Bagchi, 1982.

Handler, Richard. "An Interview with Clifford Geertz." *Current Anthropology* 32, no. 5 (1991): 603–13.

Harvey, David. *The Condition of Postmodernity.* Oxford: Blackwell, 1989.

Hefner, Robert W. *The Political Economy of Mountain Java.* Los Angeles: University of California Press, 1990.

Hempel, Carl Gustav. *Aspects of Scientific Explanation.* New York: Free Press, 1965.

Hindley, Donald. *The Communist Party in Indonesia.* Los Angeles; University of California, 1966.

Honderich, Ted. *The Oxford Companion to Philosophy.* New York: Oxford University Press, 1995.

Hughes, John. *Indonesian Upheaval.* New York: David McKay, 1967.

Hunter, Helen L. *Indonesia—1965: The Coup that Backfired.* Washington, DC: Central Intelligence Agency, Directorate of Intelligence, 1968.

Jameson, Frederic. *Postmodernism, or, the Cultural Logic of Late Capitalism.* Durham: Duke University Press, 1992.

Kahin, Audrey R. and George M. Kahin. *Subversion as Foreign Policy: The Secret Eisenhower and Dulles Debacle in Indonesia.* New York: New Press, 1996.

Kaplan, Abraham. *The Conduct of Inquiry: Methodology for Behavioral Sciences.* San Francisco: Chandler, 1964.

Kennedy, Donald E. *The Security of Southeast Asia*. New York: Praeger, 1965.

Kroef, Justas Maria van der. *The Communist Party of Indonesia*. Vancouver: University of British Columbia Press, 1965.

Langenberg, M. van. "Gestapu and State Power in Indonesia." In *The Indonesian Killings of 1965–1966*, edited by Robert Cribb, 45–65. Clayton: Centre of Southeast Asian Studies, Monash University, 1991.

Lev, Daniel S. *The Transition to Guided Democracy: Indonesian Politics, 1957–1959*. Ithaca: Cornell University Modem Indonesia Project, 1966.

Liddle, R. William. *Ethnicity, Party and National Integration: An Indonesian Case Study*. New Haven: Yale University Press, 1970.

Lubis, Mochtar. "The Indonesian Communist Movement Today." *Far Eastern Survey* 23, no. 15 (1954): 161–64. DOI: 10.2307/3024011.

Lucas, Anton, trans. "Survival: Bu Yeti's Story." In *The Indonesian Killings of 1965–1966*, edited by Robert Cribb, 227–40. Clayton: Centre of Southeast Asian Studies, Monash University, 1991.

Lyotard, Jean-François. *The Postmodern Condition: A Report on Knowledge*. Minneapolis: University of Minnesota Press, 1984 [1979].

Mackie, J.A.C. *The Problems of Indonesian Inflation*. Ithaca: Cornell University, Modern Indonesia Project, 1967.

Marcus, George E. "After the Critique of Ethnography." In *Assessing Cultural Anthropology*, edited by Robert Borofsky, 40–52. New York: McGraw Hill, 1994.

Maynard, Harold. "The Role of the Indonesian Armed Forces." In *The Armed Forces in Contemporary Asian Societies*, edited by Edward Olsen and Stephen Jurika, Jr., 18–39. Boulder: Westview, 1986.

McGehee, Ralph. "Foreign Policy by Forgery: The CIA and the White Paper on El Salvador." *The Nation* 232, no. 14 (11 April 1981): 423–25.

McVey, Ruth T. "The Comintern and the Rise of Indonesian Communism." PhD Dissertation, Cornell University, 1961.

———. *The Rise of Indonesian Communism*. Ithaca: Cornell University Press, 1965.

Miller, Richard W. *Fact and Method: Explanation, Confirmation and Reality in the Natural and the Social Sciences*. Princeton: Princeton University Press, 1987.

Mortimer, Rex. *Indonesian Communism under Sukarno*. Ithaca: Cornell University Press, 1974.

Palmier, Leslie. *The Communists in Indonesia*. New York: Doubleday, 1973.

Reiman, Jeffrey H. *Justice and Modern Moral Philosophy*. New Haven: Yale University Press, 1990.

Robinson, Geoffrey. *The Dark Side of Paradise: Political Violence in Bali*. Ithaca: Cornell University Press, 1996.

Scott, Peter Dale. "The United States and the Overthrow of Sukarno, 1965–1967." *Pacific Affairs* 58, no. 2 (1985): 239–65. DOI: 10.2307/2758262.

Sejarah, Dinas. "Crushing the G30s/PKI in Central Java." In *The Indonesian Killings of 1965–1966*, edited by Robert Cribb, 159–69. Clayton: Centre of Southeast Asian Studies, Monash University, 1991.

Southwood, Julie and Patrick Flanagan. *Indonesia: Law, Propaganda and Terror*. London: Zed, 1983.

Sundhaussen, Ulf. *The Road to Power: Indonesian Military Politics, 1945–1967*. New York: Oxford University Press, 1982.

Time, "The West's Best News for Years in Asia." 15 July 1966.

Weber, Max. *Economy and Society.* New York: Bedminster Press, 1968

Wertheim, W.F. "Suharto and the Untung Coup-The Missing Link." *Journal of Contemporary Asian Studies* 1, no. 2 (1970): 50–57. DOI: 10.1080/00472337085390151.

———. "Whose Plot? New Light on the 1965 Events." *Journal of Contemporary Asia* 9, no. 2 (1979): 197–215. DOI: 10.1080/00472337985390191.

Wright, Erik Olin. "Class Boundaries in Advanced Capitalist Societies." *New Left Review* 1, no. 98 (1976): 3–41. Accessed December 8, 2016. https://newleftreview.org/I/98/erik-olin-wright-class-boundaries-in-advanced-capitalist-societies.

Wright, Georg Henrik von. *Explanation and Understanding.* Ithaca: Cornell University Press, 1971.

Young, Kenneth R. "Local and National Influences in the Violence of 1965." In *The Indonesian Killings of 1965–1966,* edited by Robert Cribb, 63–100. Clayton: Centre of Southeast Asian Studies, Monash University, 1991.

chapter five

✸ Perpetual Peace?
Dreaming in the Time-Being of Empire

The republican constitution, besides the purity of its origin ... also gives
a favorable prospect for the desired consequence, i.e., perpetual peace.
—Kant, *Perpetual Peace: A Philosophical Sketch*

Kant's views in *Perpetual Peace: A Philosophical Sketch* (1795) have been a root of democratic peace theory, a major theoretical position in liberal political science, and a source of legitimation for US government policies of democratic globalization. Political progress, according to Kant, was movement toward a system of governance resembling a "league of nations" (1795: 102). "Perpetual peace" could be found in this "league," as the quotation that begins this section articulates, if its component states shared "republican constitutions," by which Kant is interpreted to have meant democracies. It is the judgment that a world of democracies is a world of perpetual peace that is at the heart of democratic peace theory.

What happened after Kant died? Germany, in the century that followed Kant, reunified and through warring created the Second Reich—an empire that in World War I challenged the British and French empires for global imperial domination, which led to a Third Reich and the butcheries of World War II. It was (effectively) perpetual war. In fact, Field Marshal von Molke, one of the military elites responsible for the warring, declared, "Perpetual peace is a dream, and not a nice one" (1880). However, it might be observed that the nineteenth century actually supported Kant's view that democracy would promote perpetual peace because it was a time of undemocratic empire and so no peace should have been expected. Rather, it might be argued that the present—when the old nineteenth-century empires are considered extinct and the actually existing US democracy dominates—offers a better test of whether "Perpetual peace is a dream."

This essay challenges democratic peace theory not by showing it to be wrong (though evidence is presented challenging it) but by arguing its irrelevance. This is done, arguing from a critical structural realist standpoint, by formulating, and validating, an entirely different theoretical position, global warring theory (GWT), which is premised on the assertion that empires never went away and that a major form of warfare, global warring, occurs or does not occur, according to imperial exigencies. My argumentation is as follows. Section one formulates GWT, in which warfare is accounted for as the result of reproductive fixes intended to address contradictions. Section two offers evidence from US warring in twenty-four cases from 1950 through 2015. The conclusion explores critical implications of dreaming in the time-being of empires.

Global Warring Theory

Recall that the ontology in critical structural realism is a reism—the view that only things, or somethings (as argued in the "What Is Theory" chapter) exist. Specifically, this reism is a structural one—the view that whatever is out there in the starry night of being is some form of structure. The first two rules of such a reism are, first, to decide upon what is to be explained (the explanandum) and, second, to then seek the explanans—the time-being that will contain structural things that will do the explaining. The explanandum in the current analysis is global warring; the explanans is different properties involved in imperial operations in the time-being of the New American Empire. These properties include those of contradiction, reproduction, and reflexivity, as they pertain to public *délires*, hermeneutic puzzles, and security elites.

GWT is a generalization necklace that connects the different imperial properties with global warring and, in so doing, explains why this type of warfare occurs. Contradiction, reproduction, and global warring are conceptual jewels in this generalization necklace, because they are joined in a relationship such that alteration in the first variable produces alterations in the others: increased coalescence and intensification of contradictions result in more severe reproductive vulnerabilities that ultimately cause global warring.

However, hermeneutic politics and public *délires* are two further conceptual jewels that link the first two concepts to the third. They are reflexive concepts in the sense that they involve imperial elites reflecting upon contradictions and their fixes in competition with other elites in a hermeneutic politics to establish the meaning of the contradictions and the problems they provoke. The more peaceful fixes fail; the more hermeneutic politics will lead to implementation of public *délires* that produce global warring. The following parts of this section first present the different conceptual jewels in GWT and, then, explicitly formulate it.

Empires and Imperialism

Empires are important. They are old, having been around since at least Sargon of Akkad (2334–2279 bc), who conquered part of Iraq and the Yellow Emperor, who in the Battle of Banguan (c. 2500 BC) faced his foes in China. Since then, they have metastasized, spreading—since the rise of the Euro-American empires at the beginning of modernity (c. AD 1500)—to encompass the entire world. Contra Wallerstein (1974), empires have not been replaced by world systems during the rise of modernity. They are the anatomy of those systems. Nor, contra certain political scholars (e.g., Mann 1993), have empires been replaced by nations–states during this time. Rather, so-called nations–states have become components of empires—either as core or client states. Consequently, forget world systems; forget nation–states. Time-being since Sargon and the Yellow Emperor is that of the vicissitudes of empire, the largest and most powerful social beings ever to exist.

So what are empires and their imperialism? Social forms make strings that have logics, with the former being what a social form actually does over time-being, and the latter general and abstract accounts of strings.[1] The strings and logics of social forms are exercise of forces that create powers. *Forces* are causes; *powers* are effects. Empires, composed of a core state and transcore territories, are flexible and changeable, but two key structural slots—those of economic and governmental institutions—generate the strings and logics of imperial force and power. *Imperialism* is the operation of the strings and logics of empire. Imperial operations work to accumulate value for favored elites in economic and political slots.

Empires are either formal or informal. *Formal* empires are ones in which core elites take possession in some legal manner of transcore territories so that they become colonies. These same elites implement policies in the colonies intended to facilitate value accumulation. *Informal* empires are ones in which core elites do not possess transcore territories but do exercise powers there intended to facilitate value accumulation. Transcore territories are neocolonies or client states. Rome was a formal empire; the United States is currently an informal empire.[2]

Both formal and informal empires exhibit a logic of negative reciprocity, in which core elites extract, or try to extract, greater value than is returned to actors in noncore regions. Imperial government forms to facilitate negative reciprocity and exercise violent force to enable value accumulation. Security elites are important imperial actors because it is they who initiate and manage the exercise of violent force. Much of this violence is a global warring, which is discussed next.

Global Warring

Global warring, GWT's explanans, is an exercise of violent force managed by imperial states' security elites in a colony, neocolony, or region of interest someplace else on the globe; so the fighting is literally all over the globe.[3] Global warring includes direct or indirect hostilities. *Direct* hostilities are those in which the core state commits its own military force to combat. *Indirect* hostilities are those in which the core state uses proxies to fight its fights.

Two types of simple and complex, indirect hostilities can be distinguished. *Simple* indirect warring is where core elites explicitly arrange for a proxy to conduct hostilities. For example, it was reported that elite British troops (the SAS [Special Air Service]) were "operating under US command" in the 2015 warring in Syria (*Russian Times* 2015). These soldiers were American proxies. *Complex* indirect warring is where core elites exercise force that is not violent but is intended to induce proxies to become violent in support of the core elites. For example, starting in 1992 the United States spent 5 billion dollars, ostensibly promoting democracy, but in reality delegitimizing the Ukrainian government and suggesting the need for its change. In February of 2014, antiregime forces violently overthrew the government of President Yanukovitch (Quinn 2015).

Global warring includes overt and covert aggressions. *Covert* warring occurs when the hostilities are kept secret by core elites. *Overt* warring happens when hostilities are publically announced by core elites. Global warring is not restricted by the numbers killed or wounded. If violence occurs, regardless of numbers killed or wounded, it is a global war. Global wars do not have to be formally declared. If combat occurs, regardless of whether core elites have legally begun it, it is a war.

Global warring is important for imperial reproduction when security elites perceive—correctly or incorrectly—that they can "make a killing," in the sense that they believe they can implement violent force to benefit the empire, often by creating, maintaining, or enlarging its transcore territorial powers to assist in value accumulation. Global warring is *colonial* where there is formal imperialism and *neocolonial* where there is informal imperialism. I now discuss the concepts that do the explaining, beginning with a reflection upon contradiction.

Contradiction

Most analyses of social forms concern how they work. Fair enough; it is important to know how something operates. But as everybody knows, systems—be they a child's beloved toys or a potentate's treasured empire—always, everywhere, eventually do not work, warranting a branch of social theory that might be termed "disorderly studies." Here a critical topic for analysis is *contradiction*, which concerns certain ways that social systems can come *not* to work. Contradictions are important in GWT's explanans because certain of their variations effect movement toward global warring.

Contradictions are logics whose component strings move systems toward their "limit of functional compatibility" (Friedman 1994: 48). Incompatibility and disorder are inversely related: the greater a systems' incompatibilities, the less their order. Marx's analyses of contradictions emphasize those in the economy. I maintain (Reyna 2016) that contradictions occur throughout social forms and that they exhibit structural irony: the more their power, the greater their contradictions and the less their order, with the irony here that becoming stronger is becoming weaker, prompting the question: why? Response to this takes us to an exploration of what is meant by functional incompatibility.

The notion of *incompatibility* refers to the existence of conditions in a structure of force resources in which parts that formerly interacted in some exercise of force to produce some power are less and less able to achieve their former power. The parts in a structure of force resources are the land, action, instruments, and various forms of cultural and authoritative choreography. They are in contradiction when one or more of the parts are in a state such that when an exercise of force occurs they work with fewer efficacies than in the past. In slash-and-burn farming, the force resources are a field, the farmer, his or her hoe and machete, and the cultural messages that choreograph when and how to string together the clearing, planting, weeding, and harvesting of the field over space and time. Over the years, the exercising of the forces of slash-and-burn cultivation reduces the field's fertility. The different forces in this farming may be said to be in contradiction that leads to reduced harvests, which is to say that the power of the farming system has been reduced. When contradictions become worse, they *intensify.*

Contradictions can also *coalesce,* which refers to an increasing cooccurrence of contradictions within a structure, or group of structures of power, intensifying their reproductive difficulties. Coalescence increases incompatibilities by having more strings in more places that hamper each other's output in the different parts of a social form. Sometimes coalescence may be so extensive that social form–wide incompatibilities emerge. For example, a conundrum of Marxist thought has been to explain why the 1917 revolution against capitalism came in Czarist Russia, the least capitalist of European states. One answer to this puzzle was that Russia was a site of a considerable coalescence of contradictions. There were contradictions pertaining to feudalism (between lords and serfs), those pertaining to capitalism (between capital and labor), and those pertaining to colonialism (between the imperial core and its colonies; see Althusser 1977). Next, certain types of contradictions are identified.

Many contradictions arise within, and between, political institutions. These contradictions will be called "political." Additionally, there may be contradictions between states themselves. Very often contradictions existed between competing empires, when the operations of one empire are functionally incompatible with those of other empires. For example, the Norman Empire's aspiration for the land in the English Empire in the eleventh century was incompatible with the English desire for the same land. Contradictions between empires will be termed "imperial."

A second variety of contradictions includes those that exist within or between economic institutions. These contradictions will be called "economic." Two sorts of economic contradictions exist. The first are those with *cyclical* effects, in which the contradiction results in alternation between growth and stagnation or decline. The second are those with *systemic* effects, in which contradiction is such that their intensification threatens the ability of global economic systems to reproduce. The following sections concern what happens when contradictions coalesce and intensify, beginning with a discussion of reproduction.

Reproductive Vulnerabilities and Fixes

Social forms exhibit two elemental logics: what they do and what they do to do it again. The first is a productive, the second a reproductive logic. *Production* in any system is what it does, its outcome, the power it produces. In economic systems production consists of strings making goods and services. In capitalist systems production strings make goods and services that have surplus value and lead to capital accumulation. *Reproduction* in any system is doing what needs to be done to do it again. Reproduction in capitalist systems is doing what needs to be done to make surplus value the next time. Critically, Marx showed that production and reproduction were vulnerable to contradiction. This leads us to a discussion of reproductive vulnerabilities and their fixes.

An inverse relationship is obtained between contradiction and reproduction: as contradictions intensify, reproduction becomes more difficult, that is, as the inability of systems to work increases, the ability of those systems to work again decreases. Marx appears to have offered no specific concept to address the notion of reproductive difficulty. I suggest use of the term "reproductive vulnerability." Vulnerabilities demand resolution. *Reproductive fixes* are those resolutions. This leads to a key question: how do actors respond to reproductive weaknesses and create fixes? The answer is that they get reflexive.

Getting Reflexive

Getting reflexive is actors being "thrown" (a term that was originally Heidegger's) into something and reflecting upon it with already-existing interpretations. The something can be any reality: a black American confronting a white police officer, a CEO confronting declining profits due to production costs. Reproductive fixes are choreographies—often derived from hermeneutics—that actors use having reflected upon contradictory being to organize force resources to resolve reproductive pickles. *Choreographies* are particular organizations of force resources over space and time. *Hermeneutics* are derived from preexisting cultural information —ideologies, worldviews, technical cultures—and consist of perceptual and procedural interpretation, that is, messages about what is and what to do about what is.

Perceptual messages tell actors what needs to be fixed. Procedural messages tell them how to choreograph it—that is, what forces to use in what ways—to achieve the fix. In the Trobriands, the interpretation of a necklace as a *soulava* was a perceptual cultural message; giving it away in the *kula* for a *mwali* armband was a procedural cultural message. For the CEO, declining profits is a perceptual message; offshoring is a procedural message choreographing what to do about it.

Fixes pertaining to large sections of structure in polities may be called "public *délires*." What are these? Answering this question takes us into the realm of desire and what might be grasped as its most potent form, *délire*. When thrown into contradictory realities, humans try to fix them. Exactly how they do so requires understanding cognitive and affective neuroscience, which is beyond the scope of this chapter. However, for the purposes of the present discussion, it can be said that fixing pickles involves inputting information about actualities into peoples' nervous systems by their senses, and it is clear that humans think and emote based upon this information. Let us call this "emotional and cognitive calculation." The calculation is based upon hermeneutics derived from lifeworld, ideological, and technical cultural messages stored in neural networks.

Following calculation people arrive at something to do, some choreography. They desire this choreography. Desires live a double life. On the one hand, they are something private—embedded within a person's neurons. Nonetheless, they become public when they are "out there," shared by a number of people in verbal or written discourse. Elites, with their larger windows of authority, face problems—some trifling, some grave—that they resolve in some authoritative way. These fixes are not simply desires. They are desires based upon authority that is "out there"—as laws, decrees, regulations, or administrative fiats—and as such they are *délires*. So a distinction is made between public desires and *délires*.

Both public desires and *délires* are "means of interpretation" because desires and *délires* have their hermeneutics in the sense that they contain certain perceptual/procedural pairs informing actors of "what is" and "what to do about it." A key difference between public desires and *délires* is that in the former case a group of ordinary people perceives what is and have desires as to how to proceed with regard to it. But these people lack choreographies to tell them how to proceed and resources to allow them to do so. Full of desire, they lack force to have power. While elites in various positions perceive what is and on the basis of their perceptions institute laws, decrees, and so on about what to do vis-à-vis what is. Instituted are public *délires*—that come with instructions of how to do things and the resources to do them. Then when elites are thrown into situations they perceive whether it is relevant to a public *délire* and, if it is, they implement the *délire*.

The fixes of public *délires* often do not initially work or only partially work. When such a situation occurs elites tend to become involved in "try-and-try-again" situations. Long ago Lewis Henry Morgan said that people doing this were applying "experimental knowledge" (1985 [1878]: 258). Such situations, in which there are recurring interpretations and repeated fixes of a particular pickle are ones of "experimental fixation" with elites involved in such events said to be "fixated." US security elites in the 1960s fixated on the bitter problem of not losing the Vietnam War.

Actors achieve reproductive fixes by solving hermeneutic puzzles; actors have awareness that there are pickles out there that need fixing. They are solved generally through politics. *Hermeneutic politics* are struggles between actors, or networks of actors, over the desirability of different interpretations. Global warming presents a serious reproductive pickle to economic elites. The puzzle of how to resolve it has led to a hermeneutic politics and experimental fixation dominated on one side by those interested in market and on the other by those attracted to government fixes. It should be clear, not all actors are equal with regard to the force resources they bring to hermeneutic politics, and so it is time to consider the effects of actors' positionality, which leads to a discussion of elites.

Elites and Classes

Elites are actors who enjoy substantial agency because they occupy the highest positions in social forms and are authorized to utilize large amounts of force resources in those forms, including instituting and implementing public *délires* to fix reproductive vulnerabilities. So they are *the* actors with a forceful advantage in any hermeneutic politics bearing upon hermeneutic puzzles.

It has been argued that elite and class analysis were opposed (see Higley and Pakulski 2000) Certain classic elite thinkers—Pareto (1900), Mosca (1897), and Michels (1915)—saw themselves as anti-Marxists, believed that actors did not become elites for reasons of class, and believed that elites governed society. However, others argue for the convergence of elite and class theory (Etzioni-Halevy 1997: xxvi). This position is adopted here, in which elites are considered to be class actors, though the notion of class used is broader than in classical Marxism, in which it is restricted to only economic actors.

Class relations in critical structural realism are those between actors due to their differences in the control of force resources in the structures of force and power of social forms, with elites actors occupying the missionary position (i.e., on top) in these structures. As such, elites have large *windows of authority,* areas over which they are authorized to intervene with the resources at their control. In contemporary social forms, capitalist elites are those in the highest levels in economic force structures (CEOs, CFOs, etc.), political elites are those in elevated positions in government force structures (presidents, ministers, etc.), and cultural elites are those in elevated positions in the force structures of cultural institutions (religious and media heads). Security elites are a variety of political elite whose windows of authority allow them to participate in hermeneutic politics over interpretations that create or implement public *délires* involving the exercise of violent force. This prompts the question: when are security elites likely to favor violent fixes in their hermeneutic politics?

Getting Violent

Up to a point, elites are a bit like the central character in Munro Leaf's classic children's book *The Story of Ferdinand* (1936). Ferdinand was a big, strong bull who did not enjoy fighting. He liked to sit in the sun and smell flowers. Elites, like Ferdinand, enjoy basking in the warmth of privilege, smelling the flowers of their valuables. In part, this is because raging bulls can get hurt, due to the high risks and costs of violence. However, make no mistake about it, elites are not total Ferdinands. They can get ferocious, especially when their privileges and valuables appear threatened. When this occurs it is time to kill.

Elite violence so understood is a function of the elimination of the usual, peaceful ways of reproducing elite classes. The relationship between elite reproduction and violence can be expressed as follows: the more security elites choreograph peaceful reproductive fixes that falter, the more such fixes become known as unworkable, the greater the desirability of violent fixes. Uncertain fixes are likely as contradictions intensify and coalesce, because intensification and coalescence are states of systems in which existing ways of reproducing are increasingly not working well. So the intensification of contradiction is a situation in which normal reproductive fixes falter, leaving as the alternative violent ones.

George Shultz, one of President Ronald Reagan's secretaries of state, commenting upon an occasion when the Reagan administration resorted to violence, put the matter baldly: "If nothing else worked, the use of force was necessary" (1993: 678), with "force" understood to mean violent force. Let us call this "Shultzian Permission," the principle that security elites will transform into raging bulls, granting themselves permission to exercise violent force as a reproductive fix when peaceful fixes appear to them to have failed. Violence in this optic is the failure of peace. Thrown into a hermeneutic puzzle of failed peaceful fixes, what are fearful elites to do? Nothing, or confer upon themselves Shultzian Permission? This occurs because when peaceful fixes fail, actors on different sides in a hermeneutic politics converge on the understanding that their welfare depends upon giving violence a chance. The preceding discussion of the concepts in the explanans provides information to explicitly formulate GWT.

So why is global warring likely to occur? Intensifying and coalescing contradictions produces reproductive vulnerabilities, these lead to hermeneutic puzzles and their attendant politics to fix them, and these fixes lead to public *délires* instituting global warring. When peaceful fixes fail Shultzian Permission is granted and global warring public *délires* are implemented. Expressed more formally, the theory consists of six statements:

1. Intensification and coalescence of an empire's political and economic contradictions increase its reproductive vulnerabilities.
2. The greater these vulnerabilities, the greater the hermeneutic puzzles they pose and the more the hermeneutic politics of imperial elites create hermeneutics and public *délires* whose choreography fixes the vulnerabilities.
3. Because of the high costs and risks of violent fixes, initial fixes are likely to be peaceful, but the more there are fixless peaceful reproductive fixes, the more hermeneutic politics of imperial elites will grant Shultzian Permission to institute public *délires* that exercise violent force to achieve reproductive fixes.
4. The selection of a particular public *délire* to implement is aided if there has been a hermetic seal favoring that *délire*.
5. The instituting of violent public *délires* turns colonies, neocolonies, or regions of interest into violent places, producing global warring.
6. When the spatial dimensions of intensifying and coalescing contradictions rise, the number of violent places throughout the globe grow, producing an increased incidence of global warring.

Evidence supportive of the GWT from twenty-four US global wars between 1950 and 2015 is presented next.

"Now I Am Become Death"

Now I am become Death, the destroyer of worlds.
—J. Robert Oppenheimer (a developer of nuclear weapons, following the first successful test of an atomic bomb, quoting Hindu scripture)

We will return to the above quotation to end this section, after narrating a story of US warring since the end of World War II. Studies of the frequency of US military operations since the end of World War II are limited. No research systematically includes direct and indirect as well as overt and covert US military operations, especially because of the secrecy surrounding indirect, covert warring. Consequently, estimates of the extent of US governmental violence are approximate but likely to be low due to underreporting.

Istvan Kende (1971), who analyzed existing data from the end of World War II through the late 1960s, reported that in that period the US warred more frequently than any other country in the world. Richard Lebow, forty years later, corroborated Kende, finding that the United States was the "world's most aggressive state" measured in terms of war initiation (2011). Kevin Drum claims the United States launched a significant overseas assault every forty months over the last fifty years (2013). Drum's estimate is conservative because he acknowledges that it excludes covert operations.

John Tures (2003) has used a US Military Operations data set generated by the Federation of American Scientists to estimate the frequency of US military activities since 1945. He finds that the United States has engaged in 263 interstate military operations between 1945 and 2002, which is on the order of 4.6 operations per year. However, 176 of these operations occurred in the eleven years between 1991 and 2002, that is, about sixteen operations per year. One conclusion from these findings is "that there has been a sizeable jump in the number of U.S. military actions since the end of the Cold War" (Tures 2003: 8). Military sources concur, reporting, "The number of military deployments has dramatically increased" after 1989 (Castro and Adler 1999: 86–95).

Two points can be made concerning the preceding. First, the military actions identified above were "interventionist" (Kende 1971: 5). Interventionist armed forays occur overseas and are global warring. This means, second, the United States has waged perpetual war in the form of global warring (4.6 interventions each year) since the end of World War II, raising the question: Is this warring consistent with GWT?

Nature of the Evidence

The response to this question is based upon a sample of American global wars in twenty-four countries between 1950 and the present. The evidence consists of reports of observations of the properties of the concepts composing the theory prior to, or at the time of, global war. The *property* of a concept is the condition it is observed to be in. For example, a property of water above 32 degrees Fahrenheit is as a liquid, while below that temperature it is as a solid. Mass killings in the United States in 2014 exhibited the property of being "on the rise" (Follman 2014).

First considered is the explanandum, with the evidence presented being the type of global warring that marked the aggression. Four basic properties of global warring, and their combinations, are considered:

1. Overt (O): in which there is open exercise of US military force (though not necessarily formally declared)
2. Covert (C): in which there is secret exercise of military force (including those involving coups, assassinations, sabotage, and false flag operations)
3. Direct (D): in which the United States' own armed services exercise violent force
4. Indirect (I): in which allies of some sort act as proxies and exercise violent force
5. Overt/Covert (O/C): in which the US armed services performed both overt and covert military operations
6. Direct/Indirect (D/I): in which the United States was involved in both direct and indirect military operations

Next presented are the properties of the contradictions in the explanans prior to the global warring. Two contradictory situations are examined: those bearing upon the states of the nature of the contradictions and those concerning their severity. Two basic sorts of economic and political contradictions are considered. These include the following:

1. Intraimperial, dominator/dominated contradictions (Pdd): in which the contradiction is between dominators (core elites) and the dominated (those in some way controlled by elites in other areas of the empire and beyond)
2. Interimperial contradictions (Pii): in which the contradiction is between empires
3. Cyclical economic contradictions (Ec): in which the contradictions provoke alternations between growth and no growth in capital accumulation
4. Systemic economic contradictions (Es): in which the contradictions push economic activity toward its limits

Two subtypes of systemic economic contradictions are distinguished:

5. Land/capital systemic contradiction ($Es_{[l/c]}$): in which the contradiction is between capitalist production relations and the productive force land
6. Oil company/petrostate contradiction ($Es_{[oc/ps]}$): in which the contradiction is between enterprises producing oil and the states in which the oil is found

Four different levels of the severity of contradictions are identified:

1. Potential intensification (Ip): in which prior to hostilities a contradiction existed, with the potential for intensifying and reducing reproductive capacity
2. Intensifying (I): in which prior to hostilities a contradiction was intensifying and potentially reducing reproductive capacity
3. Rapid onset intensification (Ir): in which prior to hostilities there was a sudden, rapid onset of a contradiction, with negative reproductive possibilities
4. Coelescence (Coel): in which there were two or more intensifying contradictions cooccurring

The hermeneutic politics that led to global warring involved debates between security elites who interpreted the contradictory situations facing the United States as either requiring, or not requiring, exercise of violent force. These debates were not conducted in a discourse about contradictions. So presidents did not say, "Wow! The contradictions are intensifying, we gotta go to war." Rather, they were conducted in terms of the hermeneutics by which the contradictions were understood. Thus, the intensifying interimperial contradiction during the Vietnam warfare was interpreted as "dominos falling," with elites asserting, "The dominos are falling, the dominos are falling, we have got to go to war to prevent this."

Elites who participated in these (deadly) politics were "hawks," those favoring violence, and "doves," those against violence. The states of the hermeneutic politics among US security elites prior to the global warring are threefold:

1. Do not know (DNK): in which the record of the hermeneutic politics is not clear
2. Hawks versus doves (HvD): in which there were hawks (proconflict security elites) versus doves (conflict security elites), with the former prevailing and setting in motion the implementation of global warring public *délires*
3. Hermetic seal (HS): in which there was a situation of hermetic seal, and the significant security elites were all effectively sealed into approving global warring public *délires*

Hermeneutic politics resulted in the implementation of different public *délires*. Those relative to global warring since 1950 are discussed next.

In 1950, during the administration of President Harry S. Truman, the National Security Council issued a document known as NSC 68. It is argued to be a key post-World War II, foreign relations public *délire*. It was US security elites' response to the intensifying interimperial contradiction between the United States and the Soviet Empire. They interpreted the situation as one in which "dominos" had been falling (really fast) since 1945—Eastern Europe gone, China gone. The American way of life at risk, meaning elite privileges and treasures were threatened due to the communist "menace." This understanding was enough to metamorphose security elites from tranquil Ferdinands into raging bulls. NSC 68 expressed this furious *délire*. It declared opposition to the Soviet Empire's, and their clients', expansion. This hostility included going to war when necessary. The communist menace at this time was the sole force between the United States and global leadership. By seeking to frustrate the Soviets, NSC 68 effectively set Washington on the path of global supremacy. It, then, may be termed a "global domination" public *délire*.

The data will suggest that US overseas interventions since 1950 have been different applications of the global domination public *délire*. However, there have been a number of iterations of it, depending upon which contradiction, or coalescence of contradictions, were most in evidence prior to the intervention. During the Cold War these iterations—most importantly that of the *domino theory*—tended to address different ways of reducing reproductive vulnerability due to the interimperial contradiction. After the Cold War economic contradictions became more important. In the situation of increasing and coalescing cyclical economic and systemic contradictions following 1989, with economic elites unable to provide clear fixes to these vulnerabilities, security elites suggested that by controlling petroleum energy resources, they could control the states requiring them, thereby maintaining global supremacy. This led to the institution of an oil control public *délire*.

Additionally, starting in the 1970s, it became clear that the United States was the leading imperial power in the world, dominating peoples and regions in ways that provoked opposition. Opposition was expressed as anti-American resistance that took the form of terrorism. Growing terrorism meant an intensifying dominator/dominated contradiction. This contradiction was met by the institution of an antiterrorist global domination *public délire*.

The following four were those whose implementation committed the United States to some form of global war:

1. Cold War iteration of the global domination public *délire* ($GD_{[cwit]}$): implementation of the public *délire* due to US–Soviet interimperial rivalry
2. Oil control iteration of the global domination public *délire* ($GD_{[ocit]}$): implementation of the public *délire* in order to facilitate US control over oil
3. Antiterrorism iteration of the global domination public *délire* ($GD_{[atit]}$): implementation of the public *délire* in order to facilitate US attempts to eliminate terrorism

Finally, four forms of Shultzian Permission were observed. These included:

1. +: In which security elites sought Shultzian Permission, in the sense that global warring occurred subsequent to attempts to find peaceful alternatives to violence (at least in the I-spaces of US security elites)
2. –: In which security elites did not seek Shultzian Permission, in the sense that the global warring occurred in the absence of attempts to find peaceful alternatives to violence
3. –$_{[co]}$: In which Shultzian Permission was irrelevant because the conflict was already in progress when the United States entered it
4. ?: In which the situation with regard to the securing of Shultzian Permission is not known

A word is in order about the sample of wars forming the database for judging the GWT's validity.

Representativeness

The sample consists of cases in which it is generally acknowledged that the United States intervened militarily in another country. The twenty-four conflicts analyzed are *not* a random sample. Nevertheless, if not randomly selected, they are characteristic, in the sense that they are examples of the different sorts of conflicts (overt, covert, direct, and indirect) the United States has engaged in since 1950. Moreover, they are conflicts—ranging from the covert Iranian coup, with relatively few casualties, to the overt Vietnam War, with millions upon millions of casualties—that influence, or continue to influence, global geopolitics. The wars are grouped into two temporal categories: Cold War hostilities, those from 1950 through 1989, when US security elites worried about the USSR while wrestling with the interimperial contradiction, and post–Cold War hostilities, from 1990 through the present (2016, when the United States wrestled with cyclical and systemic economic contradictions. Next up, evidence![4]

The New American Empire

First, the GWT is supposed to occur within empires, so it is important to establish whether the United States has been an empire since the end of World War II.

New American Empire

Chapters 4 and 5 in Reyna (2016) document the shifting shape of the American polity. The United States is argued to have exhibited some form of empire since its foundation. First, in the years from 1786 through the 1870s, this empire was a territorial one. Subsequently, in the years following the 1870s it experimented with different extraterritorial, formal, and informal imperial forms. Finally, subsequent to World War II, consequent upon adoption of NSC 68 as a global domination public *délire*, it became an informal, three-tiered one that on occasion paid strategic rent to its clients. Other scholars may differ on how they conceptualize empire; however, there is a convergence on the left (Harvey 2003), center (Schlesinger 1986; Lundstad 1986; Gaddis 1997; Darwin 2008), and right (Ferguson 2004) that post-World War II America has been an imperial social form, one with global ambitious. Next, conflicts of the Cold War are explored.

Cold War I: 1950–1974

The early Cold War period corresponds to a time of robust, global capitalist growth, with US capitalism the dominant economic force in the world. The central contradiction in the world was that between the United States and Soviet empires. Six conflicts are examined: the Korean War, the Iranian coup, the Guatemalan coup, the US invasion of Cuba, the Vietnam War, and the Chilean coup.

Korean War, 1950–1953

O, D/I: The Korean War was one in which US military force was overtly exercised in a direct and indirect fashion, with the South Korean and UK soldiers, most importantly, acting as proxies.

Pii: The war was in response to North Korea's invasion of South Korea. North Korea was a client of the Soviet Union and China. South Korea was a client of the United States. The North's invasion intensified the interimperial contradiction.

Ir: The North's invasion was a sudden, rapid intensification.

HS: The fact of the surprise invasion united the hermeneutic politics of relevant security elites into the intention to oppose communist aggression. They were effectively hermeneutically sealing into a common hawk position.

$GD_{[cwit]}$: Truman, US president at the time, led the United States into a war to oppose communist expansionism, thereby implementing NSC 68, the first iteration of the global domination public *délire*.

$-_{[co]}$: Peaceful alternatives to the conflict were not pursued, because the war was already ongoing when the United States entered into it.

Iranian Coup, 1953

C, D/I: The Iranian coup was a covert operation. Some US personnel from the CIA were directly involved, assisted by certain British and Iranian proxies.

Pii, ES$_{[oc/ps]}$: There were two contradictions operative prior to the Iranian coup—one was the interimperial contradiction. This was because Iran's leader at the time, Mohammad Mossadegh, was to the left, raising the possibility that Iran might be lost to communist subversion. The other contradiction was the oil company/petrostate contradiction, which intensified due to the Iranian government's nationalization of their oil sector, so that less of its oil revenues would go to the forerunner of the company that would become British Petroleum.

Coel, Ip: There was potential coalescence and intensification of the Pii contradiction as well as coalescence of the Pii and ES$_{[oc/ps]}$ contradictions.

HS: The British, who stood to lose oil revenues to Iran's oil nationalization, requested US assistance in overturning Mossadegh's regime. Under President Truman this request was denied. However, it was reconsidered under President Dwight D. Eisenhower. His security elites were united in their disapproval of the nationalization and, thus, were hermetically sealed into a plan to overthrow Mossadegh with a secret coup.

GD$_{[cwit]}$: The coup was implemented as part of the Eisenhower regime's policy of "rollback" of communism, a Cold War iteration of the global domination public *délire*.

+: The coup was only implemented after peaceful negotiations to change Iranian nationalization policy failed.

The Guatemalan Coup, 1954

C, I: The Guatemalan coup occurred a year after that in Iran. It too was covert and indirect, with the United States using elements of the Guatemalan military to overthrow the democratically elected government.

Pii: The Eisenhower administration believed that the Guatemalan government of Jacobo Arbenz was "going communist."

Ip: If Guatemala had become a Soviet satellite, it would have intensified the interimperial contradiction in favor of the USSR. Thus, a potential for intensification of this contradiction existed.

HS: The relevant security elites in the Eisenhower administration were all favored in the Guatemala coup. They were effectively hermetically sealed into it.

GD$_{\{cqit\}}$: The coup was implemented as part of the Eisenhower administration's policies of Soviet rollback, which were a Cold War iteration of the global domination public *délire*.

+: Attempts were made, US security elites believed, to peacefully ameliorate the situation in Guatemala. These were unsuccessful.

US Invasion of Cuba, 1961

C, D/Is: The John F. Kennedy administration's invasion of Cuba in the Bay of Pigs, an attempt to overturn the Fidel Castro regime, was initially a covert, CIA operation. Though conceived and managed by the CIA, it relied heavily upon the recruitment of Cuban proxies to do the actual fighting, whose immediate and decisive defeat ensured its secrecy was compromised.

Pdd, Pii: Two sorts of contradictions preceded the Bay of Pigs Invasion. On the one hand, US security elites were afraid that Cuba would join the Soviet Bloc, intensifying the interimperial contradiction. On the other hand, prior to the Castro government, Cuba had been a neocolony of the United States—with US elites dominating the Cuban economy, which meant that Cubans of different social standing were dominated by the Americans. This meant that the United States and Cuba were in a dominator/dominated contradiction.

Coel, I: The Cuban revolution weakened US economic interests in Cuba, intensifying the dominator/dominated contradiction. The considerable incorporation of Cuba into the Soviet Bloc intensified the interimperial contradiction.

HvD: There was some opposition to the Bay of Pigs Invasion (largely from Senator J. William Fulbright). This, however, was insufficient to stop the operation.

CD$_{[cwit]}$: The operation was an implementation of the global domination public *délire* as interpreted by President Kennedy's security elites.

+: It was believed that the Castro government had been given peaceful opportunities to mend their anti-United States policies but had neglected to do so, so Shultzian Permission was granted.

Vietnam War, 1961–1975

O, D/I: Vietnam was part of the French Indochinese Empire in Southeast Asia. After France had been defeated and driven from there in 1954, the area was divided into a communist North Vietnam and a noncommunist South Vietnam, with South Vietnam a client of the New American Empire. The United States overtly fought in Vietnam to prevent North Vietnam from conquering South

Vietnam. It did so with its own forces and with proxies largely from its client states (especially South Korea and Australia).

Pii: If South Vietnam was lost during the conflict, a large amount of land would become communist, either falling into Soviet or Chinese orbits. Consequently, it was an instance of the interimperial contradiction.

I: The continual and considerable loss of territory to communist forces during the conflict meant that the interimperial contradiction was intensifying.

HvD: The hermeneutic politics that US security elites became embroiled in during the Vietnam War was considerable. President Lyndon B. Johnson's national security advisor, McGeorge Bundy, his secretary of state, Dean Rusk, and his secretary of defense, Robert McNamara, were all strong hawks. George Ball, undersecretary of state, was the foremost security elite dove. Over time those favoring less violence were eliminated from positions with authority vis-à-vis the conflict.

GD$_{[cwit]}$: The conflict was implemented as a result of a Cold War iteration of the global domination public *délire*. This iteration has been called the "domino theory," which insisted that if one country fell to communism it might lead to other countries falling, like dominos, to opposing imperial formations.

−$_{[co]}$: Shultzian Permission was not granted because when the United States entered the Vietnam War it was already under way.

Chilean Coup, 1973[5]

C, D/I: Chile had long had a reputation prior to the 1970s of democratic governance. In 1970 Salvador Allende was elected president. There was a problem. He was a Marxist and a leader of Chile's Socialist party. President Richard Nixon, and his National Security Advisor Henry Kissinger, sought his elimination. In 1973 he committed suicide in a coup led by Augusto Pinochet. The United States worked covertly to make the coup. CIA operatives were inserted in-country to worked clandestinely with different elements of the Chilean military, intelligence services, and civil society opposed to Allende, making these elements proxies of US imperial intentions. By and large their activities involved sabotaging, and blockading Chilean economic life making the country ungovernable.

Pii: Allende's victory meant that another country in the Americas had gone, or could go, communist, which meant intensification in the interimperial contradiction.

I: Because Cuba had earlier joined the Soviet camp, because Allende was a Marxist, and, finally, because Chile was an important country in Latin America whose politics might influence other South American countries, the Pii contradiction can be judged to have intensified.

HS: What debate there was over policy toward the Allende government appears to have been over the degree of secrecy of the destabilization. Some felt the United States should be especially covert because, the United States overtly supported democracies, and Chile's government was democratic. However, all the relevant security elites were hermetically sealed in the view that Allende had to go.

GD[$_{cwit]}$: The conflict was implemented as a result of a Cold War iteration of the global domination public *délire*. This iteration was the domino theory, which insisted that if one country fell to communism it might lead to other countries falling, like dominos, to opposing imperial formations.

$-_{[co]}$: When Nixon learned of Allende's electoral victory, he is supposed to have screamed, "That son of a bitch, that son of a bitch," which led to a seven-minute dialogue on how he was going to "smash Allende" (in Grandin 2006: 59). Richard Helms, Nixon's CIA director testified that Nixon personally ordered Allende's overthrow (Hersh 1974). No Shultzian Permission appears to have ever been granted.

Cold War II, 1975–1989

The final phase of the Cold War—from the end of the Vietnam Conflict until the fall of the Soviet Union—was marked by a shifting relative importance of contradictions threatening the New American Empire. Attempts to reduce confrontation with the USSR and China meant, though a communist threat still existed, that US security elites worried a bit less about the interimperial contradiction. A coalescence of cyclical and systemic contradictions began during this time. Oil nationalizations throughout the developing world intensified the oil company/petrostate contradiction. Further, recognition of an oil crisis during the Nixon administration (1969–1974) might be taken as the beginning of the recognition of intensification of the land/capital contradiction.

The United States was still the largest economy in the world, but European, Japanese, and South Korean economies had substantially recovered from their post-World War II lows to compete with that of the United States. The three conflicts of this period analyzed below reflect in different ways the changing contradictions; these include Afghanistan I, the Iran–Iraq War, and Libya I.

Afghanistan I, 1979–1989

C, Is: In 1979 the Soviet Union invaded, and occupied, Afghanistan to ensure that it remained its client. A powerful resistance movement, the mujahideen (sacred warriors), formed to drive the Russians out of Afghanistan. The United States, under President Jimmy Carter, entered this conflict on the resistance's side. It did so covertly. Its participation involved providing Afghan resistance forces with the military wherewithal to oppose the Soviets. Thus, these resistance forces—some of whom would become Al Qaeda and Taliban—were employed as proxies against the Soviet Empire.

Pii: If Afghanistan fell to Russia, it would be another domino in the Soviet Empire, meaning that the Russian aggression was an instance of the interimperial contradiction.

I: Moreover, the Soviet invasion intensified the interimperial contradiction.

HvD: There were hawks and doves in the hermeneutic politics leading up to US participation in Afghanistan I. These pitted President Carter's national security advisor, Zbigniew Brzezinski, against his secretary of state, Cyrus Vance. The former was a hawk, the latter a dove. Brzezinski developed what he termed an "Islamic card" policy against the Soviets. This involved using Muslim peoples in the USSR to rebel against Moscow when it did un-Islamic things.

$GD_{[cwit]}$: Afghanistan was another domino that could drop to the Soviet Empire. US participation in the conflict played the Islamic card in the sense that it allied with the mujahideen against the atheist, invading Soviets and was a implementation of the Islamic card iteration of the global domination public *délire*.

$-_{[co]}$: Hostilities were already under way when the United States entered Afghanistan I. Consequently, Shultzian Permission was not granted.

Iran–Iraq War, 1980–1989

O/C, Is: The Iran–Iraq War began in 1980 when President Saddam Hussein of Iraq invaded Iran in an attempt to acquire Iranian territory where there were rich oil deposits. The United States entered the conflict initially covertly and toward the end overtly. At times it aided both sides, though by the end of hostilities it sought to make Saddam Hussein a US client. US participation came in the form of the provision of military equipment, so that Iranian and Iraqi soldiers fought, at least in part, as proxies of the United States.

$ES_{[l/c]}$, $ES_{[oc/ps]}$: Iran and Iraq were two major oil producers. If one acquired control over the other's petroleum resources, they would control a large amount of the world's oil. This would intensify the oil company/petrostate contradiction. At the same time, the increasing consumption of oil was increasing the amount of CO_2 in the atmosphere, increasing the land/capital contradiction.

Coel: The $ES_{[l/c]}$ and the $ES_{[oc/ps]}$ were intensifying and coalescing together.

HS: While there was debate over with whom to ally in the Iran–Iraq War, there was little controversy over participation in it. Consequently, the key security elites were hermetically sealed into an interpretation that there should be US participation in the hostilities.

GD$_{[ocit]}$: The Carter Doctrine (1978) and the Reagan Corollary specified that the United States would go to war to control, if need be, its oil interests. In effect, they were a judgment that the New American Empire could persist if it controlled the energy resources that other countries—clients and foes—required. They were, thus, constitutive of an oil control global domination public *délire*. The United States implemented this public *délire* when it entered the Iran–Iraq conflict.

−$_{[co]}$: Hostilities were already under way when the United States entered the Iran–Iraq War. Consequently, Shultzian Permission did not have to be granted.

Libya I, 1980s

O/C, D/Is: Libya became an oil producer in the 1970s. Muammar Gaddafi, Libya's ruler at this time, nationalized this oil, reducing the United States', and its clients', ability to accumulate oil wealth from there. During President Reagan's regime, the United States attacked Libya a number of times in the 1980s. Some of these attacks were overt; others were covert. At times American Navy and Air Force personnel were directly involved in the combat. At other times Libyan and Chadian proxies were trained and armed by the United States.

Pdd: Throughout the 1970s, there was recognition in the developing world that the United States had replaced the old European empires as the major imperial force in the world. Resistance, in the form of guerrilla movements, formed among dominated peoples, especially in the Middle East. Gaddafi was a strongly anti-imperialist leader. He used oil revenues to support a number of these movements. The United States interpreted these movements as "terrorist." The Brotherly Leader's support of terrorism was an example of the dominator/dominated contradiction.

I: The growth of "terrorism" throughout the 1970s meant that the Pdd was intensifying.

HS: It is clear that the relevant security elites in the Reagan administration interpreted Gaddafi as a terrorist menace, whose rule should be terminated. As such, they hermetically sealed into warring against him.

GD$_{[atit]}$: The hostilities against Libya were the first instance of the implementation of the antiterrorist iteration of the global domination public *délire*.

–: There do not appear to have been any attempts by the Reagan regime to resolve its differences with Libya peacefully. It seems to be a case in which no attempt was made to achieve Shultzian Permission.

Post–Cold War, 1990–Present

The US–Soviet interimperial contradiction relaxed during the post–Cold War period, though it began to reintensify during the 2013 Ukrainian regime change. However, distinctive of the period has been intensification of both the cyclical and systemic economic contradictions, responsible since the mid-1970s for a slackening of "capital accumulation," which is consistent with a "long slowdown" (Durand and Légé 2014: 35). Associated with these economic problems, it has become clear, at least to scientists, that a sixth global mass extinction (Eldridge 2001; Kolbert 2014) is under way, with *Homo sapiens* a possible candidate for extinction. This extinction is caused in good measure by climate change (Cabollos 2015), a manifestation of the land/capital contradiction.

While the sixth mass extinction proceeds, the New American Empire has busied itself warring in five theaters—the Middle East, Central Asia, Africa, Latin America, and the Pacific—meaning that the United States has warred on a worldwide basis. Global warring has become world warring. Fifteen global wars of this period are analyzed below: in Iraq, Iran, Libya II, Syria, Yemen, Israel, Afghanistan II, Pakistan, Kosovo, Chad, Sudan, Somalia, Uganda, Colombia, and the Philippines.

The Iraq War, 1991–2011

O, D/Is: The Iraq War was a twenty-year conflict that went through three phases of hostility. First, there was Gulf War I (1991) in which President G.H.W. Bush invaded Iraq to force Saddam Hussein out of Kuwait following Saddam's invasion of his neighbor. Then, during President Bill Clinton's administration there was a war of blockades (1991–2000), during which the United States exercised its Air Force to prevent goods from entering Iraq to induce regime change. Finally, President G.W. Bush reinvaded Iraq in Gulf War II (2001–2011). Though there were covert operations, for the most part the United States fought overtly in Iraq. Its military was at all times directly involved in the hostilities. However, Washington also formed "coalitions of the willing," consisting of its clients, who fought as proxies beside the Americans.

Ec, Es[I/c]: The Iraq War happened when cyclical contradictions were active. Similarly, it occurred during a time of intensification of the land/capital systemic contradiction.

Coel, I: Consequently, during the years of the Iraq War the United States faced coalescing and intensifying contradictions.

HvD: During most of the three phases of the Iraq War, most security elites interpreted the Iraqi situation as requiring US armed intervention. So, a large majority of security elites were hawks. However, prior to the onset of the conflict's third phase, a major debate flared between the vice-president, Dick Cheney, and the secretary of state, Colin Powell. The vice-president's interpretation of the situation was that it justified immediate military action. The secretary of state constructed a more nuanced interpretation that emphasized exhausting peaceful diplomatic steps before resorting to violence. The president resolved this hermeneutic politics in favor of his vice-president.

$GD_{[ocit]}$, $GD_{[atit]}$: Iraq has enormous quantities of oil. Saddam Hussein was judged a dangerous "terrorist" with WMDs (weapons of mass destruction)—a judgment that, subsequent to hostilities, proved false. Nevertheless, throughout the three phases of the war, US security elites went to war implementing the oil control and/or the antiterrorist iterations of the global warring public *délire*.

+: Global warring occurred in the first and the third phases of the conflict after Saddam was given warning to cease his disapproved of behavior.

Iran, 1994–2014

C, Is: As far as most Americans are concerned, since the 1979 shah of Iran's overthrow (the US replacement for Mossadegh), there has not been a US–Iran War. This is incorrect. At least since 1994, covert operations have been under way throughout Iran that are intended to destabilize the Islamic Republic of Iran. These have largely been indirect forays organized by the CIA and US Special Operations Forces. They have relied upon proxies—especially Iranian dissidents and Israelito conduct assassinations and sabotage.

Ec, $Es_{[l/c]}$: These hostilities have occurred under the prevailing cyclical as well as the land/capital contradictions.

Coel, I: It has been a period of coalescing and intensifying contradictions.

DNK: It is unclear precisely what the hermeneutic politics regarding Iran were during the 1990s and the first decade of the twenty-first century.

$GD_{[ocit]}$, $GD_{[atit]}$: Iran, like Iraq, has enormous quantities of oil. The United States was no longer able to control these after the shah's demise. Additionally, Iran provides assistance to Hezbollah, which the United States classifies as a terrorist group. Due to this assistance, Iran has itself been designated a state sponsor of terrorism. Consequently, hostilities against Iran have included implementation of the oil control and/or the antiterrorist iterations of the global warring public *délire*.

?: The situation regarding granting of Shultzian Permission is unknown owing to the covert nature of US operations against Iran.

Libya II, 2011

O, D/Is: As part of the Arab Spring rebellions in the Middle East, dissidents rebelled in 2011 against the regime of Gaddafi. The New American Empire, in concert with its clients, immediately and openly decided upon regime change. The US Air Force, Navy, and certain Special Operations troops were directly involved. Also involved were US clients' militaries in NATO, acting as proxies in the combat.

Ec, Es$_{[l/c]}$: These hostilities have occurred under the prevailing cyclical as well as the land/capital contradictions.

Coel: It has been a period of coalescing and intensifying contradictions.

HvD: There was considerable hermeneutic politics over the decision to attack Libya. The secretary of state, Hillary Clinton, and the UN envoy, Susan Rice, were hawks, interpreting the situation as one requiring intervention. The vice-president, Joe Biden, the secretary of defense, Bob Gates, and the chairman of the Joint Chiefs of Staff, Admiral Mike Mullen, were doves, convinced that the situation did not warrant such an interpretation. President Barack Obama, who interpreted the war as a "turd sandwich" (Swanson 2011), nevertheless in the end favored the hawks.

GD$_{[ocit]}$, GD$_{[atit]}$: Libya, like Iraq and Iran, floats on oil. Under Gaddafi, control over that oil was always problematic. Similarly, the hawks continually emphasized that Gaddafi was a terrorist—against his own people, against the US Empire. Consequently, hostilities against Libya were an implementation of the oil control and/or the antiterrorist iterations of the global warring public *délire*.

+: US security elites believed that Gaddafi had been offered a way to peacefully resolve his dispute with the New American Empire, which he spurned, so Shultzian Permission was granted.

Syria, 2011–ongoing as of 2016

O/C, Is: As part of the same Arab Spring rebellions that led to Gaddafi's downfall, dissidents rebelled against the regime of Bashar al Assad in 2011. Assad's government did not fall and the ensuing civil war has dragged on until the present, with increasing numbers of external military forces entering the hostility, most important among these being the "terrorist" organizations Al Qaeda and ISIL. The New American Empire in concert with its clients has entered the hostilities against Al Assad and, supposedly, against the "terrorist" organizations. US operations began covertly and have become increasingly overt. However, these operations have been for the most part indirect, involving the use of proxies.

Ec, Es$_{[l/c]}$: These hostilities have occurred under the prevailing cyclical as well as the land/capital contradictions.

Coel, I: It has been a period of coalescing and intensifying contradictions.

DNK: The hermeneutic politics of the security elites with authorities vis-à-vis the Syrian war are opaque. Clearly, there has been debate. Equally clearly, this concerns interpretations of who is the enemy and how much to intervene. By 2014, one of the rebel groups opposing Assad's government, the Islamic State of Iraq and Levant (ISIL), an extremely violent terrorist group, declared itself a state in parts of Syria and Iraq. Thereafter, the United States had two foes in Syria—ISIL and Assad.

GD$_{[ocit]}$, GD$_{[atit]}$: Security elites have generally understood Al Assad as a terrorist tyrant who needs to go. Further, while Syria does not itself produce great quantities of oil, the United States by controlling the government in Damascus can enhance its control over Middle Eastern oil. Consequently, hostilities against Syria have been an implementation of the oil control and/or the antiterrorist iterations of the global warring public *délire*.

−$_{[co]}$: The conflict was already under way when the United States entered it; thus peaceful alternatives to it were not possible.

Yemen, 2001–ongoing as of 2016

O/C, D/Is: Yemen is the poor, rugged outback of the Arab world, whose central government maintains only tenuous control. All in all, it is a suitable place to seek safe haven. Among other organizations, Al Qaeda has used Yemen as a place of refuge, especially since 2001 and 9/11. The New American Empire has waged both covert and overt warfare there. Some of the warfare has been direct, involving US Special Operations teams and Air Force drone operators. Other warfare has been indirect and has involved training and supplying Yemeni soldiers to combat terrorists opposing the government. In 2015, Saudi Arabia invaded Yemen and attacked the Houthi regime that had come to dominate much of Yemen. The United States has supported the Saudi intervention, suggesting the Saudis serve as proxies of the New American Empire.

Ec, Es$_{[l/c]}$: These hostilities have occurred under the prevailing cyclical as well as the land/capital contradictions.

Coel, I: It has been a period of coalescing and intensifying contradictions.

DNK: The nature of the hermeneutic politics bearing upon Yemen is unclear. Security elites interpret Yemen as a place where terrorism needs to be confronted. Further, the Bab al Mandab is a narrow strait between Yemen on one side of the Red Sea and Eritrea and Djibouti on the other side. This strait is of geopolitical significance because most of the Middle East's oil passes through it. Control over the strait confers control over much of the world's oil distribution.

$GD_{[ocit]}$, $GD_{[atit]}$: Evidence suggests that US military activities in Yemen result from implementation of oil control and/or the antiterrorist iterations of the global warring public *délire*.

?: It is unclear whether or not Shultzian Permission was given in Yemen.

Israel, 1985 and ongoing in 2016

O, Is: Israel has always been an ally of the United States. Since 1985 that alliance has involved Washington providing on the order of 3 billion dollars annually of foreign assistance mostly for Israel's armed forces. Israel uses its military to fight its own wars and to serve as a proxy of the United States throughout the world, especially in operations against Iraq, Iran, and Syria.

Ec, $Es_{[l/c]}$: These hostilities have occurred under the prevailing cyclical as well as the land/capital contradictions.

Coel, I: It has been a period of coalescing and intensifying contradictions.

HS: Though there are those who are critical of US support of the Israeli military, these are rarely found among security elites. Israeli operations are understood to strengthen the empire's struggle to control oil and eliminate terrorism. The vast majority of these elites interpret support of Israel as geopolitically essential. Thus, Washington appears hermetically sealed into support for Tel Aviv.

$GD_{[ocit]}$, $GD_{[atit]}$: Evidence suggests that US military collaboration with Israel is an aspect of implementation of oil control and/or the antiterrorist iterations of the global warring public *délire*.

?: It is not known how often Shultzian Permission was given prior to Israel operating as a US proxy.

Afghanistan II, 2001–2014

O, D/Is: The New American Empire invaded Afghanistan immediately following 9/11 because Al Qaeda, headquartered in Afghanistan, had attacked the twin towers and because the Taliban, who then governed most of Afghanistan, refused to hand over Osama bin Laden, Al Qaeda's leader. The American invasion was overt and directly involved its own military personnel. Equally, mujahideen paramilitaries opposed to the Taliban fought as proxies for the US Empire.

Ec, Es$_{[l/c]}$: These hostilities have occurred under the prevailing cyclical as well as the land/capital contradictions.

Coel, I: It has been a period of coalescing and intensifying contradictions.

HS: The shock of the destruction caused by the terrorist attack upon the twin towers was interpreted by all security elites in President G.W. Bush's administration as requiring violent punishment of the perpetrators. Security elites also believed that Afghanistan would be a good place to construct a pipeline to evacuate Central Asian oil. Such a pipeline would stand little chance of being built if the Taliban were in control of Afghanistan. Consequently, US security elites were hermetically sealed into the intention of punishing Al Qaeda by invading Afghanistan.

GD$_{[ocit]}$, GD$_{[atit]}$: Evidence suggests that US intervention in Afghanistan was an aspect of the implementation of oil control and/or the antiterrorist iterations of the global warring public *délire*.

+: The Taliban were issued an ultimatum to deliver Osama bin Laden to Washington. If they did so, they were promised peace. If they refused, they would be attacked. They refused. It is in this sense that Shultzian Permission was given.

Pakistan, 2001–2014

C,D/Is: The New American Empire intervened in Pakistan in support of its warring in neighboring Afghanistan. This was necessary because the mujahideen opposing the American occupiers in Afghanistan used Pakistani territory as refuge areas. The Americans largely fought covertly in Pakistan, though they additionally directly employed their Special Operations troops and Air Force personnel to conduct drone warfare. Soldiers from Pakistan's own military were also employed as proxies to attack the mujahideen in the refuge areas.

Ec, Es$_{[l/c]}$: These hostilities have occurred under the prevailing cyclical as well as the land/capital contradictions.

Coel, I: It has been a period of coalescing and intensifying contradictions.

HS: US security elites were hermetically sealed into fighting in Afghanistan, and as the ability to fight there depended upon eradicating refuge areas for Afghani mujahideen, these elites were equally sealed into operations in Pakistani refugee zones.

$GD_{[ocit]}$, $GD_{[atit]}$: Because the Americans fought in Pakistan for the same reasons they warred in Afghanistan, the US intervention in Pakistan was an aspect of implementation of oil control and/or the antiterrorist iterations of the global warring public *délire*.

$-_{[co]}$: The securing of Shultzian Permission was not an option because combat was already under way when Washington began operations in Pakistan.

Kosovo, 1998–1999

O,D/Is: Serbia invaded Kosovo toward the end of the 1990s civil wars that re-Balkanized the Balkans. Washington insisted that Serbia cease its attacks upon Kosovo. Slobodan Milošević, the Serbian leader, refused. The New American Empire, together with its NATO allies, conducted extensive bombing operations against Serbia. This was an overt case of global warring, with US armed services directly participating, aided by NATO proxy forces.

Ec, $Es_{[l/c]}$: These hostilities have occurred under the prevailing cyclical as well as the land/capital contradictions.

Coel: It has been a period of coalescing and intensifying contradictions.

HvD: There were different interpretations of the desirability for American intervention in Kosovo. Initially, President Clinton, along with a number of other security elites, was hesitant. However, his wife, Hillary Clinton, and the secretary of state, Madeleine Albright, strongly favored intervention. Their interpretation of the situation was based upon an understanding that Milošević was a dastardly terrorist. The president's wife carried the day.

$GD_{[ocit]}$, $GD_{[atit]}$: Kosovo did not produce oil. However, an oil pipeline was planned to deliver Central Asian oil to Europe. Kosovo was situated so that, if it were to become a client of the New American Empire, it would facilitate control over this pipeline. Consequently, intervention in Kosovo against Serbian terrorism was an aspect of implementation of oil control and the antiterrorist iterations of the global warring public *délire*.

+: Milošević was issued a series of ultimatums instructing him to leave Kosovo. He did not, which led to the granting of Shultzian Permission.

Chad, 1980s–Present

C/O, D/Is: Chad is a former French colony located immediately south of Libya, which since its independence (1960) has been involved in continual civil wars. It became an oil producer at the turn of the twenty-first century. Since the

1980s, when it assisted the Reagan administration in its campaign against Libya, it has been an ally of Washington. Both covertly and overtly the United States has militarily assisted the government of Chad against those opposing it. Occasionally American forces have directly aided the Chadians. Sometimes French military forces, permanently garrisoned in Chad, have operated as proxies for American interests.

Ec, Es$_{[l/c]}$: These hostilities have occurred under the prevailing cyclical as well as the land/capital contradictions.

Coel, I: It has been a period of coalescing and intensifying contradictions.

DNK: The precise nature of the hermeneutic politics bearing upon Washington's relationship with Chad are uncertain. Nevertheless, since Chad has become an oil producer, the US government doubled down on its support of any regime in power, even though—like those of presidents Hissène Habré and Idriss Déby—these are brutally authoritarian. Recently, Washington has enlisted the Chadian government in the fight against terrorism in the Sahel and Sahara.

GD$_{[ocit]}$, GD$_{[atit]}$: Exxon/Mobil controls Chadian oil production. Intervention in Chad has been an aspect of implementation of oil control and/or the antiterrorist iterations of the global warring public *délire*.

?: Information concerning the granting of Shultzian Permission in Chad is lacking.

Sudan, Late 1990s–2011

C, D/Is: The New American Empire's politics in Sudan has been nearly the reverse of those in Chad. Sudan, like Chad, is an oil producer. However, the United States lost control over Sudanese oil production in the early 1990s. Thereafter, it participated largely covertly, though with some of its forces on the ground and with other African states as proxies, to destabilize Sudan. It has done so in two ways. The first was to support a breakaway rebellion of the south region of the country, the area where the oil was located. The second was to demonize Sudan's President Omar al-Bashir as a terrorist who conspired with other, archterrorists, such as Osama bin Laden.

Ec, Es$_{[l/c]}$: These hostilities have occurred under the prevailing cyclical as well as the land/capital contradictions.

Coel, I: It has been a period of coalescing and intensifying contradictions.

HvD: There were those security elites who did not believe US aggressive action was justified in Sudan. However, a security elite network, called the Council, formed in the 1990s, whose most important member was Susan Rice, who would become Obama's national security advisor. Its members interpreted

President al-Bashir's regime as evil, so their politics demanded southern independence. This meant militarily supporting the southern rebels. The Council's interpretations prevailed.

GD$_{[ocit]}$, GD$_{[atit]}$: Intervention in Sudan has been an aspect of implementation of the antiterrorist iterations of the global warring public *délire*. The severance of the oil-producing area of Sudan from the rest of the country allows the United States a chance to reestablish control over Sudanese oil, and so intervention also contributes to the implementation of the oil control iteration of the global warring public *délire*.

?: Information concerning the granting of Shultzian Permission in Sudan is lacking.

Somalia, 1992–Present

C/O, D/Iis: President Siad Barre, Somalia's first president, was overthrown in 1991. This led to the descent of the Somali state into civil war between various warlords seeking central government control. The New American Empire intervened in Somalia in 1992 and has continued intervention since then. Its military activities have been overt and covert, direct and indirect, involving both the CIA and Special Operations Forces there as well as soldiers from different African countries as proxies.

Ec, Es$_{[l/c]}$: These hostilities have occurred under the prevailing cyclical as well as the land/capital contradictions.

Coel, I: It has been a period of coalescing and intensifying contradictions.

DNK: Information concerning the hermeneutic politics involved in US decision making regarding Somalia is obscure. Security elites have continually worried that the country has been a place nurturing terrorist paramilitaries, especially Al Shabaab, which has been affiliated with Al Qaeda. These same elites also interpret what is happening in the country in terms of control over oil resources. There are two reasons for this. The first is that Somalia borders the sea-lanes of oil being transported out of the Middle East. Loss of influence within Somalia could threaten control over those sea-lanes. Second, while no oil has been discovered in Somalia, there is reason to believe that it exists. Consequently, security elites understand Somalia to be a place worth fighting to defend the empire's interests.

GD$_{[ocit]}$, GD$_{[atit]}$: Intervention in Somalia has been to reduce the capabilities of Al Shabaab and Al Qaeda and as such has involved implementation of the antiterrorist iterations of the global warring public *délire*. Further intervention in Somalia reduces threats to the oil transport sea-lanes and protects the United

States' ability to control Somalia oil should it be found. Accordingly, US military action in Somalia is an aspect of the implementation of the oil control iteration of the global warring public *délire*.

?: Information concerning the granting of Shultzian Permission is lacking.

Uganda, 1990–Present

O, D/Ies: Uganda had a turbulent and violent postcolonial history until 1986, when Yoweri Museveni captured the presidency. Since then, as a skilled antiguerrilla fighter, he has governed Uganda with an authoritarian hand. The United States since the 1990s has provided the Ugandan military with arms and training. In return, Museveni has committed his troops to fighting terrorists throughout Africa, especially in Somalia. Thus, Washington uses Ugandan soldiers as proxies for its antiterrorist policies. Between 2002 and 2007 commercially exploitable reserves of oil were discovered in Uganda. A number of armed skirmishes occurred in the area where there was oil. A detachment of US Special Operations troops was sent to Uganda in 2011, presumably to assist with instabilities, due to the discovery of oil.

Ec, $Es_{[I/c]}$: These hostilities have occurred under the prevailing cyclical as well as the land/capital contradictions.

Coel, I: It has been a period of coalescing and intensifying contradictions.

DNK: The hermeneutic politics surrounding military activities in Uganda are opaque. However, it is clear that during the Clinton administration, especially at the State Department, Museveni was interpreted as the sort of leader who could be a strongman and a regional leader who would defend US interests. So, efforts were made to recruit him as an ally by providing him with the military hardware to become "strong."

$GD_{[ocit]}$, $GD_{[atit]}$: Uganda's military was used as a proxy to fight terrorism. US troops were sent as boots on the ground immediately after oil was discovered. Thus, intervention in Uganda appears as an aspect of implementation of the antiterrorist and oil control iterations of the global warring public *délire*.

?: Information concerning the granting of Shultzian Permission is lacking.

Colombia, 2000–Present

C/O, Is: Colombia is an oil producer, whose production is substantially controlled by US oil companies. Additionally, it has since the 1960s been locked into a civil war, with two left-leaning movements—the Revolutionary Armed Forces of Colombia (FARC) and the National Liberation Army (ELN)—opposing the central government and, as part of this opposition, attacking the country's oil infrastructure. The United States, especially since 2000, has entered the civil war on the side of the central government. US interventions have been covert and overt, direct and indirect. Its personnel have on occasion conducted military operations in the countryside, though for the most part Washington has provided both arms and training to the Colombian military.

Ec, Es$_{[l/c]}$: These hostilities have occurred under the prevailing cyclical as well as the land/capital contradictions.

Coel, I: It has been a period of coalescing and intensifying contradictions.

DNK: The hermeneutic politics of security elites bearing upon Colombia are unclear. Nevertheless, Colombia has been interpreted by influential elites in the Clinton and G.W. Bush administrations as a "weak state," one with petroleum resources in which the United States had an interest.

GD$_{[ocit]}$, GD$_{[atit]}$: Both FARC and the ELN were classified as terrorist organizations, so military intervention in Colombia continued the US fight against global terrorism. Coincidentally, fighting against terrorism was a way to support US control in the Colombian oil section. So intervention in Colombia has been an aspect of implementation of the antiterrorist and oil control iterations of the global warring public *délire*.

$-_{[co]}$: Hostilities were already ongoing when the United States began intervening in 2000, so that Shultzian Permission was not granted.

Philippines, 2009

O/C, D/Ies: The Philippines have been both a formal and an informal colony of the United States. The American military has stationed troops there since the end of the nineteenth century. These were, by the turn of the twenty-first century, a detachment of Special Operations Forces. Since World War II the United States has directly provided support and training to Manila's military. Oil was discovered on one of the Philippines's southern islands in 2005. This was an area where certain antigovernment movements operated, which the United States classified as terrorist. By 2009, though the operations were in principle covert, it was discovered that US Special Operations troops had been directly committed against one rebel movement.

Ec, Es$_{[l/c]}$: These hostilities have occurred under the prevailing cyclical as well as the land/capital contradictions.

Coel, I: It has been a period of coalescing and intensifying contradictions.

DNK: The hermeneutic politics that led to committing Special Forces are unknown. It is likely that security elites interpreted the presence of antigovernment terrorists as a threat to potential US control over the newly discovered oil.

$GD_{[ocit]}$, $GD_{[atit]}$: There was oil to be controlled in the Philippines and terrorists who threatened this control. Military force was needed to confront these challenges. Consequently, intervention in the Philippines has been an aspect of implementation of the antiterrorist and oil control iterations of the global warring public *délire*.

?: It is unknown whether or not peaceful alternatives to intervention were presented to the rebels.

Discussion

The following states of the concepts constituting the GWT need to be observed if the evidence supports the theory:

> For each case, there should be contradictions that increase the US Empire's reproductive vulnerability, followed by hermeneutic politics that lead to the implementation of global warring public *délires* and the granting of Shultzian Permission, which is designed to fix the reproductive difficulties posed by the contradictions.

The evidence reported indicates, first, that the United States has been an empire during the period under examination, second, that the twenty-four cases examined experienced some form of global warring, and, third, that the years between 1950 and 2016 were dominated by two sorts of contradictions. The prevailing contradictions during the Cold War (1950–1989) were political, with the most important being the interimperial contradiction, followed by the dominator/dominated contradiction. The most important contradictions in post–Cold War times have been economic, with both cyclic and systemic contradictions. The land/capital contradiction has been the most significant systemic contradiction. The severity of the contradictions has varied. During the Cold War, the political contradictions were potentially intensifying or clearly intensifying prior to the onset of global warring. In the post–Cold War period, the economic contradictions were both intensifying and coalescing prior to the onset of global warring.

The existence of contradictions led to hermeneutic politics among security elites. These politics were waged along a hawk/dove axis, pitting those who interpreted the situations imposed by the contradictions as requiring the exercise of violence against those whose interpretations were skeptical of this view. In each case the hawks won. Consequent upon hawk victory, some iteration of a common public *délire* was selected to implement the global warring. The common public *délire* was that of global domination authorized by NSC 68, which committed the New American Empire to seeking a world empire. From

1950 through 1989, various Cold War iterations—such as the domino theory and the Islamic card—of the global domination public *délire* were operative.

From 1990 through 2016 the oil control and the antiterrorist iterations of the global domination public *délire* were especially operative. The granting of Shultzian Permission is the least clear in the evidence, in part because it is difficult to know what transpired among security elites prior to the onset of a global war. However, it does seem, unless the conflict was ongoing, that security elites did try to offer their opponents a peaceful way out. Of course, these offers were US offers and may have been unacceptable, or unimplementable, to their opponents. Nevertheless, the evidence is consistent with the GWT.

Two potential criticisms of the preceding inquiry should be addressed. First, it might be suggested that GWT is a crude oil or antiterrorist determinism. I think not. It is not oil or terrorism that directly causes global warring. Rather it is a particular US imperial system caught in reproductive trouble due to contradiction that provokes the warring as a way of addressing the vulnerability.

Second, it might be argued that GWT is a crude form of determinism based upon contradiction. There are two responses to this criticism. First, those who doubt the role of contradiction in social forms are often those who have decided equally that Marxist theory has no place in social or cultural theory. My sense is that, regardless of whether one believes it or not, the reist reality is this: all things fall apart. "Contradiction" is the term for a particular state of social forms—when they are subject to forces leading them to fall apart. Because when things are falling apart they change, contradictions have a telluric role in social forms, and the analysis of this article has argued for one such role with regard to US global warring.

Second, those attacking a theory as crude usually mean that it posits a direct, linear causality: A causes B, end of theoretical story. The relationship between contradictions and global warring in GWT is not crude in this sense. Rather, contradictions occur; then human reflexivity steps in. Those who experience the contradictions reflect upon them. Reflection leads to hermeneutic politics in which actors interpret what it is that they experience in contradiction and what to do about what is. Security elites, in their hermeneutic politics, reflecting on contradiction, provide understandings of what the contradictions are and what to do about them. These are understandings that eventually become instituted as public *délires,* some of which call for global warring. Then, some situation occurs over which the security elites have responsibility due to the authority they possess in the public *délires* they administer.

Again a hermeneutic politics occurs among security elites with responsibilities toward the situation over how to interpret it. What this chapter shows is that in situations in which contradictions threaten, or produce, vulnerabilities, security elites tend in their hermeneutic politics to interpret the situation as one requiring the implementation of a global warring public *délire*. This is not a crude causality. Rather, it involves a complex interplay between forces of contradiction immanent in social forms and forces of governance within those forms, with the play between the two forces mediated, at least in part, by reflexivity. There is determinism here. It is not so much crude as playful.

Finally, recall that the second methodological guideline of critical structural realism's reism was to discover the time-being that contains the structural somethings that explain what needs explaining. The time-being examined has been Earth 1950–2015. The structural something discovered was the New American Empire with its proxies, reproducing itself in the face of contradictions and reflecting upon these through hermeneutic politics in which interpretations are guided by iterations of a global domination public *délire*. Contemplate reality: Wham, bang, rip and roar, economic, political, and social things blasted to smithereens across the globe, millions upon millions upon millions of persons killed, wounded, sickened, and driven into refugee flight. Reality for the time-being of the New American Empire is of "Death, the destroyer of worlds." Time to consider some dreamers.

Dreaming in the Time-Being of Empires: Of Democracy and Dodos

Old von Molke can relax. A world of democracy is not a world of perpetual peace. Democracy's ability to guarantee perpetual peace is a dream if empires are around, and, currently, the New American Empire is around everywhere. The United States went to war against democracies three times in our sample: when it intervened in Iran (1953), Guatemala (1954), and Chile (1973). These interventions were covert. Perhaps there was guilt about attacking a democracy? I think not. Empires have to do what empires do—respond to what threatens them. Eisenhower and Nixon, and their security myrmidons, interpreted Iran, Guatemala, and Chile as threats. They acted against them, regardless of their democratic status.

The preceding has a critical implication. There is a real world out there. It is a world of empires. These have economic and political slots. Since the beginning of modernity the economic slot has been increasingly filled by capitalist institutions seeking gratification of capitalist desire. The political slot has been filled by militaries with growing killing force, with that capability presently to kill everybody in a nuclear holocaust, should it be their desire. In this world, the New American Empire currently faces an intensifying land/capital contradiction coalescing with an intensifying cyclical contradiction.

An irony of capitalist imperialism is that what it does to reproduce itself, kills it—through ecological devastation consequent upon exhaustion of natural resources resultant from their overconsumption during reproduction and through imperial governance to assist capitalist reproduction that produces hermeneutic politics and public *délires* that promote global warring that kills people globally. That is the real world out there. Its imperial logic—through the global warming and warring documented in this essay—rushes toward bad times.

In this optic, liberal dreamers who insist that democracy will bring perpetual peace are like dodos, heads stuck in the sand avoiding the actualities of imperial logic. Making democracies will do nothing to stop the land/capital contradiction and global warring. Eliminating imperial social beings with their capitalist economic slots is required, along with their replacement by global organizations of governance that utilize force resources in a manner that relaxes the land/capital contradiction and eliminates global warring, all the while treating everyone equitably. This may seem utopian. Utopian or not, if this does not occur humans are likely to experience first hell, then nothing. Because they, like dodos, are extinct, bones fossilizing in an eternity of starry nights.

Notes

1. Selling goods is a string that may exhibit a capitalist logic.
2. Empires are rarely purely formal or informal. Often they may possess elements of both formality and informality, as was the case for the British Empire in the nineteenth century.
3. Mary Kaldor has argued that the period following the end of the Cold War was characterized by a form of warfare that she calls "new wars" (2007). Shaw has called this perspective the "most … illuminating representation of contemporary warfare" (2000: 1). "New wars" are civil wars dominated by nonstate actors. I (Reyna 2009) am skeptical of this approach.
4. Fuller presentation of the evidence bearing upon the GWT can be found in Reyna (2016: chs. 7–11).
5. The assertions in this section are supported by a set of US government documents pertaining to the Chilean coup (Kornbluh 1995–2011).

References

Althusser, Louis. *"Lenin and Philosophy" and Other Essays*. London: New Left Books, 1977.

Cabollos, Gerardo, Paul R. Ehrlich, Anthony D. Barnosky, Andrés García, Robert M. Pringle, and Todd M. Palmer. "Accelerated Modern Human-Induced Species Losses: Entering the Sixth Mass Extinction." *Science Advances* 1, no. 5 (2015): e1400253.

Castro, Carl A. and Amy B. Adler. "OPTEMPO: Effects on Soldier and Unit Readiness." *Parameters* 29, no. 3 (1999): 86–95, accessed 4 May 2014. http://strategicstudiesinstitute.army.mil/pubs/parameters/articles/99autumn/castro.htm.

Darwin, John. *After Tamerlane: The Rise and Fall of Global Empires*. New York: Bloomsbury Press, 2008.

Drum, Kevin. "How the Rest of the World Views the American Military." *Mother Jones*, August 2013, accessed 4 May 2014. http://www.motherjones.com/kevin-drum/2013/08/how-rest-world-viewsamerican-military.

Durand, Cédric and Philippe Légé. "Over-Accumulation, Rising Costs and 'Unproductive Labor:' the Relevance of the Classic Stationary State Issue for Developed Countries." *Review of Radical Political Economics* 46, no. 1 (2014): 35–53.

Eldredge, Nils. "Sixth Extinction." *ActionBioscience.org*, 2001, accessed 1 September 2015. http://endangeredink.com/programs/population_and_sustainability/extinction/pdfs/Eldridge-6th-extinction.pdf.

Etzioni-Halevy, Eva. *Classes and Elites in Democracy and Democratization: A Collection of Readings*. London: Routledge, 1997.

Ferguson, Niall. *Colossus: The Rise and Fall of the American Empire*. New York: Penguin Books, 2004.

Follman, Mark. "Yes, Mass Shootings Are Occurring More Often." *Mother Jones*, October 2010, accessed 9 October 2015. http://www.motherjones.com/politics/2014/10/mass-shootings-rising-harvard.

Friedman, Jonathan. *Cultural Identity and Global Process*. London: Sage, 1994.

Gaddis, John Lewis. *We Now Know: Rethinking Cold War History*. Oxford: Oxford University Press, 1997.

Grandin, Greg. *Empire's Workshop: Latin America and the Roots of U.S. Imperialism*. New York: Metropolitan Books, 2006.

Harvey, David. *The New Imperialism*. Oxford: Oxford University Press, 2003.

Hersh, Seymour. "Helms Said Nixon Sought Chilean Coup." *New York Times*, 10 February 1975, accessed 4 April 2016. http://timesmachine.nytimes.com/timesmachine/1975/02/10/80126939.html.

Higley, John, and Jan Pakulski. "Elite Theory versus Marxism: The Twentieth Century's Verdict." In *Elites After State Socialism*, John Higley and G. Lengyel, 229–4. Lanham MD: Rowman & Littlefield, 2000.

Kaldor, Mary. *New and Old Wars: Organized Violence in a Global Era*. Second Edition. Cambridge: Polity Press, 2007.

Kant, Immanuel. "Perpetual Peace: A Philosophical Sketch." In *Kant: Political Writings*, edited by H.S. Reiss, 93–131. Cambridge: Cambridge University Press, 1970.

Kende, Istvan. "Twenty-Five Years of Local Wars." *Journal of Peace Research* 8, no. 1 (1971): 5–22.

Kornbluh, Peter. "Chile and the United States: Declassified Documents Relating to the Military Coup, September 11, 1973." *National Security Archive Electronic Briefing Book No. 8*, George Washington University, accessed 6 September 2015. http://nsarchive.gwu.edu/NSAEBB/NSAEBB8/nsaebb8i.htm.

———. "Chile and the United States: Declassified Documents Relating to the Military Coup, September 11, 1973." *National Security Archive*, George Washington University, 1995–2011, accessed 11 September 2015. http://nsarchive.gwu.edu/NSAEBB/NSAEBB8/nsaebb8i.htm.

Leaf, Munro. *The Story of Ferdinand*. Harmondsworth: Penguin, 1936.

Lebow, Richard Ned. "Aggressive Democracies." *St Antony's International Review* 6, no. 2 (2011): 120–33.

Lundestad, Geir. "Empire by Invitation? The United States and Western Europe, 1945–1952." *Journal of Peace Research* 23, no. 3 (1986): 263–77.

Mann, Michael. "Nation-States in Europe and Other Continents: Diversifying, Developing, Not Dying." *Daedalus* 122, no. 3 (1993): 115–40.

Michels, Robert. *Political Parties: A Sociological Study of the Oligarchical Tendencies of Modern Democracies.* Piscataway, NJ: Transaction Publishers [2009] 1915.

Molke, Helmuth von. "Letters and Historical Writings of Molke." In *The German Classics of the Nineteenth and Twentieth Centuries.* Edited by Kuno Francke, vol. 10, accessed 4 April 2016. http://www.fullbooks.com/The-German-Classics-of-The-Nineteenth-andx23821.html.

Morgan, Lewis Henry. *Ancient Society.* Tucson: University of Arizona Press,[1985] 1877.

Mosca, Gaetano. *The Ruling Class.* New York: McGraw Hill [1939] 1897.

Pareto, V. *The Rise and Fall of Elites.* New Brunswick, NJ: Transaction Publishers [1979] 1900.

Quinn, Joe. "Euromaidan: Anatomy of a Washington-Backed Coup d'Etat." *Sott of the Times,* accessed 3 August 2015. http://www.sott.net/article/292842-Euromaidan-Anatomy-of-a-Washington-backed-coup-d-etat.

Reyna, Stephen. "American Imperialism: 'The Current Runs Swiftly.'" *Focaal: European Journal of Anthropology* 45 (Summer, 2005): 129–51.

———. "Taking Place: 'New Wars' versus Global Wars." *Social Anthropology/Anthropologie Sociale* 17, no. 3 (2009): 291–317.

———. *Deadly Contradictions: The New American Empire and Its Global Warring.* New York: Berghahn, 2016.

Schlesinger, Arthur, Jr. *The Cycles of American History.* Boston: Houghton Mifflin, 1986.

Shaw, Martin "The Contemporary Mode of Warfare: Mary Kaldor's Theory of the New Wars." *Review of International Political Economy* 7(2000): 171–80.

Shultz, George. *Turmoil and Triumph: My Years as Secretary of State.* New York: Scribners, 1993.

Russian Times, "Special Forces Disguised as ISIS Fighters Operating in Syria—Military Sources." 3 August 2015, accessed 3 August 2015. http://www.rt.com/uk/311430-isis-fighter-sas-disguise/.

Swanson, David. "Our Billion Dollar Turd Sandwich." *Veterans Today,* 30 March 2011, accessed 1 September 2015. http://www.veteranstoday.com/2011/03/30/our-billion-dollar-turd-sandwich/.

Tures, John A. "United States Military Operations in the New World Order: An Examination of the Evidence." *American Diplomacy,* April 2003. Accessed April 6, 2016. http://www.unc.edu/depts/diplomat/archives_roll/2003_01-03/tures_military/tures_military.html

Wallerstein, Immanuel. *The Modern World System I.* New York: Academic Press, 1974.

Index

30 September Movement. *See* Gestapu
Adorno, Theodor, 13–14, 126n1
Aidit, Dipa Nusantara, 148, 151–52, 159
Althusser, Louis, 3, 9, 97, 103–4, 112–13, 127–28, 171
autopoiesis, 105, 114–15, 119, 123, 128n12

Bacon, Francis, 30, 33, 108
biasing, 79, 80, 82
    external, 79, 80, 86
    individual, 80, 82
    internal, 80, 82, 86
Boas, Franz, 2, 10, 75, 79, 127n6
    Boasian (follower of Boas), 2, 15
    Boasian/Neo-Boasian anthropological theory, 2–3

causal moral analysis, 138, 141, 143, 146, 159, 162. *See also* moral: judgment
change
    iterational, 95, 122, 125–26
    transformational, 95, 122, 124–26
choreograph, 12, 108–9, 110, 123, 124, 172, 173
CIA (Central Intelligence Agency), 129n24, 141, 148–152, 154, 159, 162n1, 163n11, 183–86, 190, 197
class, 120–21, 129n24, 143, 174–75
Clifford, James, 15, 25, 28, 45–46. *See also* Writing Culture
conceptual
    biases, 6, 7, 82
    blindness, 7, 8, 64, 119, 125–26
    bloat, 6, 8, 61
    blur, 7–8, 10, 16, 44, 64, 76, 85, 102–3

contradiction, 16, 62, 63, 95, 96, 97, 170–72, 178, 200, 201–2
    coalescence, 113, 123, 126, 168, 171, 172, 175, 176, 180, 183, 189–200
    cyclical, 112, 172, 178, 180, 186, 189, 200, 202
    economic, 112, 172, 176, 178, 180–81, 189, 200
    intensification, 63, 68, 78, 112–13, 123–24, 126, 168, 172, 175–76, 179, 183, 189–200
    interimperial, 178–187, 189, 200
    intra-imperial (dominator/dominated), 178, 180, 200
    land/capital, 112, 116, 118, 126, 200, 203
    limits, 113, 122
    oil company/petrostate, 178, 183, 186, 187
    political, 178, 200
    systemic, 172, 178, 180, 186, 189, 200
    vulnerability, 118, 122
Crapanzano, Vincent, 25, 28, 43–44, 83. *See also* Writing Culture
critical structural realism (CSR), 2–4, 8–16, 18, 55, 85, 110
criticisms of science, 27, 58, 60
cultural neurohermeneutic systems (CNHS), 107, 119
culture
    discursive, 107
    ideological, 107, 116, 173
    neuronal, 114–15, 123
    perceptual/procedural, 107–8, 110, 116–17, 119, 129n23, 173
    technical, 107, 116, 173
    worldview, 62, 107, 116, 128n19

www.ingramcontent.com/pod-product-compliance
Lightning Source LLC
Chambersburg PA
CBHW060037030426
42334CB00019B/2366